# ROOKIE SMARTS

**ALSO BY LIZ WISEMAN**

*Multipliers*

*The Multiplier Effect*

# ROOKIE SMARTS

*Why Learning Beats Knowing*
*in the New Game of Work*

# LIZ WISEMAN

**HARPER**
BUSINESS

*An Imprint of* HarperCollins*Publishers*

HarperCollins books may be purchased for educational, business, or sales promotional use. For information, please e-mail the Special Markets Department at SPsales@harpercollins.com.

FIRST EDITION

*Designed by Kris Tobiassen of Matchbook Digital*

Library of Congress Cataloging-in-Publication Data has been applied for.

ISBN 978-0-06-232263-0

19   ov/LSC   10 9 8 7 6 5

*To Larry, who has never lost his sense
of adventure and childlike wonder.*

You shall not cease from exploration and
the end of all our journeying will be to
arrive where we started and know the
place for the first time.

—T. S. ELIOT

# CONTENTS

# ROOKIE SMARTS

# INTRODUCTION

When is *not* knowing more valuable than knowing?

Why are you often at your best when you are new to an undertaking, doing something for the first time?

I've often wondered about these questions, too. At the age of twenty-four, just a year out of business school, I was thrown into a management role, due more to circumstances than to capabilities. I was working at Oracle, at the time still a young, maverick software company that was doubling in size each year. After a year of teaching Oracle software to new recruits, I was put in charge of company-wide training and charged with building a new corporate university—a task about which I knew absolutely nothing. The job felt more than a few sizes too big for me. Nevertheless, it seemed unwise to begin my career by turning down a promotion.

With only a little direction from my supervisors, I went to work—with no grand vision and no clue how to build a corporate university. And yet I understood that my task was critical to the company's future: If our sales force and field consultants didn't know our new product inside and out, it would probably break the young company. So, it was critical that I figure out how to get it right. My own ignorance, coupled with the harsh reality that my work mattered because it was directly linked to the company's future, prompted me to talk with everyone and anyone I could in order to close this knowledge gap. Mine was a humility born of desperation.

My team was made up of recent college graduates who were also new to corporate education—all of us lacking experience but sharing a hunger to make our marks. Together, we went to work seeking out conversations and interviews with product bosses and senior field managers, trying to understand what information needed to be taught to whom by which dates. With few resources and tight timelines, we kept our model simple: The university would mobilize existing experts and resources and create a learning environment where technical knowledge could be transferred to those working with customers.

We decided to co-opt space on the current campus rather than to build a stand-alone facility, a costly, time-consuming process that was the norm at the time. Without a stand-alone location, our campus-within-a-campus needed an even stronger identity and gravitas, so we decided to adopt an official crest and a Latin motto. Knowing no Latin myself, I phoned nearby Stanford University and asked to be connected to the humanities department. Within a minute, I had a professor of Latin on the phone. I explained our need, and asked him to translate our chosen motto, "Knowledge Is Power," into Latin. He seemed amused, if not exactly delighted, by my naïve but sincere request and carefully spelled out *Sapere Est Valere* (literally, "to know is to have power"). I thanked him for his time, hung up the phone, and called the company's T-shirt vendor to order several hundred T-shirts with our collegiate crest. Oracle University was now official.

Within a year, I was asked to expand Oracle University to serve more than one hundred countries around the world. Once again, none of my bosses seemed concerned that I didn't have international work experience and had, in fact, never traveled outside the United States. When I mentioned that I lacked a passport, I was told to get one, fly to Europe, and figure things out.

Our team was scrappy, but we continued to move fast. From my perspective, everything seemed to be working well. That is, until the day my immediate superior, the director of human resources, sat me down and explained that due to the company's fast growth, we now needed an experienced manager to lead Oracle University. He told me that a candidate for the job was coming in the next day to interview with a few senior executives. *Ouch.* I was devastated. But I could certainly understand the wisdom in hiring a more experienced manager. The next day a man named Jay, who looked every bit the experienced training executive I'd expected, met with me and then interviewed with the senior executives. Meanwhile, I weighed my options: Should I leave the company or stay and learn from the person who had been brought in to replace inexperienced me?

It turned out that my ruminations were unnecessary. The following day, my boss came to my office and announced emphatically but rather awkwardly, "We've decided not to hire Jay or anyone else to take over Oracle University. We'd like you to continue in the job." *What?* While I was still reeling, he apologized with dignity and grace that I still admire today, "I misjudged. When I solicited feedback from the executives, they were perplexed that I wanted to hire someone else. They assured me that you and your team are doing a great job and they were adamant that we not hire someone else."

Their vote of confidence was reassuring, but I still wondered why they would want to keep a rookie like me on in such an important role. Further reflection clarified what, at first, seemed to be a counterintuitive decision: Because I had no agenda of my own, I eagerly sought guidance from both product experts and senior leaders; because I lacked experience, I worked cautiously, staying close to my stakeholders, reporting on progress and outcomes, and continually seeking feedback. The obvious gap between the size of the job and the length of my experience forced me to leverage any and all available resources around me. My value didn't derive from having fresh ideas; it came from having *no ideas at all.* What my team and I lacked in experience and conviction we compensated for with our willingness to learn, to think creatively, and to deliver quick wins to prove ourselves.

This experience—simultaneously scary, exhilarating, unpredictable, and extremely rewarding—shaped my outlook as I continued to lead Oracle's corporate university for the next fifteen years. My boss Bob would occasionally tease me and mention to others how underqualified I was for my job. I reminded him that I didn't actually want a job I was qualified for—there'd be nothing to learn. I came to realize that the best jobs are often the ones we're not fully prepared for. Eventually my learning curve flattened, and I came to a troubling realization: I was, at last, legitimately qualified for my role. I had ascended the steep slope of ignorance and found myself on a plateau of accomplishment, gazing at a flattened landscape. Like others stuck on a plateau, I was relying on routines and building on past successes. Honestly, my work had become mediocre. Determined to recapture these earlier feelings of exhilaration, I left the cradle of my career in search of something I didn't yet know how to do. Sure enough, in this foreign, virgin terrain, I once again began to do my best work.

Sometimes not knowing is more valuable than knowing. A certain genius gets sparked in our rookie state and a learner's advantage kicks in.

Is it possible that we can be at our best when we are underqualified, doing something for the first time? With the right mindset we can. When we are stretched to reach beyond our current capabilities, we can open ourselves up to learning from everyone and everything around us and tap into a different mindset—what I have come to call rookie smarts.

While coaching executives and teaching leaders around the world in my post-plateau, post-Oracle life, I've seen rookie smarts at play over and over again; I've seen people on fire, doing their best work while closing massive knowledge and capability gaps. Sometimes a young professional has been given the chance to hit above his weight class. Other times an executive has taken on a new assignment outside her area of expertise. Once out of their comfort zone, these rookies experience a sense of challenge and exhilaration. One executive described his first month at his new job: "It's so much fun to be doing something new and invigorating. I have to turn my brain on and have to really think again. I felt so stale in my last job, and I welcome the challenge." Whether the rookie is a new college grad or a seasoned executive, behind them you will likely find a manager who took a risk and bet on their ability to learn quickly.

In other organizations, I've seen bright, driven people idling away at a job they've been doing for years. These veterans have been around the block more than a few times, and they tend to approach their work with the same level of mindfulness we give to our daily shampooing ritual—lather, rinse, repeat. When it is time to run the annual customer satisfaction survey, they pull up last year's project plan, update a few names and dates, and present the same, warmed-over program. They confess that they've become stale in their jobs, working well past their sell-by date. They feel themselves wasting away, anxious that their hard-earned knowledge and skills will become obsolete, wondering if they will be fit to work anywhere else. It is painful to watch, and even more painful to experience.

As I've worked with various organizations and individuals over the past ten years, the contrast between these scenarios has raised a host of questions in my mind: When does experience become a burden? Why are we so often at our best when we are newcomers, when logic tells us we might be underskilled, underqualified, clueless, and potentially dangerous? And, why do some people thrive in these conditions while others disengage or operate disastrously?

Curious, I determined to study these issues and understand the implications for managing talent inside organizations. After scouring the existing literature, I assembled a team to investigate how inexperienced people approach work differently than their experienced counterparts. Over the course of two years, we interviewed and surveyed more than one hundred managers asking them to contrast the two approaches and to assess the performance of each. We then surveyed more than two hundred professionals to better understand how they worked when they had experience and when they were brand-new to a task. Lastly, I conducted in-depth interviews with dozens of high-performing rookies. What we found was often surprising.

While experience provides a distinct advantage in a stable field—like the realms of bridge building, ballet, or concert piano performance—it can actually impede progress in an unstable or rapidly evolving arena. When the world is changing quickly, experience can become a curse, trapping us in old ways of doing and knowing, while inexperience can be a blessing, freeing us to improvise and adapt quickly to changing circumstances. In the new world of work, where knowledge is fleeting and innovation cycles spin so quickly that many professionals never face the same problem twice, rookies are often top performers, drawing on the power of learning rather than falling back on their accumulated knowledge. If rookies now have the home court advantage, where does that leave us veterans? Fortunately, even the most experienced professionals and organizations can tap into their rookie smarts. Those who choose to live and work on a learning curve will experience greater vitality in their careers and will be well positioned in the new game of work.

## THE NEW WORKSCAPE

The theme of a recent Human Capital Institute annual conference intrigued me: talent management in a VUCA world. While the term might sound like Klingon, VUCA is an acronym commonly used in the military to describe an environment of Volatility, Uncertainty, Complexity, and Ambiguity. These sorts of environments require heightened awareness and situational readiness because conditions can change quickly, mistakes are easy to make, and surprises lurk around every corner. It is the stuff of high-stakes military missions, suspense thrillers—or a typical day with toddlers!

The term VUCA closely approximates the reality under which many, if not most, leaders now operate—conditions that are far more complicated than when they began their careers. Some of this change is seen in how we talk about work: Work has become less of a place to go—a building to check into in the morning and out of in the evening—and more of a landscape to which we contribute. The shift is from a workplace to a "workscape" characterized by three fundamental shifts—vast, fast, and fleeting—that necessitate new ways of working and a different type of intelligence.

## Vast: An Abundance of Information

Everyone in the wired world can already feel it: We have a lot of data streaming at us. To understand the magnitude of this deluge, consider the astronomical rate at which humans generate new knowledge:

- The total amount of information in the world doubles approximately every eighteen months.

- New biological data doubles approximately every nine months.

- In the field of medicine, knowledge doubles every two to three years.

- More video is uploaded to YouTube in two months than the three major TV networks in the United States have created in the last sixty years.[1]

One might argue that there is too much "content," but there can be no doubt that the amount of content will continue to grow, and at an ever-increasing rate. The question then becomes how to manage this glut of information. How can we process this data, converting it into information, then knowledge and insight, and eventually wisdom? Mastering the data will prove futile. When there is too much to know, the only viable strategy is to know where and how to find information you need when you need it.

More and more people around the world are joining the knowledge

economy. By the year 2000, information workers composed the majority of the workforce (growing from 37 percent of workforce in 1950 to
59 percent in 2000).[2] This transition is impacting nearly every job in
every profession.

As work shifts from the physical to the knowledge realm, what are
the implications for mastery? While physical virtuosity requires practice, might brilliance in the world of ideas demand mental agility?
When there is too much to know, having the right question may be
more important than having a ready answer.

## Fast: Work Cycles Spinning Faster

As more tasks get automated and productivity tools abound, we can
finish our work faster, allowing us to complete more work in the same
amount of time. Improved tools supply the grease that allows the
wheels of work to spin at higher RPMs. Instead of closing the accounting books quarterly, we can now report monthly, daily, or in real time
on online dashboards—and we can work 24/7, so the business day
never ends. Work can begin to feel like a never-ending Spin class with
an overzealous instructor.

The "lean" mentality that optimizes customer outcomes while minimizing waste is compounding the effects of increased automation in
shortening the work cycle. With the lean approach, nothing extraneous
is kept on the manufacturing floor, and nothing extra is kept on the
intellectual shelf, either. New functionality is currently created, tested,
and iterated faster than past projects could have been planned. Work
cycles are spinning so fast that managers and professionals find themselves in uncharted territory daily. The implication for professional ex-
cellence is clear: When work spins faster, learning cycles must spin
faster, too.

## Fleeting: Disposable Knowledge

While truth may be eternal, knowledge is fleeting: not because we forget, but because as the pace of discovery quickens, what we learned yesterday may no longer be relevant today. In the 1970s it was estimated that the annual rate of knowledge relevance decay was over 10 percent across all industries. A more recent study in 2005 estimated that knowledge becomes obsolete at a rate of 15 percent per year. Another recent study reports that the annual rate of decay in high tech is 30 percent.[3] As technology permeates every industry, we are likely to see increased rates of decay in all arenas. We used to spend a week in a training class to learn to use a software program. Now, with new functionality being introduced via "the cloud" weekly (if not daily), we must constantly update our skill sets.

If the amount of information in science doubles every nine months and decays at 30 percent a year, how long does one's expertise last? Without constantly updating your knowledge base you could end up with as little as 15 percent of your technical knowledge relevant within just five years. However, when you can google just about anything, knowledge acquisition becomes more important than knowledge retention. We must learn to operate like our mobile devices, all data-processing power and negligible data storage.

Not only is the shelf life of information decreasing, but institutional memory has shrunk as well. Over the last couple of decades, there has been a migration of talent away from large organizations and toward self-employment. In his book *Free Agent Nation*, Daniel Pink reported that there are as many as 25 million free-agent workers in the United States alone. A recent survey by *Inc.* found that 20 percent of small businesses prefer hiring independent contractors to full-time employees.[4]

Like our electronics' reliance on cloud storage, many companies are turning to crowdsourcing to solve complex problems. In this fluid staffing model, project teams come together like flash mobs of talent. They assemble, learn, contribute, and then disband. This model of work demands heightened levels of collaboration and learning. To contribute, individuals must swiftly ramp up their understanding of the situation, the problem, the players, the options, etc. They must then learn how to quickly assemble expertise, without the benefit of long-term relationships. When the flash of collective brilliance ends, they must let go and move on to the next rapid-learning, rapid-contribution cycle. Business strategist Jennifer Sertl has observed, "Our role as conduit is more vital than our role as source in this knowledge economy."[5] Much like I found with my research for the book *Multipliers*, the critical skill of this century is not what you hold in your head, but your ability to tap into and access what other people know. The best leaders and the fastest learners know how to harness collective intelligence.

Today we work in an environment where information is vast, fast, and fleeting. While this technology-based reality has utopian overtones, many would claim a more dystopian existence. Those trying to cling to the mastery model in today's world will surely struggle. Many will feel overwhelmed and exhausted as work expands like a gas taking up all available space. The overwhelmed may yearn for the day when work was merely a place we went and then left, whether at the end of the day or the end of a career. They may take a break, lingering too long on a learning plateau, and get left behind.

Others will cling to their amassed body of knowledge and expertise, trying to hold their own in a culture that no longer values their brilliance. When their ephemeral knowledge becomes obsolete, they will be left faking a mastery they no longer possess. As the great physicist Stephen Hawking said, "The greatest enemy of knowledge is not ignorance, it is the illusion of knowledge."

## GETTING ON THE CURVE

For experienced, midcareer professionals exhausted from climbing a career ladder or just stuck on a learning plateau feeling bored, *Rookie*

*Smarts* offers renewal. For those who wonder if younger upstarts will upend their careers (or their whole company), *Rookie Smarts* offers a competitive edge. If you are stuck climbing your way up a corporation, it might be time to get off the career ladder and get onto a learning curve. The ladder leads to stagnation while the curve promises renewal, both for you and the corporation.

This book is about living and working perpetually on a learning curve. It is about why we do our best work when we are new to something, striving up that steep ascent. As the pace of work quickens, you don't need to move into the slow lane or disengage; you can speed up along with it. As Jonathon Colman, the leader of the content strategy team at Facebook, blogged as he started his new role, "I'm energized. And since life doesn't slow down, I'm going to speed up."[6] You can even take the benefit of your experience with you.

*Rookie Smarts* is also for leaders of organizations who must ensure their workforce remains vital and competitive. It is for corporate talent management, learning, and coaching professionals who must ensure the talent inside their organizations is engaged and vibrant. Wise leaders leverage the rookie smarts on their team, not out of an obligation to "enlightened" management practices, but because of the value rookies bring to the table: new practices, expert networks, agility, tireless improvisation, and a greater sense of ownership. Managers who ignore this pool of talent, which is often exiled to the outer edges of the organization, may find themselves and their teams left behind.

In Silicon Valley, an epicenter of technology innovation and birthplace of many new companies, cafés brim with talk of the newest, hottest company to work for. But, when a company is white-hot, why can you almost be sure that eighteen to twenty-four months later it will be stone-cold? At the end of 2011, game maker Zynga had just offered an IPO and was on fire. By the spring of 2013, they were desperately fanning the flickering flames of their former success.[7] What happened? Is it hubris? Complacency? Or a sluggishness and bureaucracy that come with size? Surely some combination of these forces is at play. As companies mature and grow, many become caught in the trappings of success and lose their rookie smarts—the twin powers of naïveté and chutzpah that germinated their initial success. Large organizations, even more than growing start-ups, need an injection of rookie thinking to maintain their competitive edge. Perhaps the most important quality leaders can infuse into their organizations is a youthful metabolism and the ability to learn. Rookie smarts provide that metabolic boost to your workforce.

The promise of this book is simple: You can be the perpetual rookie. You can renew your mind and your skills and combine your hard-won wisdom and experience with the naïve brilliance and vitality of a rookie. You can live on the steep side of the learning curve, perform at your best, and create an organization or a career that never stops growing.

I still have that first T-shirt I created for Oracle University, but its message (Knowledge Is Power) is a relic of the times. It is no longer sufficient to simply *know*. Information flows in too many directions, knowledge is fleeting, and power can be perilous. The vast majority of us now work in environments where the ability to learn is more critical than what we know and where the most valuable currency is influence, not power. And so we need a new motto, one that recognizes these new realities.

Shifting into rookie mode once again, I summoned my naïveté and phoned the Stanford University switchboard. This time, I connected with Father Greg Haake, Ph.D. candidate in the language department (and a Holy Cross Father from the University of Notre Dame), who thoughtfully translated my new motto: *Quaerere Eruditionem*.[8] That's the new rallying cry for leaders who safeguard and strengthen the intellectual vitality of their workforce: "Seek Learning."

# PART ONE

# ROOKIE SMARTS: LIVING ON THE LEARNING CURVE

CHAPTER 1

# THE RISE OF
# THE ROOKIE

The ark was built by amateurs,
but professionals built the *Titanic*.

— RICHARD NEEDHAM

During the 1970s, the National Basketball Association (NBA) experienced what Alon Marcovici called "a decade of parity."[1] In this era, when the players' shorts were still short, no one team dominated. It was anyone's game. Although well respected, in 1979 the Los Angeles Lakers hadn't clinched an NBA title in eight years. At the time, the phenomenally talented seven-foot-two center Kareem Abdul-Jabbar, considered by many to be the greatest basketball player of all time, anchored the team. Despite his wicked skyhook, Abdul-Jabbar hadn't yet led the team to a victory in the finals. It was in this situation that the Lakers secured first-pick rights for the 1979 NBA draft.

Enter Earvin "Magic" Johnson II, the six-foot-eight point guard from Michigan. Johnson had played two years for Michigan State, where he averaged 17.1 points, 7.6 rebounds, and 7.9 assists per game and earned the nickname "Magic" for his ability to make every team better.[2] For Magic, life was "a joyous journey," and the opportunity to play on the Lakers and learn from Abdul-Jabbar was a thrill.[3]

While the sports world called him Magic, his teammates called him "young buck" for his childlike enthusiasm. When Magic spontaneously hugged Abdul-Jabbar after Abdul-Jabbar's last-minute, game-winning skyhook, the big guy remarked, "Take it easy, kid, we've got 81 more of these to play."[4] After thirteen games, head coach Jack McKinney sustained a serious head injury while cycling, so assistant coach Paul Westhead (who had more experience as a Shakespearean scholar than an NBA head coach) took over. Sixty-eight games later, the Lakers made it to the finals, going up against the Philadelphia 76ers.

The Sixers brought a veteran lineup led by the phenomenal Julius Erving. The Lakers took a 3–2 lead in the series with strong performances from Abdul-Jabbar and company. But the team faced another distressing setback in game five when Abdul-Jabbar, who was averaging 33 points a game, sustained an ankle injury that would prevent him from traveling to Philadelphia for game six.

The Lakers would surely get beat without their star center, so said the pundits. Experienced advisers to the new head coach suggested he send the "B team" to Philly and save his best players for the seventh game back in Los Angeles. Instead, Westhead decided to play Magic at center in game six. Coach Westhead gave Magic the news. Magic assured his team that he would not just play center, he would *be* Kareem. The team wasn't convinced. He was good, but he was a bit unpredictable, and he was just a rookie.

Boarding the flight to Philadelphia, the players were quiet as they passed Kareem's noticeably vacant seat, 1A. Even when Kareem didn't travel, no one dared sit there. But that day, Magic did. According to the *NBA Encyclopedia*, "Magic plopped himself down in the first-class seat always set aside for Abdul-Jabbar. Then he went through Abdul-Jabbar's normal routine, stretching out in the seat and pulling a blanket over his head. This done, Magic looked back at his coach and winked. 'Never fear,' he told his teammates."[5] Magic intended to carry the team, but not as Earvin Johnson; he was going into game six as Kareem Abdul-Jabbar.

The rumor mill spun at the outlandish idea that Magic might play center. Before the game, a reporter asked the rookie about his readiness to guard Erving and if he would play center. Magic responded, "I'm going to do my best wherever I play. [This season's] been a learning experience. But I enjoy challenges. And it's a challenge tonight to see what I can do."[6]

ESPN's Rick Weinberger described what happened when the rookie point guard lined up at center in Kareem's spot: "Sixers center Caldwell Jones turns to Magic and said, 'You gotta be joking, right?' "[7] Magic was unsure which foot to put into the tip-off circle, but he was grinning nonetheless. He lost the tip-off, but then took control of the game as he transformed into a smaller version of Abdul-Jabbar.[8] Playing center, forward, and guard, Johnson scored 42 points, and made 15 rebounds, 7 assists, and 3 steals. He scored 9 points in the final 2:22 and led the team to a 123–107 victory, winning the NBA finals for the Lakers and receiving the NBA finals Most Valuable Player award.[9] Many consider that game on May 16, 1980, the greatest rookie performance in NBA history. The stronger team was beat by a flash of rookie brilliance.

But, was this magnificent performance an isolated incident, a fluke? When a rookie performs exceptionally, is it magic? Is it luck? Or is it something more ordinary, more accessible?

Rookies are more capable than we might expect. We often see it on the athletic field, but it also plays out in the halls of the workplace. Is it possible that the rookies inside our companies might be our most valuable players? Research conducted by my team suggests that, in many cases, inexperience can work to your advantage. It can spark a dazzling performance, and help you compete with, if not surpass, even the most talented, experienced players. Not only does inexperience confer an advantage, but also it is desperately needed in today's rapidly evolving world of work.

## A QUESTION OF EXPERIENCE

To understand the promise of inexperience, we must first recognize the lure of experience.

Experience is the steady hands of a master craftsman, the accumulated knowledge, both broad and deep, of a venerated professor, or the wisdom of a guru atop a mountain dispensing pearls of wisdom gathered throughout a lifetime. We admire the master teacher who can tame an undisciplined classroom with a single stare. We idealize the image of an organization guided by a seasoned executive, surrounded by expert technicians and a skillful staff. We gravitate toward experts because they represent safety, comfort, and certainty.

It's not merely wishful thinking, either. As we gain experience, we accumulate a repertoire of tools, techniques, and resources that can be repeatedly leveraged. It just makes sense that a veteran sales executive with a well-worn Rolodex of contacts will outperform the new sales associate starting from scratch.

The prevailing view also holds that experienced people have better intuition—the ability to understand new problems immediately, without the need for conscious reasoning. Intuition guides a veteran firefighter to take the north stairs rather than the south stairs. He isn't sure why, but it feels right, and it later proves right. Several researchers have shown a link between experience and greater powers of intuition. One study concluded that intuition is the brain unconsciously drawing on past experiences and external clues to make decisions. Another study found that participants who possessed expertise in a particular task domain performed as well, on average, using their intuition as they did when relying on analytical means.[10] In short, experts have better intuition, because they have amassed more data points on which to base gut feelings.

We generally assume that it takes years to achieve this kind of mastery. Psychologist Anders Ericsson's oft-cited study (referred to as the 10,000 hour rule) shows that in professions such as music, medicine, and sports, mastery is achieved after roughly 10,000 hours of deliberate practice.[11] This equates to roughly five to ten years of relevant work experience. Coincidentally, to the frustration of many young professionals and career changers, five to ten years is the typical minimum experience level required just to be considered for many jobs.

For years, we've elevated experience to a position of primacy. We idolize the idea of someone at the top of his game or the peak of her career. The master is the manager, the mentor, and the teacher, who, having climbed the mountain, will guide others to the top.

But this is not the whole story. Research offers some intriguing insights into the genius locked inside decidedly average nonexperts. Indeed, studies have shown that a group of rookies can outperform individual experts. Behavioral scientists at the University of Chicago showed that expert pathologists poorly predict a cancer patient's survival time based on viewing a biopsy slide; yet when the decision of a group of less experienced individuals is aggregated, the readings are much more accurate than the predictions of individual experts.[12]

It has become clear that most jobs don't require anywhere near ten thousand hours of practice to attain mastery. Business author Josh Kaufman claims most career skills require only twenty hours of practice to master. And several studies show that practice accounts for only 30 percent of the variance in ability among those considered experts.[13] Ericsson's famous study focused primarily on violinists, surgeons, and athletes, professions requiring mastery of precise physical motions. A large workplace study conducted by the European Union in 2007 showed that the ability to mobilize the skills and competencies of the people around us has a bigger impact on our performance than does the amount of experience we have.[14] Most professions today do not require this sort of physical precision. Have we too quickly assumed that the degree of experience necessary to achieve virtuosity in physical and technical pursuits is also required in the knowledge realm?

Finally, companies are finding that the amount of previous experience an employee has is not correlated with job success. For example, when the U.S. call and customer care center for Xerox Services implemented personality testing and cognitive skills assessments in 2010, they found that a customer service person's previous experience had no bearing on either their productivity or their retention.[15] A study from the IE Business School in Spain and the NEOMA Business School in France found that CEOs in S&P 500 corporations with former experience as a CEO performed worse than those without such experience.[16]

The upside of experience may be less pronounced than once imagined, while its downside may be even steeper. What we know might actually mask what we don't know and impede our ability to learn and perform. All too often, the person doling out the advice is the one least likely to learn.

## THE LEARNED AND THE LEARNERS

January is hardly the prime time for a retreat in Seattle. But the leaders of the sales and marketing readiness group for this global company are holed up at a winter lodge for an off-site team workshop and strategy session. The goal of the off-site is to refocus the group's priorities for the next six months. It is this group's responsibility to ensure that sales and marketing staff thoroughly understand and can appropriately sell a new product by the time it is released. Commensurate with their importance, this group is well funded, with a multimillion-dollar budget and a staff of 140 people.

Chris,[17] the group's general manager, is a bold thinker who has been tasked with leading an important change: General management wants the sales and marketing teams to start thinking about the company's products in terms of lines-of-business (that is, which products would be useful for particular types of businesses) instead of clusters of functionality (what the products do). Chris's management team consists of veteran training professionals with a massive wealth of experience. But Chris has also recruited two new players, Sara and Angela—both of whom are experienced and successful sales leaders but complete novices in the employee-training arena.

The team has isolated themselves in this winter lodge to plan key initiatives for the second half of the fiscal year. During one exercise, each member of the management team is asked to craft a "challenge question"—a concrete objective that will focus the team's energy on quick, sustainable wins. Sara, just starting her third week on the job, suddenly blurts, "This is going to be really hard. I'm just getting started and I have no idea what I'm doing." Chris tells her this just might be her superpower.

Each person works independently and then shares their challenge question with the group. The veterans go first. Carina begins by explaining that she ignored Chris's list of priorities and came up with her own: She figures she has a better handle on what needs to be done. Another member of the team, Will, lays out an ambitious challenge, which is quickly countered by another veteran on the team: "Isn't this what we've been trying to do for years?" Will quickly explains that his team will be more inspired by his lofty vision than by a series of smaller, tactical challenges. Carlos articulates a challenge to introduce a new online program. When asked how he would engage the executives inside the company, Carlos brushes it off, declaring, "I've learned to keep the executives out of things. I usually just ask for their opinion on issues that don't really matter. I know what needs to be done." Each of these veterans has missed the mark. Each one has relied on their own expertise to craft a plan of attack independent of their colleagues.

Next come the rookies. The newest member of the group, Sara, nails it. Her challenge question aligns with Chris's priorities and orchestrates a much-needed small win that will garner attention and support from internal clients. The rest of the team is stunned. Someone comments,

"Wow, pretty good for a newbie." Next comes another rookie, Angela. Her challenge is pretty good, but it's not yet great. During the next work session, while the others work independently, Angela seeks guidance from the workshop leader. She listens carefully, takes notes, and then goes back to work. In round two, Angela nails it, too, while the veterans are still struggling. Will, who is prone to the lofty, aspirational approach, has made little progress, so the group jumps in to help him. As the challenge statement begins coming together and the excitement is building, he abruptly shuts down the conversation, saying, "I'm not really comfortable with this approach. I need to go away and think about it." The team's energy dissipates with an almost audible hiss. At the end of the day, Chris remarks, "Wow, it seems like the more you know the harder this is."

Does this scenario feel all too familiar?

Sometimes the more you know, the less you learn. Too often expertise can blind us to new possibilities and put us on the defensive. When we feel we already know what needs to be done, we are unwilling to coordinate our efforts with others or to accept outside input. Too often we play solo when we should be gathering the support of a broader team. Too often we drown out new voices with cynicism, blunt criticism, and explanations for why their ideas won't fly. Perhaps that's why so many of these off-site exercises feel routine and even disheartening. It might be why so many initiatives run out of steam. And it might explain why so many energized newcomers get frustrated and move on to more dynamic environments.

## THE RESEARCH ON ROOKIES

I'm not suggesting that experience has no place in the workplace, but I am suggesting that the value of inexperience may be a largely untapped resource. I'm also not suggesting that sheer ignorance is better than studied intelligence. I am suggesting, however, that there is something truly valuable and different in how rookies think and work to make up for their knowledge and skill gaps—a mindset and a way of behaving that more experienced workers might do well to learn.

To get some answers, my team of researchers studied almost four hundred workplace scenarios, comparing how rookies versus veterans tackled work assignments. We defined a rookie as someone who had never done that type of work and a veteran as someone who had previous experience with that type of work—both regardless of their age. We analyzed the data by performance level, looking for the key differentiators between how rookies and veterans approach their work and the situations under which they excelled (see Appendix A for a full description of the research process). Our work yielded four major surprising observations.

**First, rookies are strong performers.** Our research, conducted across a broad array of industries, gave veterans a slight advantage, but when we isolated the results specifically on knowledge industries, we found that rookies performed at slightly higher levels than veterans.[18] In particular, rookies consistently outperformed veterans in innovation and time-to-completion.

**Second, rookies have a unique success profile.** Our data showed that rookies and veterans take very different paths to success, but that they both fail in much the same way. The highest-performing rookies sought out expertise in others, connected the dots, experimented, learned from mistakes, and focused on making incremental gains. Conversely, the top-performing veterans had a distinct savvy of their own: They were fast to act, marshaled resources, found simple solutions, persisted along a path, and focused on solving the right problem. While the profile for the top performers looked different, the profiles of bottom performers looked remarkably similar. Regardless of their level of experience, bottom performers operated with a sense of invincibility and acted as if they had something to prove or a reputation to defend. The low performers shared a set of blinders while the top performers had distinctly different approaches to success.

**Third, rookies aren't always what they seem.** As you might have guessed, our research confirms that rookies listen more, are more likely to ask for help, believe they have a lot more to learn, and learn faster.[19] Our research also found that veterans are more politically savvy, use more intuition, and are more likely to default to past behavior.[20] You might also expect inexperienced rookies to be idea-wielding risk takers and veterans to be cautious, incremental workers. We found just the opposite. Veterans bring more ideas and seek greater clarity while rookies work more cautiously, biting off smaller pieces and checking in frequently with stakeholders to minimize risk. We also found that:

- Rookies have significantly higher levels of self-awareness than veterans, although we often assume they are clueless.

- Rookies seek out expertise more than veterans despite having weaker networks. And, when they do reach out, it is to a surprisingly high number of people.

- Rookies tend to deliver more timely solutions despite having a steeper learning curve.

- Rookies are more attuned to politics (although veterans possess greater political savvy).[21]

Rookies don't operate with a false bravado as much as they are driven by desperation. Their coarseness makes them porous and open to new information; they have a productive anxiety that drives them to establish themselves as players and peers. By virtue of their naïveté, rookies are unencumbered by preconceived views or deeply engrained assumptions.

**Finally, experience creates dangerous blind spots.** Our analysis identified a number of areas where experience created blinders that narrowed the veteran's focus and kept him stuck in a rut. With experience come habits, and once we form a habit our brain stops working.[22] Researchers at Duke University found that 45 percent of everyday behaviors tend to be habitual, repeated in the same location almost every day.[23] As we build (and come to rely on) experience, we also become desensitized to the world around us. Previously acquired knowledge can prevent us from seeing new developments, and as we build expertise, we often stop seeking outside perspectives. In his book *To Sell Is Human*, Daniel Pink describes the inverse relationship between power and what he refers to as perspective taking. Power or status decreases the likelihood of someone trying to understand another person's perspective. The less power we have, and the fewer resources available to us, the more attuned we become to the people and events around us. As we climb to the top of the learning curve, we also tend to stop seeking feedback. This tendency underlies Malcolm Gladwell's conclusion that planes are safer when the least experienced person is flying: the junior pilot will be open to feedback from the second, more senior, pilot if something goes wrong.[24] We also stop exploring new domains and paths. With experience inevitably come bad experiences. While these quickly scar over, we often dismiss ideas and ventures that might reopen these wounds.

## THE ROOKIE SMART MINDSET

We live and work in a culture obsessed with youth. Who doesn't want to look young and feel young? But real vibrancy comes from *thinking* young. Fortunately, no matter how old you are, no matter your level of experience, you can once again begin to think with the acuity and agility of a newcomer and generate new learning every day. You can start drinking from an intellectual fountain of youth by putting yourself into the rookie smarts mindset, which, our research shows, is characterized by four distinct modes, which I refer to as: *Backpacker*, *Hunter-Gatherer*, *Firewalker*, and *Pioneer*. Each mode is a component of how we tend to think and act when we are in a rookie assignment—doing something for the first time. We'll examine each of these modes in more detail.

**1. Backpacker**—Because rookies typically have nothing to weigh them down and nothing to lose, they are open to new possibilities, explore new terrain, and act wholeheartedly. Instead of getting stuck in yesterday's best practices, rookies find new practices to fit new realities. This unencumbered and hopeful mindset allows them the freedom to wander and explore new terrain. Rookies operate like *Backpackers*.

Richard Branson, founder and CEO of Virgin Group, captured this mindset when he said, "We have started hundreds of new businesses, in most cases knowing next to nothing about the industries we were moving into. And our inexperience has always allowed us to focus on how we can do things differently, rather than on the reasons we cannot. This gives us freedoms that other businesses don't have, constrained as they are by past lessons and industry history."[25]

In contrast, veterans can too easily act as *Caretakers*. Having accumulated a track record, a trophy case, and the spoils of success, they maintain the status quo.

**2. Hunter-Gatherer**—Because rookies are disoriented and lack know-how, they are forced into a sense-making mode that causes them to pay close attention to their environment and reach out to others for guidance. They scan the area, seek out experts, and return with ideas and resources to address the challenges they face. Instead of bringing one person's expertise to bear on a problem, rookies marshal a network of experts, garnering five times the expertise on average.[26] Alert and seeking, these rookies function much like *Hunter-Gatherers*.

An IT manager at a large financial services firm exemplified the Hunter-Gatherer mode. When Jeff was abruptly put in charge of vendor management, he had no experience and felt completely out of his element. He systematically reached out to twenty-five people with deep experience in purchasing and vendor management. Within a few weeks he had acquired a set of tools and knew the right questions to ask.

In contrast, because veterans are often confident that they understand their environment, they don't seek new information. They act like *Local Guides* who stay close to what they know, doling out advice rather than seeking out learning.

**3. Firewalker**—Because rookies lack situational confidence, they operate cautiously but quickly in an effort to close a knowledge or a performance gap. They take small, calculated steps, move fast, and seek feedback to stay on track. Because they operate in fast cycles, they build agile, lean organizations. The mindset is cautious and quick. They move like *Firewalkers*.

A former executive, now venture capitalist, described how he developed this mindset: "I was always put in jobs where I was in over my head, so I never had experience to draw on. The knowledge gap forced me to listen to people, let them teach me, and gather data as fast as I could. But I had this paranoia that I had to show leadership immediately, which forced me to quickly turn these insights into a plan."

In contrast, because veterans feel capable they tend to operate like *Marathoners*, running the long race at a steady pace. They readily revert to autopilot and either traipse along or take big, careless steps without consulting critical stakeholders along the way. It is a mindset of staying steady, pacing oneself, and plodding along, assuming one is still doing a great job.

**4. Pioneer**—Because rookies are traversing uncharted and often uncomfortable territory, they improvise and work tirelessly to provide for basic needs. They face a paucity of resources, so they keep things simple and focus on meeting core needs. Their work pushes boundaries as they take ownership and create value for others who follow in their footsteps. The mindset is one of hunger and relentless pursuit. They forge ahead like *Pioneers*.

Sara Blakely's journey to build Spanx from $5,000 in savings to a billion dollars of market value in just twelve years reflects this pioneer mentality. Sara prototyped the product herself and then bypassed the established direct distribution channels, all the while operating on a lean, scrappy infrastructure until the brand was firmly established.

In contrast, because veterans are well established and have access to more resources, they tend to behave like *Settlers*, and put down roots. Having already established themselves, they stay in their comfort zone, follow protocols, and rely on what's available. The mindset is one of comfort and consumption.

The following chart summarizes the four rookie smart modes and mindsets (our state of mind in this mode). This is contrasted with the "veteran comfort zone," or the way we tend to think and act when we have experience.

## ROOKIE SMARTS: MODES AND MINDSETS

| ROOKIE SMARTS | | VETERAN COMFORT ZONE | |
|---|---|---|---|
| **Mode** | **Mindset** | **Mode** | **Mindset** |
| Backpacker | Unencumbered | Caretaker | Protecting |
| Hunter-Gatherer | Alert and Seeking | Local Guide | Advising |
| Firewalker | Cautious and Quick | Marathoner | Steady Pace |
| Pioneer | Hungry and Relentless | Settler | Comfortable and Consuming |

These four rookie and veteran modes are not an attempt to categorize *people*; they illustrate patterns of *behavior*. They are modes we can slip into and roles we tend to assume. For example, if you read my bio, you might conclude I am a leadership expert. I have significant corporate leadership experience and have studied leaders from all around the world. People frequently seek my counsel on leadership and management issues. When I begin to think of myself as a leadership expert, I start dispensing my ideas and doling out advice—the hallmarks of a local. I can easily become a "talking head." But when I choose to see myself, more accurately, as a student of leadership, I tend to have an open mind; I am driven to research, reach out, learn, and then bring this insight back to my colleagues and clients. With a student mindset I operate in Hunter-Gatherer mode, creating greater value for others and for myself.

Rookie smarts isn't defined by age or by experience level; it is a state of mind. We shift into and out of these modes based on our situation, mindsets, and assumptions. A rookie assignment, where we face a large, uncomfortable knowledge or skill gap, will pull us toward operating in one or all of the rookie smart modes. When we are capable and often feel comfortable with our own level of competence, however, we tend to fall back into the veteran comfort zone, even when we have better intentions. Without exerting some conscious effort to counter this natural pull, the blessing of experience can become a burden—a millstone about our necks. As we travel mindlessly down the familiar path carved out by our own often hard-won expertise, we become stuck in the ruts of our past while the novice is out exploring new mountains.

Escaping this force requires deliberate thought and action. While it might be easier to operate with the hopeful, unencumbered outlook of a backpacker when we are brand-new, even those of us with years of experience can work to shed old, possibly erroneous (or even dangerous), assumptions. The role we play at any given moment in time isn't a function of our circumstances; it is a function of our choices.

Let's take a look at how one veteran business leader, Gina Warren, vice president of diversity at Nike, used rookie smarts to unleash a wave of rookie thinking across a global athletic powerhouse.

## The New Crew

Mark Parker, Nike's president and CEO, was gathering the company's top fifty executives for a corporate strategic review. Knowing that their innovative culture was key to their ability to continue inspiring and

engaging consumers around the world, they set aside the first day of
the meeting to discuss how they could continue to leverage the Nike
culture to gain competitive advantage. Gina Warren was chosen to
define and lead this "culture" day. At the time Gina was a seven-year
Nike veteran and an experienced corporate manager in the second
half of her career, but she was just six months new to this senior leadership role.

Gina came up with a framework to guide the discussion: They
would examine the past, present, and future of the Nike culture. Ideas
for the past and present came easily to Gina and the colleague she was
teaming with, yet Gina struggled to wrap her mind around the culture
as it moved into the future. She realized that if she wanted to define
the future of the culture, she would need the help of some of those who
would create that future. She called Delano Hunter, a recent college
graduate, who was working in the diversity and inclusion team at Nike,
and asked him to gather a few friends who could give her some insights.
She would buy lunch.

Gathered for lunch in a conference room on Nike's campus, Gina
confessed, "Guys, I'm stuck." The newcomers began tossing out ideas
for her to consider. She was so delighted with their fresh insights and
natural ingenuity that she asked them if they would lead the "future"
section of the day with the execs. They readily accepted the challenge,
and soon more sparks were flying. Gina was even more impressed now
and, somewhat impulsively, she offered to let the group lead the entire
day's event.

Soon, the part of Gina's mind that worries caught up and she began
to wonder if these newcomers understood the significance of the responsibility they had just been given. She interjected, clarifying the
objective and adding some gravitas: This emergent group would be responsible for a full day with the company's fifty top executives. The
executives' time was extraordinarily valuable, she explained, and there
were only three weeks to prepare. These seven new hires quickly pulled
out their smartphones to coordinate a time for their first meeting.

When Gina reached for her phone to do the same, a young man named Jordan sitting next to her put his hand on her arm and said, "It's okay, you don't need to be there. We've got this." Gina was startled and perhaps a tad anxious, but responded, "Okay, I get it, but keep me updated and plan time for rehearsal."

Then Gina let the team run. While they worked, she kept a careful watch and reassured her bosses that the team had the event well in hand. Two and a half weeks later, as the team rehearsed, her hopes were confirmed; overwhelmed, Gina began to cry. The veteran leader reflected, "I was just so blown away. I had no idea they could design such a premium experience in just three weeks."

The next day the group of seven introduced themselves to the fifty executives who had gathered in the conference center. They explained their plan without fear as they thanked the executives for the opportunity to lead: "We created the day to give you choices as a leader, because we think a culture is created by the everyday choices people make." For the first exercise, the executives would move between three breakout rooms, each with a different program, where they would experience the past, present, and future of Nike's culture. Next up was mentoring—reverse mentoring where the executives could learn from the employees. The executives would rotate, speed-dating style, between tables where two employees sat, but the organizers had a hard time getting the executives to move on because they were enthralled with the conversations. The afternoon was spent exploring the assumptions and choices that would make Nike's culture part of their strategic offense.

The young leaders' efforts resulted in a thoughtful, insightful experience for the senior executives. But this was just the beginning. This informal group was dubbed the "New Crew." As a result of the success of this inaugural crew, the process has been formalized across Nike's major divisions. The New Crew is now three hundred members strong, with top-performing employees contributing and then rotating out of the group after one year, making way for other fresh talent. New Crew members often give highly visible presentations inside the company, and executives are eager to get them into their division. The New Crew is more than a specific set of people; each New Crew member is evidence that this type of talent exists all across the organization. Senior leaders just need to continue looking inside their own teams to find it. In a creative culture like Nike, leaders know that great ideas can come from anywhere, and the New Crew is just one way that Nike taps into new, creative thinking.

Gina believes that the New Crew is special but not rare. If you look inside your organization, what new talent might you find? The genius of the rookie is special, but it's not hard to find. We just have to look for it.

It isn't hard to see why rookie smarts is a natural fit and critical intelligence for the new fast, furious workscape in which most companies operate. Given their drive to contribute and hunger to learn, where might rookies shine as your most valuable players? In which kinds of competitive landscapes could rookie smarts make a difference?

## THE RIGHT TERRAIN

While rookies can play an important role, they need to be channeled and directed toward the right kinds of terrains for top performance.

**New Frontiers.** New business ventures, no surprise, are naturally ripe for rookie smarts. Tomasz Tunguz, a partner at Redpoint Ventures, describes the nature of start-ups: "[T]here are no templates or stencils or best practices. . . . In such circumstances, the best expeditionary force keeps open minds about the way forward. They learn from each other and the market. The first step to learning is accepting we don't know everything."[27] The market is replete with examples of successful new companies built by people with no industry experience: Amazon, eBay, Netflix, Twitter. But the list isn't limited to technology start-ups; it includes Cirque du Soleil, Mountain Equipment Co-op, and Zipcar.[28] In a study of social media start-up firms, researchers found that ventures with experienced entrepreneurs on board accumulated about $66,000 less in revenue and nearly $100,000 less capital than those led by novices.[29] Rookie smarts also deliver punch in the broader innovation arena. According to the authors of *Innovator's DNA*, Clayton Christensen, Jeff Dyer, and Hal Gregersen, the best innovators demonstrate the following skills: questioning, observing, networking, and experimenting.[30] Rookies are naturals at this.

**Short Cycles.** Experts tend to outperform novices in the long game because they can recognize patterns and project into the future, but rookies are particularly well suited to deal with the immediate and the ephemeral. For example, one of the key differences between chess masters and novices is their strategic horizon. Chess masters are able to think several moves ahead while novices focus on the next one or two moves. However, in a short-cycle environment, the rules can change before you get to the second move. In this dynamic workscape, best practices don't apply, and the best conceived plans typically don't survive contact with the changing reality. As heavyweight champion Mike Tyson vividly said, "Everybody has a plan until they get punched in the mouth." When the world is changing fast, you want someone with rookie smarts in the ring. Having a rookie in your corner can offer more than just a competitive advantage; it can be a matter of survival.

**Multiple Answers.** In our interviews with more than fifty managers, the work that was most cited as the best use of rookie talent was "creative in nature, with multiple possible solutions and jobs that were more fluid." This is work where the answer "D: All of the above" is acceptable. Such work types include writing a proposal or posting a blog, building an effective lesson plan, writing software, and perhaps even prescribing a treatment course for a disease. This may be one of the reasons Mark Zuckerberg favored hiring new engineers rather than programming veterans as he built Facebook. Zuckerberg told Sam

Teller of the *Harvard Crimson*, "The job lends itself to people with raw intelligence rather than industry experience."[31]

**Too Big to Know.** In complex systems, where there is too much information for any one person to process or any one expert to know, the organizations that win will be those that tap into the greatest number of brains.[32] As journalist James Surowiecki argues in *The Wisdom of Crowds*, there are a number of situations in which the aggregation of information in a group results in decisions that are better than any one individual could have made. This is particularly the case with work involving cognition (thinking and information processing), coordination of activity, and cooperation (without central control or compliance).[33] If the challenge is too big for any one expert, the situation is ripe for a rookie operating in Hunter-Gatherer mode. Complex problems require structured, collaborative thinking, and not just random talk. Someone operating with rookie smarts provides much-needed orchestration— framing the issues, posing the question, searching for truth, and then bringing the newfound intelligence back to bear on the problem.

**Seasoned Executives; Fresh Domains.** One might assume that the quintessential rookie is a young, fresh entrant to the workforce, but we found the opposite to be true. The highest-performing rookies were most often in executive roles. These were smart, seasoned executives who had made internal or external career moves and were now leading in a new domain—a new business segment, an unfamiliar industry, or a function in which they had no experience. They brought the best of both worlds: a veteran's wisdom of experience, leadership skills, and organizational savvy and a rookie's tendency to ask naïve questions, learn quickly, build new networks, and unlock new possibilities.

But, while there is ideal terrain for rookie smarts, there is also a danger zone—free climbs up sheer cliffs or runs down double-black-diamond slopes. Without good leadership and direction, rookies can be dangerous to themselves and others. You probably wouldn't want a first-time skydiver as your tandem-jump instructor, or a rookie heart surgeon, or a beginner dentist drilling in your mouth. And you might not want a rookie installing new software on the production servers in your data center.

When a single mistake can be game ending, playing a rookie can be risky. This is where mistakes can cause irreparable damage to your organization, be truly business ending, or career ending (for themselves or you!), or life devastating. The challenge of parenting offers a useful illustration, because children encounter brand-new challenges every day. There are the obvious firsts: first steps, first words, first day of school. But the "firsts" continue through the teenage years as they navigate the complexity of school, relationships, and responsibility. Then, at perhaps the most chaotic stage of their development, we hand them the keys to the car, opening up a plethora of new possibilities and heightened risk. Most parents wrestle with how much space to give their children. We want them to learn, but we don't want them to crash and burn. As a parent, I've learned to ask myself a simple question: Is this a mistake they can recover from? If so, it's good rookie terrain—step back and let them learn from experience. If not, hover close and offer very specific guidance or coaching. If it is truly one-strike-and-you're-out (for example, drinking and driving), a wise parent might pull them out of the game.

Or, consider the case of Asiana flight 214, which crash-landed at San Francisco International Airport on July 6, 2013, killing three teenagers and critically injuring twelve other passengers. The primary pilot was receiving his initial operating experience and had only forty-three hours in the captain's seat on a Boeing 777 aircraft. This was his first time landing a 777 at SFO. Inexperienced with the plane's auto-throttle system, he set the throttles to idle, causing the aircraft to lose speed. Sitting in the copilot seat and acting in the dual role of instructor captain and pilot-in-command was the secondary pilot, who had 3,220 hours of flying experience on the 777, but this was his first flight as an instructor.[34] The secondary/instructor pilot caught the error but failed to respond quickly enough to abort the landing. Having lost sufficient speed, the plane landed short of the runway, which is mere feet from the bay waters, and the tail caught on the seawall. A rookie pilot, a rookie instructor pilot, and their first time working together set the stage for disaster. When it is a matter of life or death, rookies require a safety net (see Chapter 8 for more on this).

## RELIGHTING THE FIRE

If our rookie smarts flame has gone out, can it be rekindled? Or do some people just have it? The answer is much like the answer to the perennial question "Are great leaders born or made?" or its close cousin, "Are great athletes born or made?" The answer is both. Like athletes, some working professionals possess a *natural* advantage and inherently operate with rookie smarts (perhaps they were born with them or they learned them at their mother's knee); others without such an endowment will need to work harder.

But working harder isn't the only approach to increase learning. We can manufacture a *situational* advantage by placing ourselves into an unfamiliar, even uncomfortable, situation where we are forced to think and act like a rookie. Either way—through practice or by putting ourselves in a new situation—rookie smarts can be developed. Each of these mindsets is learnable and can be cultivated. It is best done with coaching—either with a professional coach, a thoughtful colleague, a good friend, or with deliberate self-evaluation. It is a matter of intention and work. True, there are some who will never learn. But for the most part, those who can't learn are simply those who don't wish to learn.

### The Perpetual Rookie

Something magical happens when a skilled veteran successfully relearns his rookie smarts *and* is still able to retain his veteran acumen. He can then select the specific mentality and approach that is most effective for each task and situation. Learning how to pivot between savvy veteran in some situations to rookie in others gives you the agility to climb new mountains and see new vistas.

The rookie smart modes, while being the natural approach for newcomers, aren't intended to be a permanent condition. These are states of mind we should be able to conjure up and toggle to when we need it. For example, if you are beginning a new product development cycle, you might invoke your rookie smarts by talking to outside experts, asking the naïve questions, and carefully orchestrating a quick experiment to test the viability of bold ideas. However, if your project team is floundering, dead in the murky waters of corporate bureaucracy, you might toggle to your veteran savvy—what veterans are capable of contributing when they are at their best—helping the team clarify their goals, simplifying their approach, and connecting them to the people inside the organization who can speed their progress.

The most experienced (and successful) professionals who easily and continually conjure up their rookie smarts are those I call "perpetual rookies."

Consider Jim Delaney, who did everything right but found himself on the wrong end of a corporate reorganization. An engineer at heart, Jim thrives on building stuff and learning how things work. He rebuilt cars as a teenager, then attended the U.S. Naval Academy, earned a scholarship to study in France, and learned a second language. After graduation, Jim served as a lieutenant and cryptologist in the U.S. Navy and as an engineer at Verizon Communications.

Jim then returned to school and earned an MBA from the Wharton School at the University of Pennsylvania, where he made the dean's list. During the next twenty years, he worked at a series of midlevel and senior leadership positions in technology and the financial services industry. He was climbing the corporate ladder, readying himself for a CEO role. Jim did all the right things and went to the right schools. He had just climbed another rung and was working as a divisional president when his company brought in a new CEO. The new CEO

brought in a new management team, so instead of being offered a promotion, Jim was handed a pink slip.

Jim was optimistic as he began interviewing for new positions; after
all, he had solid experience and was a well-groomed leadership candidate. However, given the emergence of social, mobile, and digital
technologies, with each interview he began to see that his years of carefully crafted experience weren't seen as an asset. As the jobs went to the
rookies, he realized his experience was a liability. The pace of innovation had accelerated and many corporations were not able or willing to
keep up. If he stayed in this world, he might not keep up, either. He
feared that his skills were becoming, at best, less relevant, or worse,
completely irrelevant.

Jim then did something that his previous years of experience hadn't
prepared him for. He stepped out of his field of expertise (big military, large corporations, and corporate ladder) and took a job as COO
(and then CEO) of a small, private-equity-backed, start-up—Sysomos,
a technology company that helps its clients cull and route the social
communications that matter most to them. Social media, a market
typically dominated by twenty-somethings, was a new frontier for Jim,
so his new job came with a steep learning curve. He had to let go of his
company-centric logic and co-create with his customers and the social
media community. He had to learn to move faster without necessarily
working harder. But Jim caught on quickly, learning something new
every day.

To grow the firm, Jim not only recruited young professionals and
digital natives but also reached out to people like him—successful
midcareer professionals eager to reinvigorate their careers and brave the
new world of social media. The eclectic mix of people came together
with the excitement of the gang in *Ocean's Eleven*, who realize they
have one more heist in them. Joanne Clarke, in her early fifties, is a
master of corporate selling and the art of navigating up and down an
organization, but she knew next to nothing about social media when
she joined Sysomos as head of enterprise sales. She dove in, learned

fast, and is now more than just social media literate; she adeptly advises clients how to use social media to optimize their customer reach. Not only is Joanne enjoying the new challenge, but her family also notices the change in her outlook. Her daughters tell her how proud they are of her, while her husband comments, "I haven't seen you this happy in years."

The company continues to grow and thrive. But perhaps most important, the people inside the company are thriving. As Jim said, "I feel great when I'm building something and when I'm learning. There's a joy and sense of accomplishment." He continued, "If you want to create an environment where people do their best, they have to be becoming." The best leaders understand that the joy of work is in the striving, not in arriving at the top of a ladder.

## THE FOUNTAIN OF YOUTHFUL THINKING

The most dangerous place to be might be at the top—whether it is the top of a ladder or at the top of your game. Bill Gates said, "Success is a lousy teacher. It seduces smart people into thinking they can't lose." Business growth adviser Verne Harnish has noted a similar pattern in the entrepreneurial world. In their freshman venture, entrepreneurs know nothing, so they make mistakes and learn. When they win, they win big. This experience kills them the second time around. Confident that they know what needs to be done, they often misread markets and miss important signals. "They make a lot of money in their first venture and they're lucky if they don't blow it all in their second," says Harnish. Experience plus hubris makes for a deadly combination.

When we rely too heavily on our past experience, we can quickly become irrelevant. Those who cling too tightly to the past may hear the dreaded words that were uttered so unemotionally by straight-talking Simon Cowell to the *American Idol* contestant: "You're just not relevant." We may be experienced, but we're not marketable. Those who find themselves irrelevant will wonder how they wound up in this seeming dead end. You see, the experience trap isn't a spring-loaded claw that inflicts painful wounds as it snares its victims. We are caught by comfort. We become victims of ease and habit and choose to stay on the familiar path. Too many of us are living in the past tense—talking about what we learned, experienced, did—when what we really need to do is start living in the present tense or even the future tense—talking about what we're learning and what we're planning and where we're heading—as if the adventure is still on.

If you are at the top of your game, it might be time to position yourself at the bottom of a learning curve. The unease that accompanies a new venture offers the promise of renewal and vibrancy. It is on this steeper learning curve that we can rekindle our rookie smarts.

When the world is changing fast, you want a rookie on the job. Not just any rookie—you want someone with rookie smarts. You want someone who can free herself from the past, mobilize the expertise of others, operate cautiously but quickly and then forge ahead into new territory. In short, you want someone who can learn. A former Oracle executive said, "If you are going to start with ignorant people, you need to start with people who want to learn." Most people want to learn, but are you learning faster than the world is changing?

When rookie Magic Johnson stepped in for the Lakers' star center, Kareem Abdul-Jabbar, the basketball community didn't expect much. But Magic expected more from himself, and he rose to the occasion. My hope is that we begin to see the term *rookie* as a badge of honor, rather than a burden. Instead of lowering our expectations, perhaps we should raise them in acknowledgment of a brilliant new way of working and thriving in today's changing world of work.

## CHAPTER SUMMARY

### Research Findings

1. Rookies are surprisingly strong performers, performing on par with experienced colleagues in many situations and at higher levels in innovative and urgent work.

2. Rookies have a unique success profile, with top-performing rookies operating very distinctly from their top-performing experienced colleagues.

3. Rookies operate in a number of ways that counter conventional logic.

4. Experience can create several blind spots. As habits form, people often stop seeing new possibilities, seeking new perspectives, and going down new paths.

### Rookie Smart Modes and Mindsets

| ROOKIE SMARTS | | VETERAN COMFORT ZONE | |
|---|---|---|---|
| **Mode** | **Mindset** | **Mode** | **Mindset** |
| Backpacker | Unencumbered | Caretaker | Protecting |
| Hunter-Gatherer | Alert and Seeking | Local Guide | Advising |
| Firewalker | Cautious and Quick | Marathoner | Steady Pace |
| Pioneer | Hungry and Relentless | Settler | Comfortable and Consuming |

Rookie Smarts is how we tend to think and act when we are mindful that we are doing something for the first time. The rookie and veteran modes are not classifications of people; they are modes of behavior we can slip into and roles we tend to assume. We can be in a rookie mode in one aspect of our work and in veteran mode in another.

## The Right Terrain and the Danger Zone

Rookies are highly adept in the following circumstances:

1. Exploring new frontiers and innovating

2. Making immediate gains

3. When there are multiple ways to solve a problem

4. When there is too much information for any one person to know

However, when a single mistake is game ending, putting a rookie on the job can be disastrous.

## Shifting into Rookie Smarts Mode

You can begin your journey by finding out if you are in the learning zone, operating with rookie smarts, or if you have become stuck in the veteran comfort zone. Go to www.RookieSmarts.com/quiz to take the "Are You in the Learning Zone?" quiz.

## CHAPTER 2

# BACKPACKERS: AN UNENCUMBERED MIND

Some of the world's greatest feats were accomplished by people not smart enough to know they were impossible.

—DOUG LARSON

The business computing scene in the early 1980s was dominated by what industry experts called "big iron." Mini and mainframe computers the size of delivery trucks, isolated in AC-controlled rooms in corporate data centers, looked impressive but offered little computing power for the price. In 1980, Digital Equipment Corporation (DEC) came out with a mini computer with a not-so-mini price tag ($30,000). This state-of-the-art machine boasted a robust computing platform for the time and served as the backbone of many corporate information systems. The next year, when IBM joined the computer race by announcing a personal computer with a starting price of just $1,565, most considered it a novelty. One young woman, however, saw something more. Unencumbered by the weight of industry knowledge, she saw a world of new possibilities in these low-cost computers.

Stephanie DiMarco graduated from the University of California, Berkeley with a bachelor's degree in business in 1979. She went to work as an analyst for a small money management firm in 1981 and found herself smack dab in the middle of the computer wars. Frustrated by the manual accounting, she convinced the company to develop an automated system to track the firm's trading. Like everyone else, Stephanie's firm built the information systems using state-of-the-art DEC minicomputers, but for the small firm $30,000 was a hefty price tag. Six months later, when IBM released a personal computer for $5,000 with 10 megabytes of memory (twice that of the DEC minicomputer), Stephanie spied an opportunity to build information systems on PCs for a fraction of the cost of "big iron."

At only twenty-five and with just two years of business experience, DiMarco joined forces with Steve Strand, a technologist, to create Advent Software. DiMarco reflects: "I was not a technologist. I had a business background; so as far as technology was concerned, my background was essentially nothing." With product development under way, Stephanie began hearing loud cries of objection from established technologists. "You can't do this," they said. "You can't build a rigorous information system on a PC. Everyone knows that!"

Despite the disparaging convictions of technology heavyweights, Stephanie trusted in her vision of what was possible. If the PC offered twice as much computing power at a third of the price point, the transition from big iron to PCs not only seemed possible but also inevitable. Ignoring the naysayers, she, Steve, and their growing team began to build high-performance information systems on the PC. Within one year the team created the first robust PC-based portfolio accounting system. Soon Stephanie was schlepping an IBM PC on wheels through the streets of lower Manhattan, making sales calls to financial firms and pitching the value proposition—high computing power at a lower total cost of ownership.[1]

There were still numerous naysayers in the early days. Stephanie recalled a trade show where a competitor referred to Advent as "that company from California using baby computers and run by a little girl." But the product really delivered and the company grew client by client. Stephanie and team continued to refine their business model and their plans for taking their new product to market. They decided to sell directly to investment firms, rather than going through channel partners. Stephanie recalls the sound of another chorus of cynics: "Everyone told me that you couldn't sell direct to customers at that price point." Well, it turned out, you could. And they did.

Twelve years later, in 1995, Advent went public. Today the company has a market capitalization of more than $1.5 billion, operates in more than sixty countries, and manages some $14 trillion in assets. Stephanie served as CEO until June 2012, at which point she stepped down to allow a new CEO to lead the company into the next generation. Through inexperience—because she saw a value proposition that so many of the incumbents couldn't—DiMarco created a $1.5 billion company.

To create new possibilities, we must see beyond the state of the art.

In this chapter we'll investigate two questions: *How does a lack of experience free us to rise beyond the current state? How do mastery and success anchor us in place?* We'll explore how rookies operate much like unencumbered backpackers, with little to weigh them down and with the freedom to venture out and explore new possibilities while veterans tend to stay close to base camp and protect the resources they've worked so hard to build.

## CARETAKERS VERSUS BACKPACKERS

We all know that feeling when a "relaxing" campout turns out to be more of a burden than a rejuvenating break. You set out to enjoy a peaceful weekend in the wild, but take so much stuff (just in case you might need it) and spend so much time packing, unpacking, and setting up that you have no time or energy left to enjoy nature (and then of course there's the taking down, repacking, driving home, and unpacking). What was intended to be an escape turns into the usual grind.

Too often our managers operate like the car camper, weighed down and burdened by the very experience that should embolden them. They become burdened by yesterday's ideas, today's resources, and the expectations for continued performance tomorrow. Instead of using their success as a launching pad, they become anchored in place, guarding and protecting the status quo. Professionals in this mode find themselves on a slippery slope from trophy to atrophy.

Here are three common ways experience can constrain forward thinking:

**1. Limit What Is Possible.** Once we have run a few races, we establish our own personal track record—an expected level of performance. The 4:01.4 record for the mile set by Gunder Hägg in 1945 stood for nine years and convinced experts and commentators alike that a sub-four-minute mile wasn't humanly possible. In 1954, Roger Bannister, a medical student at Oxford University with a highly unconventional training routine and two pace setters, shattered that record with a time of 3:59.4 seconds. Once broken, this artificial limit was shattered again and again as others began running sub-four-minute miles. Bannister's record lasted only forty-six days.

**2. Stay on a Path**. Defending hard-fought territory, experienced, successful professionals and companies can too easily pursue the path of least resistance. They begin to move like big-game cats living in inadequate zoo habitats, anxiously pacing back and forth along a worn pathway. Their established trails operate as invisible fences restricting them from roaming the space actually available. These are companies like Research In Motion (RIM), the Canadian maker of the once-ubiquitous BlackBerry smartphone, that become so enamored with the status quo that they cannot respond to a changing market. RIM invested so heavily in corporate data centers running on BlackBerry security and networks that they were unable to see and respond to a fundamental shift in the market. Even when consumers began favoring unified devices to both create content and consume entertainment, RIM forged ahead, improving their device and strengthening their existing network while ignoring the fact that the market was shifting to devices that enabled work-life integration. When RIM finally attempted to change course, it was too little, too late.

Defending the paths of the past can quickly constrain thinking and limit innovation. As one CEO of an Internet start-up warned, "The most lethal person in your organization is the one who thinks he has something to defend."

**3. Protect Resources and Relationships**. The spoils of success can all too easily color our thinking. As we become accustomed to the trappings of success, we begin to defend our position and protect our stance. Resource protection plays out in the business world in many different ways. Some managers cling to lofty corporate titles and measure success by the number of people reporting to them, touting head count as a proxy for their organizational influence. But defending and protecting resources isn't always about ego. Well-intentioned managers can also undermine much-needed progress and innovation simply by seeking stability and caring for decent, hardworking people.

## Taking Care of Business

I recall a meeting with Larry Ellison, Oracle's founder and CEO, in which we strategized rebuilding Oracle University around a globalized curriculum, delivered primarily through virtual, Internet-based learning. It was a positive, creative conversation until the smoke cleared and Larry asked me to drastically reduce the size of my organization—from 450 people to only 100, and then rebuild.

I was determined to do the responsible thing, both for our business and for the employees on my team. I conferred with other business executives and assembled data demonstrating the disruption this plan would cause to the existing business. I then assembled a plan recommending we eliminate only 100 employees instead of Larry's suggested 350.

A week later, Larry listened carefully to my analysis, agreed that he was probably asking too much, and acknowledged that my new plan was reasonable. I sensed a subtle disappointment behind his approval (although I don't think anyone has ever accused Larry Ellison of being subtle), but I conveniently ignored it. I was relieved to avoid such Draconian measures and considered this a victory. However, a year later, after watching my remaining team struggle to let go of the past, and attrition turn to a slow bloodletting as more people began leaving, both voluntarily and involuntarily, I realized exactly how wrong I had been. Mine had been a Pyrrhic victory. Larry Ellison was trying to build for the future; I was protecting the past.

Our workplaces need managers and professionals who operate less like Caretakers and more like Backpackers, unencumbered by their current reality and able to explore and agilely investigate beyond immediate boundaries. Rookies often don't feel the weight of experience and tend to operate without limits. They are intellectually unconstrained, without history or expected pattern to confine their thinking. They are also often socially unconstrained, without a reputation to uphold or defend.

Consider the flexibility that accompanies those who pack and travel light.

Many years ago, my husband (also named Larry), whose native outdoor genius is really wasted on this modern century, and I drove seven hundred miles to spend a week hiking through southern Utah. Our final adventure would be a three-day backpacking trek through the backcountry of Kolob Canyons, a hanging valley in a remote section of Zion National Park with scenic canyons, waterfalls, and spectacular views of the ruddy southwestern wilderness.

Off to a late start, we threw the bare essentials into our packs and began hiking at a near jog hoping to arrive at our first night's intended destination before dark. Soon we were hiking in full darkness, unable to see anything beyond the small visual clearing made by the three-foot radius of light from our flashlight. When it became too difficult to proceed, we simply plopped down for the night in a small open space just off the trail. No permits, no campsite, and no worries (except for what might be crawling outside our tent).

We awoke the next morning in a valley of wildflowers and breathtaking views. We then continued hiking until we reached our intended first-night destination—a meadow with a small creek that appeared to have been a river in its grander days. We dropped our packs, set up our tiny tent, and immediately ventured out. After exploring the waterfalls and rock formations, we returned for lunch, fired up the Bunsen burner–size stove, and perched on a rock along the creek to eat our meager rehydrated meal. When a faint but strange roar in the distance interrupted the peace, Larry, the watchful scout, yelled, "Flash flood!" Within seconds, we had sprung up, grabbed our scant gear, and scurried to a safe distance just fifty feet away. We watched in amazement as a torrential wall of water swept through the riverbed, slashing the surroundings and consuming anything along its path that was not deeply rooted.

Our light packing not only gave us greater range to explore this wilderness; it also gave us the flexibility to change plans, move in new directions, and respond quickly. Similarly, newcomers, unencumbered by know-how and history, are able to see above and go beyond established practice.

## Rising Above the Establishment

Consider how one freshman legislator's ability to see beyond the privileges of power is helping a system rise above political and economic turmoil.

In 2011, Greece was grappling with a colossal political and economic crisis fueled by widespread tax evasion and high debt. While leaders in Greece imposed austerity measures and layers and layers of cutbacks, citizens protested forcefully in the streets. As the situation escalated and began to teeter toward catastrophe, leaders in the European Union debated bailout options, seeking to constrain the crisis, while the rest of the world watched, anxiously pondering the implications for the intricately linked global economy.[2]

Earlier, Hara Kefalidou, an Athens resident and daughter of a retired politician, had been persuaded by the majority Pasok party to return to her hometown of Drama and seek office. Forty-six years old and pregnant, Kefalidou won handily and took public office.

Ironically, just as average Greek citizens were receiving lower wages, paying higher taxes, and having their government benefits cut, public officials were enjoying the privilege of elected office and excessive perks. For this freshman legislator, something seemed unjust: "It seemed obvious that lawmakers needed to sacrifice, too."[3] In a letter she wrote in a conservative daily newspaper, she called on her three hundred fellow legislators to relinquish many of these perks, including paid cars, double pensions, free rail passes, and the additional $425 legislators were paid for each committee meeting they attended (something Kefalidou assumed should be considered part of their core job).

Though citizens warmly welcomed Kefalidou's letter, incensed party leaders responded with condescending lectures. Senior colleagues in Parliament scorned and shunned the junior lawmaker from Drama. Alone in her tiny office in Athens, Kefalidou waited for any sign of a thaw from her colleagues. With none forthcoming, she announced that she, herself, would give up her allotted Mercedes and would forgo receiving fees for attending committee meetings. That same day, a member of the opposition party gave up his car as well. Other members of smaller parties made similar moves in the next few weeks. Soon after, the Speaker of the House announced that fees for attending meetings would be cut in half. Eventually lawmakers began to experience salary cuts similar to those of other state workers.

Why were so few politicians able to rise above the establishment? Perhaps the established politicians' entrenchment in the system blinded them to the flaws inherent in the way things were done. Without the blinders of experience, Kefalidou could see the barriers separating the privileged politicians from the populace—and began to envision a better way. To rise above, we must first be able to *see* above.

## THE BACKPACKER'S WAY

The rookie has an unencumbered mind that allows him to question the establishment, and a hopeful mindset that allows him to see new possibilities. Because rookies can see new opportunities, they are driven to explore new terrain, and because they are not weighed down, they operate wholeheartedly. Here's how those with rookie smarts do it.

### Practice 1: See New Possibilities

Rising above the current reality doesn't typically require a heroic leap. Like a hiker who trudges obliviously past a snake lying quietly in the brush, rookies simply walk past the obstacles they don't see. And because they don't know what they are supposed to be looking for, they can end up seeing what others fail to notice.

How do rookies identify new possibilities? They ask fundamental questions, see new patterns, and find mistakes.

**Ask the Fundamental Questions.** Newcomers, without the weight of knowledge, ritual, and rule to constrain their thinking, often ask questions that cut to the core of an issue. It isn't that experienced people don't recognize problems. After all, they've been living with them the longest and know them best. But the longer we live with a problem, the less likely we are to think we can do anything about it. People fresh to a problem haven't convinced themselves that they can't solve it.

Consider the product design team at iconic sneaker maker Converse, which had been working obsessively on speed. Not speed on the basketball court (the heritage of classic yet youthful Chuck Taylor sneaker), but speed-to-market. Reducing the lag time between concept and shelf would allow Converse to bring their fashion-forward customers the latest trends faster. The design team (headquartered in North Andover, Massachusetts) could already produce a sample sneaker in a single day, but their factories in China and Vietnam weren't as agile. Peter Hudson, the vice president of design, was eager to introduce a new mindset—what he referred to as a "straight to making" mentality—to the entire production process. This challenge was issued to Bryan Cioffi, vice president/global creative director of footwear: Figure out how to scale up their one-day sample production capacity worldwide, particularly in their factories.

Bryan, who dresses all in black, shaves his head, and sports ear gauges and tattoos, looks as much like a street artist as a corporate manager. At fifteen, Bryan left home to begin supporting himself. Naturally brilliant, Bryan finished high school with honors and attended college in Boston on an academic scholarship, where he experimented with the latest 3-D digital printing and prototyping technology before graduating with a degree in engineering. His work caught the attention of the Converse team who hired him to start a rapid-prototyping group. Having struggled to make his way in the world, Bryan was blown away when the hiring manager told him, "We don't care how old you are. [He was twenty-three.] Your work is amazing. We'll give you a small budget, and then let's see what you can do." No one had ever taken a chance on him, and now someone was asking his opinion. Bryan would have worked for free. Once at Converse, Bryan was offered a series of opportunities and promotions. Every time someone took another chance on him, Bryan extended similar opportunities to others whenever he could. As a leader, he loved to see what people were capable of doing.

When Bryan assumed a new leadership role on the innovation team, the process for how the design team collaborated with the factory staff was well established. As he pondered their speed-to-market, he began asking the most basic questions: Why do the design samples need to be made at headquarters? Could the teams move faster if the sample sneakers were made directly by the craftsmen in the factories? His simple questions opened up new possibilities.

Bryan traveled with a team to Guangzhou, China, to work directly with the factory team. He explained to the factory staff that he wanted to unleash some creativity and asked them to design and make a unique prototype using the materials he had brought with him. He then asked, "Can you make a sample sneaker in one day?"

Bryan reassured the factory craftsmen who were contemplating this new challenge, "Nothing you can do is wrong. Whatever you bring back to me is perfect, I want to see your creativity." Bryan handed over the materials and asked if they could make just one sneaker by the end of the next day. The meeting calmly adjourned, and the factory floor became charged with energy and action. The next morning Bryan was presented with not just one sneaker but four pairs of beautifully crafted sneakers. Their designs were thoughtful, unexpected, and excellent.

Converse president and CEO Jim Calhoun observed, "Bryan is intellectually curious, reflective. He asks the questions that get us all thinking." Bryan has noted, "Some people assume we stumble onto our success, but the path of discovery is paved with interesting questions." Rookies simply ask the question.

Can the simplest questions prompt the most sophisticated thinking? Are you asking the most fundamental questions, the questions a newcomer might ask? By asking extremely naïve questions, rookies not only rapidly acquire situational understanding; they also can assist their stakeholders in clarifying their needs and articulating new ideas.

A few caveats are in order: Bryan's questions weren't based in bravado or a feigned intellectualism; he asked earnest, innocent, and humble questions. Bryan knew he didn't have the answers, but he knew he could rely on other people to contribute to finding the solutions. A humble ask can prompt an amazing feat. Similarly, naïve questions are different than stupid questions. Naïve questions are natural, innocent, and unaffected. A naïve question has no preconceived assumptions or answers and often cuts to the core of an issue. Stupid questions lack intelligence and common sense. Their insensate tone reflects a lack of awareness and due diligence on the part of the asker. Asking naïve questions refreshes and invigorates thinking. Asking stupid questions is simply annoying.

**See New Patterns and Find the Mistakes.** When we conducted our comparative study of experienced and inexperienced professionals, we asked managers what inexperienced people bring to their work. The most frequent answer was "openness." Rarely did managers say that these newcomers brought a bounty of new ideas. In reality, most rookies bring an absence of knowledge and ideas, which makes them open to the possibilities that exist around them. Sometimes the less you know, the more you can see. Driving past a cemetery, a five-year-old girl delightfully exclaimed, "Look, Mommy, a sculpture forest!" Having no previous association with this strange collection of stones, the child formed a new pattern—an enchanting art project nestled in nature.

When we have identified a pattern, it becomes difficult to ignore the pattern and to see what actually exists. We fill in the blanks, mentally forcing reality to conform to the pattern we expect to see. For example:

It deson't mttaer in waht oredr the ltteers in a wrod aepapr, the olny iprmoatnt tihng is taht the frist and lsat ltteer are in the rghit pcale. The rset can be a toatl mses and you can sitll raed it wouthit pobelrm.

S1M1L4RLY, Y0UR M1ND 15 R34D1NG 7H15 4U70M471C4LLY W17H0U7 3V3N 7H1NK1NG 4B0U7 17.[4]

No doubt your mind extracted meaning from the two previous paragraphs. Using minimal clues, your mind forced the nonsense words to conform to the preset word recognition patterns you have honed over a lifetime. Marta Kutas, a cognitive neuroscientist and the director of the Center for Research in Language at the University of California, San Diego, studies the importance of context for language comprehension. In her research Kutas has found that, to varying degrees, people use context clues to predict what the next words on the page are in a process that she calls pre-activation. Kutas explains,

"Pre-activation entails unconsciously building representations for up-coming concepts, features or forms that may never be encountered in the input."[5] In other words, our brains recognize patterns and jump to conclusions about what comes next.

A woman was trying to explain to a friend that her distance vision was starting to fail. Lacking an official diagnosis from the optometrist, she explained anecdotally, "I can still read words from a distance, but only if I already know what it says!" She explained that when driving in familiar territory she can recognize the street name from a block away, but it is only because her mind fills in what her eyes can't really see. In other words, her vision was perfectly adequate if she only went places she'd already been before. So it goes for far too many experienced leaders.

This skill in quickly recognizing patterns and making rapid inferences can speed decision making, but it can also cause experts to overlook mistakes. Researcher Thomas Wolf describes an experience Boris Goldovsky, opera commentator and renowned piano instructor, had while teaching piano.

Some years ago, a student whom Dr. Goldovsky describes as "technically competent but a poor reader" prepared a Brahms "Capriccio" (opus 76, No. 2) which she brought to her lesson. She began to play the piece through but when she arrived at the C# major chord on the first beat of the bar 42 measures from the end, she played a G natural instead of the G# which would normally occur in the C# major triad. Goldovsky told her to stop and correct her mistake. The student looked confused and said that she had played what was written. To Goldovsky's surprise, the girl had played the printed notes correctly—there was an apparent misprint in the music.

At first, student and teacher believed that this was merely a misprint in the edition they were using but upon further checking they found that all other editions contained the same incorrect note . . . the reason that countless skilled musicians had never found the mistake was because they were reading musical patterns rather than individual notes.[6]

Fundamental errors can go undetected by those with mastery. On the other hand, novices can find mistakes and logical flaws in conventional wisdom. Their lack of pattern recognition also accelerates and fortifies their learning since our brains retain what they work harder to obtain.[7] And, not yet having established a preferred route, we are more willing to blaze new trails.

## Practice 2: Explore New Terrain

As we build a body of knowledge and climb from success to success, we come face-to-face with a mighty dilemma: to stand secure in the certainty of what we already know, or to venture out into a hazy, uncertain and potentially hostile world of possibility? It is difficult to escape the gravitational pull of comfortable competence. But when we have not yet developed a body of expertise, we don't face this challenge. Without a homeland, we are free to explore new terrain and find new paths.

**Take Shorter Paths.** Freed from convention and protocol, neophytes find simple patterns and direct paths. Sometimes these paths are a straight line to the goal. Several years ago I watched my daughter Megan find such a path. It was opening day for Menlo-Atherton (Calif.) High School's girls' lacrosse season. It was also Megan's first game. She hadn't attended a single lacrosse practice yet, either, as she had been playing in an extended soccer season. She had picked up her first stick a few weeks earlier, when a more experienced player taught her some basic stick skills. With her very basic understanding of the game, Megan suited up and took the field in the forward position. Her teammate passed the ball to her, and she caught it. Not entirely sure what to do next, she did the only thing she knew for sure she was supposed to do: run down the field and put the ball into the goal box. She shot and scored! Her team won the next draw and a teammate again passed to Megan. Lacking confidence in her passing skills, she again ran the field (racing past stunned defenders) and clumsily flung the ball into the net. Again she scored. Spurred on by her amused teammates and managing some basic passing, Megan scored four more times during that first game.

Megan played four years of high school lacrosse and was a solid player, but never again matched her rookie record of six goals in one game. What happened that day? Was it beginner's luck or a rookie reflex? She hadn't learned the plays, so she pursued the logical and shortest path to a goal. As a new player, she didn't understand that she was stealing the show. She simply did what she could and what appeared most useful.

This experience raises the question: How many more victories could be ours if we didn't overprescribe the plays? Are there times when managers should simply describe the goal and turn their people loose?

**Make Bigger Asks.** Not knowing perceived limits enables rookies to score more often, and it also allows them to score bigger gains. That's what Bryan Cioffi did with his team at Converse. Or consider the experience of another Bryan: Bryan Schramm, the newcomer to a high-tech start-up company, who wasn't afraid to ask for the moon. Schramm, who has graduate degrees in both engineering and business, began his career at ExxonMobil trading and optimizing positions in commodities. He learned from very talented people who were world experts at their craft. He felt privileged to have meaningful responsibilities and to be exposed to strong leadership so early in his career. Still, he felt like he had more to learn and more to give.

Seeking opportunities to break out of his comfort zone, Schramm met Reed Jensen, a renowned scientist at Los Alamos National Laboratory. Jensen was attempting to commercialize a carbon-mitigating technology he had spent his entire career discovering, in a new company called Sundrop Fuels. Jensen invited Schramm to join as a co-founder responsible for business development. With approximately a year of postgraduate work experience, Schramm asked his wife, "What do I have to lose?" and joined Jensen as a cofounder and director of business development, responsible for finance and technology commercialization. At just twenty-seven, Schramm was the token young guy among a team of brilliant, veteran scientists.

Upon joining Sundrop Fuels, Schramm secured seed investment from Amp Capital, founded by Dr. John Stevens, a world-class and well-respected Stanford-trained cardiologist turned serial entrepreneur and investor. Sundrop Fuels operated on this seed capital from Amp but would need to secure additional funding to complete the next phase of technology development—an essential milestone that would enable them to secure the even larger funding they needed to go into full-scale production. Stevens joined the company as founding CEO, and it was soon clear that they needed more money to achieve their goals.

Jensen evaluated the situation and felt that $2 million would suffice. Schramm agreed that $2 million would allow the company to continue comfortably at their existing pace, but he felt they needed to advance the technology and development faster. So, as they made the rounds in Silicon Valley, Schramm increased the fund-raising goal to $10 million.

And guess what? Within five months Schramm, Stevens, and team had secured $20 million from two of the premier VC firms in Silicon Valley. It was the combination of a rookie, Schramm, and savvy veterans, Stevens and Jensen, that got the deal done. Today Sundrop Fuels has raised over $200 million and is ramping up to operate a 1,200-acre plant in Louisiana, another milestone on the company's path toward becoming a large-scale provider of renewable gasoline.

Schramm reflected, "My inexperience gave me the courage to make a big ask." Seven years later, his caution has grown. He says, "I now know how hard it is. It makes it a little more difficult to jump into the next unknown venture." When we don't know the limits, we aren't afraid to shoot for the moon.

Michael Fertik, CEO of Reputation.com, understands the wisdom of inexperience. He exercises restraint to ensure he doesn't preempt new employees, many of whom come straight from college. Fertik says, "I'm careful about what *not* to teach our new people. I never tell our new business development staff how to size a deal. Many of them end up bringing in far greater-sized deals than the experienced staff do. I also never tell them when or where to start in the sales process, because, in absence of knowing, they often just start the conversation at the top of the organization."

**Act Erratically.** Without a preestablished pattern, rookies can act erratically, which can confuse those with mastery and catch them off guard. One business professional with a black belt in karate reflected on the hidden dangers of "green belt syndrome," which is defined by the Urban Dictionary as "a disease common to junior martial artists. After very little experience they think they are the love child of Bruce Lee and Musashi and know everything there is to know about combat arts." The martial arts master Stephen Graham warned another seasoned business leader, "Over the years that it takes to become a black belt, you get very used to the practice of karate. You bow before and after the match, certain moves trigger certain responses, some of the match is like a chess game with some level of things being predictable. Then you get in the ring with a green belt that doesn't know all that yet and while you're trying to shake his hand, he kicks you in the head."

In their erratic, unpredictable moments, rookies are inevitably underestimated and often catch others by surprise. Sometimes they aren't only sneaking in, but they are actually breaking away from the pack. By the time anyone notices them, they are too far down the path for competitors to catch up.

## Practice 3: Act Wholeheartedly

As Brigetta Barrett, U.S. high jump silver medalist, has said, "There's something about being young and exuberant and having no pressure on you to produce a performance."[8] Without reputation, they can operate without ego or fear of falling. They have nothing to lose and nowhere to go but up, which spurs them to act boldly and reach higher.

**Act Boldly and Recover Quickly.** If anyone has volunteered on behalf of a candidate at a local election for public office, you know the scene: voter lists sorted by voting proclivity, handed to volunteers who dial for dollars and knock on doors surveying opinions and seeking commitments. Such was the scene for a local election in Cincinnati, Ohio, in 1974.

Rick Segal, a marketing executive by vocation and lifelong political activist by avocation, was campaign manager of a local legislative race. The campaign was staffed with numerous first-time volunteers, eager to be part of the political process. Thirty years later, Rick vividly remembers how the first-time volunteers' creative energy brought an intensity that fueled the larger campaign. He recalled, "They did *everything* zealously. Much of campaign work, particularly in a pre-tech world, was unglamorous repetition and drudgery. These rookies had our cause and purpose at heart and no opinion at all of what was important to do, or not do. Typically once volunteers had a campaign or two under their belts, then they were more opinionated about tactics and typically less fruitful."

So, when these new volunteers went out knocking on doors, they knocked on every one. They talked to everyone, literally everyone— including the local newspaper editor (who held opposing views) when they stumbled into him while they canvassed a block. It wasn't until their words came back to bite them that they realized they had stepped into the lion's den.

Rick conceded that their cluelessness would indeed cause problems as they made naïve mistakes—not careless, just misguided mistakes. However, they quickly fixed the mistakes with the same zealousness with which they made them. They courageously alerted the campaign manager and recovered. Rick remarked, "I recall one who had forgotten to order some bumper strips in time for an imminent campaign event. I only learned after the fact that he had called the manufacturer feigning to be from that state's governor's office to plead expedition of the shipment. None of this was in the manual, so to speak."

The campaign survived their mishaps, and through their bold action, the campaign built momentum and went on to elect a first-time Republican candidate to the state legislature ninety days after Richard Nixon resigned—not a particularly big year for the GOP.

Bold action brings mistakes and necessitates the courage to recover quickly. As innovation cycles spin faster in business and in education, might not this principle extend well beyond the world of politics? Innovation demands that we act boldly, but recover quickly.

Children, especially young children, acquire language with greater ease and rapidity than do adults. Consider how rarely we see parents in immigrant families learn to speak the new language faster than their children. Why is this? Any parent of a toddler will notice that a child will fail and retry dozens of times in order to learn a word in their would-be mother tongue. But what motivates them to carry on? Their learning is driven by the purest motivations of all—learning to speak is an efficient tool to manipulate and to interact with their environment. Fortunately, research from Daniel Curlik II has shown that new neurons are formed every day in the adult brain, too. The majority of these new cells die within two weeks. However, there is hope for the mature brain: These new cells can be rescued from death and kept alive by learning.[9] When you put your mind through the exercise of learning new things, these neurons become programmed as an integral part of your brain and they survive. Learning actually does make your brain grow, and it can happen at any point in your life. Truly, it is a "use it or lose it" scenario.

**Work Passionately.** Bono, U2 front man and global activist, said, "The less you know the more you believe." And, perhaps the less you know, the more you believe in yourself. In 1998, Navi Radjou, an Indian-born French national, emigrated to the United States after earning a master's degree in information systems from the École

Centrale Paris and having worked in Southeast Asia for three years. Living in New Haven, Connecticut, on a student visa, Navi began his MBA program at the Yale School of Management. After the first year of business school (and several massive tuition payments), he was out of money and in desperate need of a job. A newcomer to the Northeast, Navi had only a weak network to support his job search. To make matters worse, he received official notice that his student visa would be expiring in thirty days!

Despite his predicament, Navi chose not to panic. Instead he began contacting companies for a job. His application to Forrester Research secured him an interview in Boston for an analyst job doing market research on emerging technologies. After making it through the first round of interviews, Navi was asked to submit a research paper. He chose a topic about which he was naturally curious and passionate: how technology improves collaboration. His paper earned him an invitation to travel back to Boston for a performance-based interview—a presentation defending his research paper. As he prepared for the high-stakes interview he told himself, "I love this topic and I have nothing to lose. I will give it my best and if it doesn't work out I will simply go back to France."

Navi remembers: "I went in like a child—joyfully and fully myself." Navi's presentation was neither forced nor particularly forceful. It was just authentic, joyful and wholehearted. The interviewing team didn't see nervous desperation; they saw a happy guy talking passionately about a topic he loved. The hiring manager remarked that she had never seen anything quite like it. Within ten minutes of his presentation, they made him a job offer. His student visa expired two days later.

Navi continued working for Forrester for nine years in Boston and San Francisco, before joining Judge Business School at the University of Cambridge. He also became a member of the faculty at the World Economic Forum and coauthored two best-selling business books. He is now a fellow at Cambridge Judge Business School and was recently named the top innovation thinker in the world by the Thinkers50 organization. Navi's LinkedIn profile aptly reads: Uplifter, Catalyst, Connector. Navi has sought to maintain his rookie state of mind. He said, "Every problem feels like an adventure. I ask myself, 'How hard could it be?' I have nothing to lose. I face challenges as an underdog—with humility and passion. I'm content but never satisfied. When I don't feel like an underdog is the day I'm dead."

Working wholeheartedly—without reservation, without exception, without limitation—is at the very core of our humanity. Through full engagement we find deep meaning in our work and serve beyond self.

## BUILDING ROOKIE SMARTS

How do we regain our rookie smarts when we have become encumbered by success?

Consider the burden felt by a once up-and-coming writer turned superstar.

Imagine yourself a novelist who, at age thirty-seven, writes a memoir documenting your journey of self-discovery. Your book becomes an international bestseller, translated into more than thirty languages, with more than 10 million copies sold worldwide. Your book becomes a hit movie and *Time* magazine names you one of the one hundred most influential people in the world. While your success imbues you with a certain confidence, you secretly wonder if you can do it again. As you embark on your next major project, you discover your secret wonderings and self-doubt reflected in the comments of your family, friends, and everyone you meet.

Elizabeth Gilbert, author of the mega-sensation *Eat, Pray, Love*, captures the bitter torture behind the sweetness of success in her heartfelt 2009 TED talk. At forty years old she was hardly ready to watch her career fade into the sunset. Gilbert contemplated her next piece of work, what she called "a dangerously, frighteningly over-anticipated follow up to my freakish success."[10] She described the tortured conversations with friends and colleagues:

People treat me like I'm doomed. They say, "Aren't you afraid you're never going to be able to top that? Aren't you afraid you're going to keep writing for your whole life and you're never again going to create a book that anybody in the world cares about at all, ever again?" Yes, I'm afraid of all those things. Everything I write from this point forward is going to be judged by the world as the work that came after the freakish success of my last book. It is likely that my greatest success is behind me.[11]

Gilbert wrestled for many months trying to recalibrate her relationship with her work, knowing her next piece of work would inevitably be compared to *Eat, Pray, Love*. She was not only summoning courage, but also desperately searching for a psychological construct that would allow her to maintain emotional distance between herself and her work. She began to see her work not as a function of her own abilities or genius but rather as a product of an outside source or muse. She focused on being an open receptacle, available to receive and process inspiration from this source.[12] The result? Another memoir, *Committed*, in 2010 (four years after *Eat, Pray, Love*) and an acclaimed novel, *The Signature of All Things*, in 2013. Most important, she overcame the enormous burden of her success and continued doing the work she loved.

As we unencumber our minds and lighten our load, we find ourselves more able to ascend the steeper, rockier roads of truly transformational leadership. One young student conferred with a highly respected business school professor about his desire to have a deep impact and establish new progressive practices in the business world. The wise professor's singular advice: "If you want to make an impact, stay unencumbered. When you consult with senior leaders, you can't have any other agenda than to act purely in the interests of the leaders you advise."

Those unburdened by resources are free to act in the best interests of their organizations and uncover the new practices that are fit for new terrain. But how do we break the shackles of experience and escape the trappings of success? Is it possible to become less encumbered? Here are three ways to increase your mental capacity to see, explore, and discover.

1. **Ask Naïve Questions—*Ask the basic questions that simplify and clarify.*** Consult with the stakeholders for your work and only ask questions. Ask the questions that cut to the core and reveal the fundamental objectives or needs. Ask the questions that a newcomer would ask. Or even better yet, ask a novice to define the questions for you.

2. **Wipe the Slate—*Get a fresh start.*** Implement a semester system where work has a beginning, middle, and an end where victory can be claimed or defeat declared. Then wipe the slate clean and give yourself and your colleagues an opportunity to start fresh, unburdened by past performance.

3. **Let Go of the Monkey Trap—*Release your resources.*** A monkey can easily be trapped in place by placing a banana inside a basket or container with an opening large enough for the monkey to put his hand in but not sufficiently large to pull the banana back out. He'll wait captive, banana in hand, rather than release the prize and extract his hand. You might not need to actually release your entire staff, but start by rebuilding your budget from the ground up. Or ask yourself, What would I do if I didn't have any staff to consider? What would I do if my title was simply "Team Member"?

Every traveler knows what it's like to scramble after hearing the dreaded announcement that their flight has been delayed, or worse, canceled. They make it up to the counter and after the click clack of hurried typing and checking and rechecking, the gate agent asks, "Did you check bags?" Those traveling with just a small carry-on answer "no" and then hear the magic words: "We can get you on another flight." Ironically, that's how veteran travelers do it, but why, when it comes to the workplace, do so many leaders weigh themselves down with a heavy pack?

To build your rookie smarts, try ditching the heavy pack. The less you carry, the more you can truly see what is transpiring around you. As you wander and wonder, take time to enjoy the view. You might begin to see things from a new perspective.

## A WEIGHTLESS, WANDERING MIND

In *The Phantom Tollbooth*, an insightful tome disguised as a children's book, the author Norton Juster celebrates "the awakening of the lazy mind."[13] In the story, Milo, a young, bored boy, passes through a mysterious tollbooth to find himself in a strange land. He meets a king who sends him on a difficult, dangerous mission that involves a secret matter that the king will tell him about when the boy returns. When Milo returns victorious, he asks the king to reveal the secret matter at last. The king says of Milo's mission, "It was impossible. . . . But if we'd told you then, you might not have gone—and, as you've discovered, so many things are possible just as long as you don't know they're impossible."[14]

Sometimes not knowing is better than knowing. In our state of relative cluelessness, we don't yet know that a new opportunity is impossible. So, we willingly embark.

Charles Kettering said, "A person must have a certain amount of intelligent ignorance to get anywhere." This is certainly true in a workplace where the state of knowledge doesn't stand still. Just as those who seek physical vitality shed excess pounds, those who seek intellectual vitality must shed assumptions, wipe the slate, and let go of the resources that limit their actions. As we release these constraints, we can more fully embrace a healthy skepticism for the sacrosanctity of our own knowledge.

As the saying goes, not all who wander are lost. Because the less you know, the more you need. The unencumbered Backpacker can venture out, but the rookie's naïveté prevents him from wandering aimlessly. Aware of his own lack of knowledge, the rookie embarks on a desperate, focused, diligent search, hunting for experts who can teach him and guide his way.

## CHAPTER SUMMARY

**Backpackers** have nothing to weigh them down and nothing to lose, which opens them to see new possibilities, explore new terrain, and act wholeheartedly.

**Caretakers** have accumulated a track record, a trophy case, and the spoils of success, which cause them to expend their energy maintaining the status quo.

## THE MINDSETS AND PRACTICES

|  | ROOKIE SMART MODE<br>Backpackers | VETERAN COMFORT ZONE<br>Caretakers |
|---|---|---|
| Circumstance | Rookies have no history to draw from, no reputation to uphold, and no resources to hide behind. | Veterans have a past track record to maintain, a reputation to uphold, and resources to protect. |
| Mindset | With nothing to weigh them down, Backpackers have an unencumbered and hopeful outlook. | Burdened with resources and expectations, Caretakers have a defensive, protective outlook. |
| Practices | Backpackers tend to:<br><br>1) See new possibilities<br><br>2) Explore new terrain<br><br>3) Act wholeheartedly | Caretakers tend to:<br><br>1) Limit what is possible<br><br>2) Stay on a path<br><br>3) Protect resources and relationships |
| Result | As a result, they can rise above the status quo. Instead of settling in to yesterday's best practices, they find new practices fit for the new terrain. | As a result, they get trapped into approaching projects "the way it has been done," protecting the status quo, often optimizing for old realities. |

## Cultivating Rookie Smarts

You can foster a Backpacker mentality by conducting any of the following learning experiments found on page 67 or in Appendix C.

1. **Ask naïve questions**—Ask the basic questions that simplify and clarify.

2. **Wipe the slate**—Get a fresh start.

3. **Let go of the monkey trap**—Release your resources.

## CHAPTER 3

# HUNTER-GATHERERS: FINDING EXPERTISE

If we become increasingly humble about how little we know, we may be more eager to search.

—SIR IAN TEMPLETON

The Theater Pub in San Francisco is one of those local indie theaters where the players act, not in hopes of being discovered, but for the pure love of the craft. When the actors are paid, it is just enough to cover gas and drinks after the performance. Still, these actors come together for a fortnight to create something brilliant and then disband, each to find another project, and build new chemistry with a new troupe.

Among the company is Jan Marsh, a passionate actress and single mother, who exudes warmth, charisma, and intelligence both onstage and off. Actress by night, Jan is a substitute teacher by day. Many years ago, she began substitute teaching, to make ends meet when her children were young. Now that her children are grown (one working as a physicist with a Ph.D. and the other as a pediatrician), Jan has begun to think about her own future. While she loves acting, it will not pay for her retirement.

After much thought, Jan has decided to earn a middle school math and science teaching credential. Jan has always been good with numbers and logic. In fact, she entered college intending to major in chemistry. Without the necessary math prerequisites, however, Jan struggled to keep up, and ultimately chose to put college on hold. After her children were born, Jan returned to school. She would put the babies to bed and then stay up until midnight studying math and physics. She worked hard and completed calculus, bringing her grade up from a D-minus to earn the highest grade in the class. Ultimately, though, Jan decided to abandon chemistry in the pursuit of an acting degree.

Now several decades later, and a rookie again, Jan is enrolled in an online program, which will allow her to become a full-time teacher. But before that will be possible, she'll need to take English, U.S. history, health, algebra, and statistics to earn her teaching credential. Jan will tackle statistics first. Sure, Jan has a knack for numbers, but as an actress for the last twenty-five years, she has lived in the realm of scripts, lines, and words.

Jan is quick to point out that she's been out of school and out of formal learning mode for roughly thirty years. With smartphones and online tutorials, learning is a whole new world, and Jan is understandably terrified, suffering, if you will, from a student's version of stage fright. Jan begins sharing her anxiety and uncertainties with her friends, many of them on Facebook. Her first Facebook post reflects her awareness of the gap she faces:

> Graphing calculators had not been invented when I last did math. Oh
> brave new world . . .

Despite her trepidation, Jan concocts a plan, complete with support systems and supplemental resources, and she begins slaying the dragon of Stats 101. Her string of posts over a nine-week period suggests that she's becoming unstuck and that her plan is kicking in:

> You know that Statistics homework that has been kicking my butt these last two weeks? Well, I'm kicking back and today it's going down. Just sayin' . . .
>
> That which we persist in doing becomes easy to do; not that the nature of the thing has changed, but that our power to do has increased. Emerson/Heber J. Grant.
>
> I'm a discriminating woman. Meaning I know the difference between a discriminant and a determinant . . . and how to use them.

Unlike her early college days, Jan doesn't just hunker down alone and work harder; she reaches out to experts for help, and she builds a support network around herself. She finds free tutoring at nearby College of San Mateo and attends tutoring sessions weekly. Meanwhile, her friends at the theater, at church, and on Facebook form a cheering section that erupts into a roar at her next post:

> I got a 95% on my Statistics midterm!!!! HOW DID THAT HAPPEN??!?! Uh, uh . . . uhn-belief!!!!! Relief.

A month later, she posts:

> Dear Facebook cheering section: I got 120 out of 120 points on the proctored portion of my Statistics final. Color me grateful.

Six weeks later the all-important multiple-subject CSET (California Subject Examination for Teachers) prompted this post:

> Guess who passed all three parts of the Multiple Subject CSET?!?!?! Uhhuh, uhuh!!!!!

Not only did Jan slay the stats dragon, earning an A in this daunting class—she earned an A in every class she took that semester. Several months later, another post captured her sentiment after climbing a steep, grueling learning curve:

*I just finished 37 units in 6 months. Coursework, Pre-Clinical Experience, and Demonstration Teaching, all done. 6 months. I'm in shock.*

Jan, who has a deep faith, said, "With help, I can do anything." Jan has finished her student teaching and her credential is in the works.

In this chapter we will meet more people like Jan and explore the practices that help people excel despite a lack of experience. We'll see why rookies who possess a combination of a large knowledge gap, heightened self-awareness, and access to connections learn faster and build expert networks that serve them well throughout their development. This powerful combination propels rookies into a hyper-learning mode that produces a 5X effect—that is, through their scouting efforts, rookies bring back five times more expertise to a problem than does a single expert.

## LOCAL GUIDES VERSUS HUNTER-GATHERERS

The echo chamber is a pervasive disease of our time. This term captures our tendency to customize and configure our environment so that we only hear and see our own thoughts and beliefs echoed back to us. This ability to manipulate our data stream is hailed as a feat of technological virtuosity, allowing us, for example, to limit our newsfeeds to sources that conform to our biases, and then sit back and "like" it all. While this ability might be comfortable, it's a trap.

Similarly, as a weary business traveler on yet another client visit, you may have contracted a case of what I call "geo-blivion." It's a condition characterized by a total lack of awareness of the immediate environment. You could be in any airport, any city, any hotel, or any conference room. And you don't really need to know where you are because your smartphone conveniently tells you what you are supposed to be doing at every moment and how you're supposed to get there. You blindly obey, turning left and right without even looking at the street names, and you don't need to stop and ask for directions. Our phones are so smart that they can make us deaf, blind, and dumb. Likewise, in our work lives, we run the risk of falling back on old tricks and short-cuts and feeling like we have all the answers even when the questions have changed.

Veterans, brimming with opinions formed by years of experience, can insulate themselves in this echo chamber and begin acting like small-town locals—old codgers sitting around Joe Bob's coffee shop, having the same conversation they've been having for the last twenty years. Their opinions are predictable, their observations routine. In this mode, we are confident that we understand our surroundings, and we stop asking questions and seeking guidance. Old ideas and opinions reign supreme while new ideas and information bounce off the walls. In such a situation, we might not even notice a new development in town or, worse, that the barbarians are at the gate.

As their confidence gives way to arrogance, veterans operating in this mode tend to:

**1) Look for Data That Confirms What They Already Know.** People are pattern seekers. We form beliefs about the world based on our ex-perience. Then we ignore or disregard data that challenges these beliefs and give priority to information that confirms the patterns we think we've seen. The result: opinion stasis. Lisa Lahey, of Harvard's Gradu-ate School of Education, observed, "One of the things that happens when we unquestioningly hold our big assumptions as truths is that we pay attention to only that which confirms them. We don't seek out counter-examples to our big assumptions because we are so sure they are correct."

**2) Entrench Within Their Tribe.** The better angels of our nature may espouse diversity as a core value, but the harsh reality is that our brains actually prefer familiarity. Apparently, like does attract like. Christian Crandall of the University of Kansas has studied how people choose friends and the people with whom they surround themselves. In a large study involving several college campuses, he found that, given a larger student body, students are more likely to become friends with people who are similar. The larger the student body, the easier it is for students to be selective in their choice of friends and the more likely they are to surround themselves with like-minded people.[1]

Not only do we prefer familiarity, but our brains also respond differently to strangers, sending off "stranger danger" signals. We have dramatically different physiological reactions when we encounter someone we consider similar than when we encounter someone we deem different. Adrianna Jenkins and J. P. Mitchell have demonstrated that when we meet someone we believe shares our values, personality, or background, the region of the brain associated with empathy (medial prefrontal cortex) becomes active. When we meet someone we find foreign or strange, this region of the brain remains at its baseline level of activity. Our brains literally light up when we encounter someone similar.[2]

However comforting the familiar may be, when we entrench ourselves in our well-acquainted hall of mirrors, we limit our perspective. We begin to operate with a 90-degree view of the world and get blindsided. Effective navigation of today's workscape requires a complete 360-degree view.

**3) Disseminate Their Knowledge.** Without access to disruptive information that threatens their worldview, veterans tend to broadcast their views without adjusting for new information or ideas. The one-way flow of information and ideas parallels the geometry of a medieval arrow slit. Arrow slits built into thick castle walls allowed archers to kneel and shoot at enemies outside the wall, with very little risk of getting hit by return fire. Their unique design—a horizontal trapezoid with a narrow slit facing the exterior of the castle, but a wide opening on the inside—provided a very small target for outside arrows to hit while allowing the archer a wide angle from which to launch their arrows. In other words, it's hard for arrows to get in but easy for them to get out. This setup directly parallels the flow of information and ideas to and from many experts (and most senior executives).

Stephanie DiMarco, the former founder and president of Advent Software described in chapter 2, captured this challenge as she reflected on her transition from rookie to veteran technology executive: "If you are successful, it is so much easier to give advice than to take the advice yourself. It is easy, and tempting, to take this route." What can happen to senior leaders who are sought-after mentors but no longer seek out mentors of their own?

## A Textbook Approach

Andres,[3] who has twenty-five years of experience in learning and development, was one of the cornerstone members of the training team at a global nongovernmental organization. His colleagues describe Andres as "the ultimate tutor. Brilliant. It's like having the Smithsonian museum at your fingertips." But they also say that he can be closed and hard to read.

Andres was tasked with creating a much-needed training program for top talent—an important group, and he wanted to deliver the best possible result for them. He knew what needed to be done and he set out to do it. He began by forming a design team, including training professionals and stakeholders. But, even as he launched this team, one could see his core assumptions at work: *I'm the expert and the designer. There's a right way to do this, and I already know what it is.* A colleague observed, "He took a textbook approach. He had it envisioned in his mind based on what he had done in the past." He convened the team and listened to their input. He took some advice, but most fell by the wayside.

Then Andres went into "a cave" and created a design document for a training program that was beautifully crafted and technically sound. He sent the document out for review and asked people to react to his ideas. When one reviewer opened the document, however, it became clear that his reactions were not actually welcome. The document was password protected and, to the dismay of its recipients, there was no way for the reviewers to add, edit, or comment. The feedback process had been co-opted into an opportunity for Andres to showcase his design, disseminate his knowledge, and seek support for the decisions he had already made.

Andres proceeded to assemble a team of trainers, present his plan, and brief them on their role. They delivered the program. The reviews were ordinary at best. Yes, some participants loved it, but many more felt frustrated by the experience. A colleague said, "Andres collaborates alone. He takes your input and then considers it by himself." This expert shared his knowledge and sought feedback, but only to confirm what he knew. As a result, the organization got a program designed by one expert. Andres's strategy got it right for some but very wrong for others.

In what conditions does one person's expertise suffice? When you ask an expert, you get one expert. When you ask a rookie, you get a network of experts.

**From Dazed to Dialed In**

Now consider how another training professional went about building a leadership development program for World Vision, a global relief and child-development organization. Anne is a very smart, make-it-work professional with thirteen years of experience in a variety of roles (including the training department) but was entirely new to the arena of leadership development, with literally zero experience in this field at the time of her hire. The hiring manager saw beyond Anne's lack of experience and hired Anne for her curious, thoughtful, reflective work style and her track record of getting results across the diverse roles she had held.

Anne dove headfirst into the project. Initially disoriented, Anne never froze. Instead, her uncertainty fostered an attitude of fearlessness. She was a learner unafraid to make mistakes. While she never passed herself off as an expert, she managed to convince her colleagues that she was in the lead and accountable. Instead of assuming she had all of the answers, she operated from a position of profound inquiry (for example, *I wonder what is possible? Who are the people who know more than I do? What can they teach me?*) and began scanning the team for those who could offer insight. Her manager said, "She asked a million questions of anyone she could." As she sought out stakeholders and experts, Anne asked: Why is this important? What would success look like? What would you like to see? How would you approach it? And, if you were doing it, where would you start? She then sought out likely participants, asking them what they needed from the program. As she listened, she began to draw people in.

She quickly drafted a design document based on her newfound insights and potential participants' desired outcomes. She circulated the document for feedback from her colleagues and prospective participants. To be sure, her draft design wasn't perfect. Her manager assessed, "It was about sixty to seventy percent right. But she puts stuff out there saying, 'Here's what I'm thinking,' and then gets rapid feedback." While she asked for input, she never waited for it. Her typical offer was "I'd love to have your input on this so I can work on it over the weekend." But if she didn't receive it, she just kept moving.

Anne continued designing and building the program one module at a time, pulling resources from the half dozen "go to" experts in her nascent network. With each new module she developed, she solicited input and iterated until it was ready to pilot. As she climbed the learning curve, each new module became better than the last. She managed to develop the program so it could be delivered both in person and virtually—a critical success factor for any organization operating broadly in the developing world. Unlike most training programs, Anne didn't need to twist any arms or wrangle any cats to secure a pilot location for her program, because in the process of creating the program she had reached out to, listened to, and collaborated with the same network of leaders who were now invested in and excited about the work she allowed them to help shape. Not only was there an abundance of pilot sites, but there was also a growing pool of people who wanted to be trainers and facilitators of the program. Through her practice of asking stakeholders questions and implementing their suggestions, Anne built a brain trust of invested individuals three times the size of her original resource pool.

While the process was scrappier than Andres's, the results were stellar. The program launched to rave reviews, and demand exceeded expectations. Anne turned her nascent team of facilitators into a true community of practice, continually improving the state of this art. Anne was successful because she relied on a multitude of people. Without a storehouse of tools of her own, she had to seek out and build a network of experts.

When dropped into a new environment, rookies become disoriented: not terminally confused, but unsettled and somewhat dazed. With much out of focus, they zoom in on the immediate problems, driven to make sense of their surroundings. While many of us might think that newbies are bumbling, clueless clods, we found the opposite to be true—rookies are keenly aware of where they stand and see their deficiencies to a far greater extent than their experienced colleagues (our study showed 2.5 times higher levels of self-awareness in rookies).

## Traveling on High Alert

This disorientation, when coupled with a sense of humility (either born of circumstance or of choice), puts rookies into a heightened state of alert. Can you recall the first time you visited a foreign country? For most of us, the thrill (or terror) of this is still vivid. For me, it involved five hungry days finding out how far a hundred dollars could stretch in Europe.

I was twenty-five years old when I first ventured outside the United States. The trip was part of phase two of my rookie challenge at Oracle: globalize Oracle University. I knew little more than that I needed to

build connections with the managing directors who ran each of Oracle's
European subsidiaries. I scheduled two-hour meetings with each country manager, and naïvely arranged to visit one country every day!! Even
more naïvely, while in a train station in the city of Utrecht, Netherlands,
I let my guard down and a band of boys stole my wallet. Fortunately, I
had been cautious when I packed and had tucked away an emergency
$100 and my pristine passport in another compartment of my bag. At
the pace I was traveling, there would be no time to receive a money
transfer from home and I figured asking my new colleagues to give
me a wad of cash probably wouldn't result in a good first impression. I
secured an emergency credit card to use at hotels, but I would have to
pay cash for everything else. (This was well before the days where every
cabdriver accepts credit cards via a little payment device on their smartphone.) In my desperation, I made a simple calculation: With four more
countries to go, I would have to make it through each country on $25,
including the money exchange fees required in pre-euro days.

Unable to "buy my way" through Europe by riding in taxis and
handing out tips, I became very resourceful, figuring out how to navigate public transportation, schlepping bags in and out of subway
stations, and eating on the cheap. I studied everything and asked for
continual guidance, knowing I had no room for major mistakes or
further mishaps. But, just as I started to get my bearing in the Netherlands, for instance (yes: scraping by on $25), it was time to fly to
France. I was tired, hungry, and very humble. I flew into the Charles
de Gaulle Airport in Paris and made my way to my hotel, and to
the office the next morning. After my meeting, I headed back to the
airport, only to find that my flight was actually departing from Orly,
Paris's other airport. Who knew Paris had two airports? With no
money to spare, I began asking for help. A wonderfully generous man
overlooked my unintelligible French and diligently helped me find a
cheap shuttle between the airports. I made the flight.

Next on to Spain: I would need to make three bus transfers to get to
the Oracle office in Madrid's La Florida suburb. By the final transfer, I

was disoriented and lost, so I used my meager Spanish to ask for guidance from an older woman who appeared to be headed to the market. Sensing both my plight and ineptitude, she took my hand, led me off the bus, and stood with me at the bus stop until the right bus came. She put me on the correct bus, helped me pay the fare, waved, and nodded in confirmation as I made my way to my destination. I arrived with five minutes to spare—just enough time to wipe the perspiration from my brow. Next stop: Munich, where I landed at 10:30 p.m., too late to change my last $25 into deutschmarks. A sympathetic man paid my bus fare to the main square, and, after a thirty-minute frantic search, I found a taxi driver who would allow me to pay her the fare to my hotel in Spanish pesetas.

I arrived at the hotel in Munich at midnight only to learn that the desk clerk had given away my hotel room. I would need to sleep in the only room available, a hospitality suite complete with a bar and a disco ball, but unfortunately no bathroom. The next morning, I showered at the spa downstairs—a lively hub with an enormous indoor lap pool, massage rooms, and an inviting sauna. I felt victorious at the end of the day: I had navigated in and out of five countries on $100 while making it to every meeting on time (and somewhat composed). I breathed a deep sigh of relief—my first in a week—and decided to retreat to the sauna to relax.

It was then that I let my guard down. I walked into the women's sauna and collapsed in near exhaustion. But ten minutes later, when five men walked in and sat down near me, I learned the naked truth! This was definitely not the women's sauna. I suspect they could tell by my reaction that I wasn't a local.

That was nearly twenty-five years ago, but I can still tell you what the woman on the bus in Madrid looked like, and that in Munich the bus was blue, the taxi was a light tan Mercedes, and that I stayed at the Holiday Inn on the Hochstrasse. I had been on high alert for five grueling days: I paid close attention to everything. I scanned for navigational clues like a lost sailor and I noticed everyone, especially those who looked like they could help a struggling, novice traveler.

I'd like to think that I was an open-minded, humble-hearted global citizen at twenty-five, but in reality, I was simply desperate. Disorientation and uncertainty trigger a state of high alert. In this state of high alert, we focus intensely on our situation, seeking clues to help us move forward. In our work, are we keenly alert to our surroundings, looking for signals of change and seeking support and navigational guidance? Or, have we become numb to what is happening around us, retreating to our secure and familiar corner of the world?

In his delightful blog, The Folly of Age as a Number, tech start-up CEO Brian Wong asks, "When was the last time you walked out of a subway station somewhere in the world and had an almost 'woosh'-ing sensation come over your head of both wonder and awe? I remember I had this feeling the first time I visited New York. The first time I visit any city, really. I strive for this feeling in every setting in life. The more times you feel wondrous, the more times you appreciate the world and what it can provide you."[4]

When veterans feel desperate, they tend to close up and confide in a few trusted colleagues (or their smartphones). Under similar circumstances, newcomers, with a heavy dose of humility, reach outward as they scan the environment, seek out experts, and mobilize ideas and resources.

## THE HUNTER-GATHERER'S WAY

Hunter-gatherers subsist in the wild on food obtained by hunting and foraging. They are a people on the move, venturing out to hunt game or forage for plants. This was how everyone on the planet lived until the advent of farming, which allowed societies to settle in one locale. In an agrarian society, the focus turned inward, toward tending and maintaining resources "owned" by the cultivator. In a hunter-gatherer system, the focus is outward, venturing forth, harvesting game and foraging for resources to bring back to the tribe.

Rookies work in Hunter-Gatherer mode because they have no existing resources or expertise to tend to or rely on. As Anne's manager at World Vision said, "She doesn't have a library of content and expertise to draw on." So she points outward, scanning the organization, foraging for information and hunting for expertise. And when she finds it, she gathers it back in to sustain the project at hand. Here's what rookies do when operating in Hunter-Gatherer mode:

## Practice 1: Scan the Environment

Sense making, or rapidly converting information into intelligence, begins with gathering data. However, this happens only when we believe our current understanding is deficient or under threat. As Epictetus said centuries ago, "It is impossible to begin to learn what one thinks one already knows." This was confirmed in our comparative study, where the data showed that rookies were two times more likely to believe that they had something to learn.

The business-to-business ad agency gyro was asked to design a campaign for Scotsman Ice Systems, a commercial manufacturer of machines that produce ice as cubes, flakes, and nuggets. Their first, and logical, action was to assign the project to a veteran ad team. That team returned with a standard recommendation: ads to the trade journals, sales literature, a campaign website, some trade show support, and publicity efforts. Meanwhile, a team of "newbies," including members of the gyro Academy (a corps of agency up-and-comers), were given the brief to see what they might recommend. Instead of applying "best practices," they first turned to the Internet to see what people were saying about ice. They were delighted to discover an existing community of ice lovers on Facebook. Posts to this group extolled the virtues of the chewable, nugget ice produced on, yes, Scotsman equipment. They launched the "Love the Nug!" campaign and there are now forty thousand people liking the Facebook page, professing their love for chewable ice and hailing the "Love the Nug" truck to visit their neighborhood. Rick Segal, the ad agency's worldwide president, said, "What began as an effort to promote the quality of the equipment was transformed by the newbies' fresh eyes into an offer to own a machine that produces ice cubes that consumers actually prefer and are passionate about. Who'd a thunk it?"

Rookies are sense-making machines. Whether they are connecting the dots between data points, connecting with colleagues across a company, or connecting with a product's fan base on the Internet, their value comes in their outward orientation. And, in this hungry search for much needed knowledge, they seek out experts to teach and guide them.

## Practice 2: Seek Out Experts

In our study, we found that rookies are four times more likely than veterans to ask for help. Steve Jobs, reflecting on his success, pointed to the importance of asking for help throughout his career. In a video interview for the Silicon Valley Historical Association, he said,

> Most people don't get those experiences because they never ask. I've never found anybody that didn't want to help me if I asked them for help. . . . I called up Bill Hewlett when I was a 12-year-old. He lived in Palo Alto, his number was still in the phone book. And he answered the phone himself. He said "yes," I said, "Hi, I'm Steve Jobs, I'm 12 years old, I'm in high school and I want to build a frequency counter and I was wondering if you had any spare parts I could have," and he laughed and he gave the spare parts to build this frequency counter, and he gave me a job that summer at Hewlett Packard working on the assembly line putting nuts and bolts together on frequency counters. He got me a job at the place that built them, and I was in heaven. . . . Most people never ask. And that's what separates sometimes the people that do things from the people that just dream about them.

Brené Brown's fascinating research on vulnerability shows that a willingness to be vulnerable is the single most important value held by people considered wholehearted.[5] Brené's research findings are a reminder that vulnerability isn't showing weakness; it is being open and courageous enough to ask for help. But many successful professionals are afraid to be vulnerable and seek the help of others. Angelina Sutin and her research associates at the National Institute on Aging, the University of Colorado, and Johns Hopkins University found that vulnerability is negatively correlated with prestige, income, and, interestingly enough, job satisfaction.[6]

Rookies, with little to lose and everything to gain, seek help and reach out to experts who can guide them and augment their deficits. Jane Wilson Mitchell and Jen Porter Anderson, relative newcomers to school management and cofounders of an innovative residential school for incarcerated young adults, report a similar strategy. Jane is a former lawyer and educator. Jen recently graduated from Harvard Business School and worked previously in venture philanthropy. They described their journey in building the Reset Foundation as follows: "We aren't the experts, but we know who the experts are. We make connections. And we are willing to learn and ask for advice. You have to be willing to find answers in strange places and go with it."

Our comparative study revealed that rookies seek out expertise 40 percent more often than experienced professionals. In addition to reaching out more often, when they do reach out, they reach out to far more people. In our study, managers reported that their rookie employees reached out to an average of six experts, compared with an average of one for their veteran employees—six times more! Interestingly enough, when professionals self-report, rookies claim an average of three reach-outs compared with one for the veterans. In other words, experienced staff perceives they are seeking input at a much higher frequency than their managers observe. Weighing the two datasets, we calculate a net effect of 5X—meaning rookies reach out to five times more experts than veterans do. This 5X multiple is the network effect of not knowing. Rookies forage for expertise. They ask the experts, and they ask a number of them.

This data might cause leaders to pause and ask, What is more valuable in this situation: having full access to one expert or getting partial access to five experts? If you want more expertise, you might just want to put a rookie on the job and tell her it is okay to not have answers herself. Tell her to go find the people who do. You might find this 5X network effect generates a multiplicity of ideas and potential solutions, allowing you to skip best practice and innovate a next practice more fit for today's realities.

But, with all this reaching and seeking, are these up-and-comers a nuisance and a drain to their veteran counterparts? Do they exhaust people with an onslaught of inquiries? It appears not. We find that not only do veterans tolerate rookie requests for guidance; they welcome the requests and want to help these protégés. Perhaps a mentoring gene kicks in. Brian Wong continues in his blog: "Many people forget that the simple statement 'I'd love to learn from you' opens more doors than anything you can imagine. It's the ultimate statement of humility, respect, understanding, and curiosity. Through (numerical) aging, many of us forget to ask to learn. Maybe it's because we think we know enough, or that we may be rejected, or that it sounds needy."[7]

It is late at night at the San Francisco office of BTS, a global consulting firm that creates business simulations to help their clients hone their strategic thinking skills. Just three years earlier, Dillon Lee had joined BTS straight out of Middlebury College. Dillon, an athletic Korean American, is the kind of person who gives his all and, if necessary, would drag himself over glass to finish a race.

When a global energy company asked BTS several months earlier to help them with their strategic planning, the client alluded to a particularly difficult component of the project—building an algorithm to determine gas prices, industry impact, and returns in California based on aggressive new regulations and global dynamics. The client made it clear to Fredrik Schuller, a vice president at BTS, that their company had never before built dynamic models like this in-house. In response, Fredrik, who has a penchant for "new and challenging," made it clear to the client that BTS actually hadn't, either. Acknowledging the probability of failure, they agreed to proceed. Nonetheless, Fredrik was confident, because he knew just the guy to lead the project—that's how Dillon got involved.

Having led only one other project, Dillon was still a bit of a novice. But determined to deliver for the client, he and his team began to attack the problem. Following the usual protocol, the team interviewed stakeholders and subject matter experts early on and mapped out the concept. Dillon maintained his game face in front of his team while he privately wondered how he would be able to solve a problem that was so out of his league.

On this particular night, Dillon stares at his computer screen. He has no idea how to predict the flows of different crudes coming into which refiners in California and a myriad of other nuances in a complex (if not crazy) distribution system. As he breaks down the problem into its component parts, it occurs to him that, although no one person in the client's company knows the answer, there might be experts who can help him build each element of the model.

First thing the next morning, Dillon calls his contact at the client, who compiles a list of in-house experts. Dillon contacts these individuals until he uncovers the six experts he needs and begins gathering the data. It isn't easy, but after three hundred thousand lines of Excel code, Dillon and his team build a functional model—the first of its kind.

With literally only hours to spare, Dillon's team pilots the model with a team of experts. With each successive iteration, the model is further refined until it becomes a powerful predictive model. In the end, Dillon's model reflects the insights from more than one hundred participants in the strategic planning sessions. Those insights then make their way to the CEO/chairman and his strategy committee and have guided the company's asset and advocacy strategy.

What happens when smart, diligent professionals are out of their league? They seek out experts. And when they do, they build a collective belief in their ability to solve hard, complex problems. And that belief can be infectious.

Dillon is only one of the dozens of examples we uncovered of rookies who became expert magnets, pulling experts in to help them solve new challenges.

When you ask one veteran, you get one expert. When you ask a smart rookie, you gain access to a team of experts. This is the network effect at work. While this knowledge accelerator may average 5X, with the hungriest and most humble rookies, that 5X network effect can become a 25X effect. Imagine what is possible when rookies reach out into vast social networks?

## Practice 3: Mobilize Ideas and Resources

The best rookies seek out and marshal expertise and bring back their newfound network, like a big-game hunting prize to feed their community. Consider how Pierre-Yves Cros, one of the directors of Capgemini Group, one of the world's foremost providers of consultancy, technology, and outsourcing services, saw the formulation of a flash mob of new talent. Pierre-Yves, with strong support from the CEO Paul Hermelin, had engineered Capgemini's presence in India, which he grew to over 57,000 people strong in 2013. In India, Pierre-Yves sees more than just a vast population; he sees resourcefulness, a hunger, and a willingness to collaborate to solve problems.

Pierre-Yves is making one of his usual trips to India, to Mumbai for a town hall meeting of their then 360 staff members. On his mind is a problem with an important client. The client's project is in danger of running over budget and over time, and the team back in Paris has yet to find a solution.

During the town hall meeting, Pierre-Yves briefly discusses the challenge the team in France is facing. He admits that they still haven't solved it. Salil, a young engineer/leader in his mid-twenties (the typical age in the office), raises his hand and asks if Pierre-Yves can tell them more about the problem. The executive explains the problem in more detail. Before the meeting even adjourns, Salil and team kick into high gear finding data and exploring options. After the meeting, Salil opens up a chat site on one of their internal networks and builds a network of approximately twenty collaborators who could help solve the problem. These aren't senior leaders or even the most experienced consultants, but worker bees. But, with a hive mentality, they work continuously and collectively. They begin with brainstorming, but when a potentially feasible solution emerges, they move quickly to problem solving and building the solution.

By the time the sun sets the next day over Mumbai, Salil and team have solved the problem. And, by the time Pierre-Yves's plane lands back in London and he arrives at his office, the file has been transferred and the solution is in his inbox. Pierre-Yves is wowed by the work of this young engineer and his flash hive. Pierre-Yves, now the chief development officer for Capgemini Group worldwide, said, "They worked fast and were flexible. The team didn't just talk about finding a solution; they solved the problem right then and there."

This young engineer didn't have a solution; he had something far more valuable: access to a network. But he didn't just consult with them; he mobilized them and put this smart, capable, and willing group of collaborators to work.

In complex environments, winning organizations tap into the greatest number of brains. When do you need to give a problem to a smart network? When is it time to remove organizational barriers, forget about organizational hierarchy, and allow a hive mentality to flourish?

Crowdsourcing is growing as a viable and efficient alternative to in-house or expert-led solutions to complex problems. Revenues for crowdsourcing firms grew 53 percent between 2009 and 2010, and 74 percent between 2010 and 2011.[8] Organizations like Makesense .org, a two-year-old, rapidly growing network of social entrepreneurs who consider themselves "gangsters," do "hold ups" where they rapidly mobilize talent to solve some of the most interesting social challenges at a municipal level.

Perhaps it is a flash mob of talent, mobilized around an immediate challenge, which then dissipates when the problem is solved. But these talent pools can extend beyond simple crowdsourcing to form lasting learning communities. For example, Nike's New Crew (discussed in chapter 1) was initially mobilized to help the executive team imagine the future of Nike culture. But the New Crew concept became a permanent fixture in the organization, with talented young professionals rotating into the New Crew team to serve for a year (while continuing to work in their day jobs). Their charge? Inject the organization with fresh ideas and create an infectious optimism across the company.

At Nike, what began as a solitary effort to reach out and get input on one issue became a tool for harnessing and mobilizing the talent on the fringes.

## BUILDING ROOKIE SMARTS

Saum Mathur, one of the chief information officers (CIO) at Hewlett-Packard and named one of the top one hundred CIOs by *Computerworld* magazine, embodies the Hunter-Gatherer mindset, even though he is a recognized expert in his industry. One of Saum's favorite mantras is never be afraid to say "I don't know." He believes that "I don't know" is the start of a learning process. When someone enlightens him, he can then share this information with ten other people. With technology changing fast and an explosion of new possibilities, Saum finds himself using his mantra more than ever—especially in the world of "big data" and analytics, where system requirements begin with what is unknown rather than with a set of facts. Recently Saum was asked to present his priorities and perspectives on big data at an industry conference. Instead of doing a typical "show up and throw up" presentation with a set of standard slides, this astute CIO posed questions to the audience. Sure, he might have worried that his colleagues would be put off, but they weren't. They applauded his openness and were drawn in. The organizers said it was the best session of this two-day conference. Furthermore, by posing questions, Saum connected with others who face similar challenges. These peers quickly formed a community and are finding answers to questions they didn't even know they had. Saum said, "It is the network effect of not knowing."

Leaders often face pressure to be thought leaders for their organizations and to have ready answers. When they reverse roles and become the one who is seeking rather than the one who is sought after, they become more alert and strengthen their rookie mindset. And, while you don't need to have all your money stolen on a five-leg trip to trigger a state of high alert, you probably need a change of perspective.

Several years ago I gave a presentation at an impressive, state-of-the-art facility. At the back of the two-story auditorium on the upper level was a control room where a team of technicians ran the audiovisual elements of the show. During a break in the seminar, one of the AV technicians ventured down from the control box to talk with me. He told me that he had run AV for a seminar I had given at this location several months earlier. He was intrigued by an assignment I'd given the group that day called the "extreme question challenge" (the goal of which is to lead a group without making any statements and only asking questions). He had decided to put it to the test at home with his young children. He wanted me to know the profound impact this exercise had on his family and how it had completely changed the way he and his wife led at home.

I was delighted to learn of their success and quickly suggested he share this experience with the executives participating in that day's seminar. He was surprised but agreed. As the executives returned from break, the AV technician stood front and center on the auditorium stage, and I handed him the microphone. As the lights came on and his mic went live he looked out at the sea of people with wide eyes. There was an awkward moment of silence and then he said, "Wow. I'm used to being up in the AV box. Things look *very* different from down here."

This young technician and father extraordinaire taught the executives a powerful lesson that day in leadership and learning. He also taught me that sometimes we need a sudden change of perspective. We need to get up from our seat in the AV box, as it were—from our comfortable seat at the head of the table or from our cushy corner office—and see what it's like up front, onstage; conversely, top leaders need a chance to listen and learn from those at the lower levels of the organization.

The following learning experiences are designed to help you swap seats, change perspectives, and learn from new sources. Which one will help you open a mental window?

1. **Teleport Yourself—** *Rediscover your newcomer, rookie state.* Transport yourself in time and place to when you were starting your first professional job after college. Remember how you felt, what you did, and how you approached the work. Use this insight to provide great leadership to your new college graduate and to renew your own work.

2. **Multiply Your Expertise—** *Build an expert network by seeking expert advice.* The next time you are faced with a challenge that falls within your area of expertise, avoid the temptation to jump in. Instead, reach out to at least five other experts with your questions, thus bringing in new expertise to bear on the challenge at hand. Ask the experts and keep asking them until you find new patterns.

3. **Reverse the Mentoring—** *Ask a junior colleague to mentor you.* Reverse the learning roles. Instead of offering your insights and expertise to a more junior colleague, find someone younger and less experienced who can mentor you. Allow them to teach you new approaches or technologies and give you insights that reflect your consumer base or employee population.

4. **Talk to Strangers—** *Expand your network and perspective.* Eliminate the distortion caused by the echo chamber. Remove your

information filters and consider views contrary to your own. For example, if you read the *New York Times*, try reading the *Wall Street Journal*. As Robert Shiller, 2013 Nobel Prize winner in economics, said, "It's like having a good friend who is a devout believer in another religion. You can learn a lot from a friend like that, even if you don't pray in his church."[9] As you change the stream of information you receive and consider contrary views, you will not only expand your thinking but also widen your network.

5. **Make a Map**—*Map your terrain.* Take a step back from your current organization and map the terrain the way a newcomer or a cultural anthropologist might. Map out: Who are players? What are the rules of the game? What is valued in this culture? Who can I align with? Where are the customers? Who are the experts who can guide me when I get stuck?

6. **Borrow a Job**—*Swap jobs for a day.* Identify a colleague in an adjacent area and swap jobs for a time period—anywhere from one day to two weeks. Use the exchange to gain new insights and to formulate the naïve questions that a newcomer might ask.

## SEEKERS AND FINDERS

The ceiling of the Sistine Chapel at the Vatican is considered to be one of Michelangelo's great masterpieces and one of the greatest works of the Renaissance. Most of us have been taught the basic story: Michelangelo painted this great work while lying on his back for four years supported by a network of scaffolding. When I dug into the history, however, I was rather surprised to learn that the Sistine Chapel was his first fresco and that he didn't do it alone.

The suggestion to commission Michelangelo for this work was whispered in Pope Julius II's ear by several of Michelangelo's rivals.

They knew that Michelangelo favored sculpture and that he had never painted using the fresco technique (painting on a plastered wall while the plaster is still damp, allowing the colors to chemically bond with the plastered walls). They proffered his name in hopes that his rookie project would be a fiasco and that Raphael, who was painting the fresco *The School of Athens* in a room down the hall from the Sistine, would be summoned to save the project.[10]

Michelangelo sought expert help. He collaborated with the learned theologians of the papal court, who suggested themes and ideas that the artist then further refined.[11] Aware of his inexperience with fresco, the great artist hired two assistants, each deeply skilled in the technique, who worked alongside him for several weeks until he had mastered the necessary skills. He then continued working essentially solo, with the minimal collaboration of assistants. The result, of course, was one of the great treasures of the Renaissance, which, like Michelangelo's other painted work, is not as much a painting as it is a two-dimensional sculpture—the creation of a sculptor who happens to be working with paint. Like the name of the technique he so rapidly mastered, *fresco*, which means "while fresh," his painting was new, unprecedented, and an innovation of his time.

Not far from the famed Sistine ceiling, which depicts the story of Genesis, is the north wall, depicting several of the stories of the New Testament. One panel illustrates a story instructive to those of us who find ourselves in the newcomer role: "Ask, and it shall be given you; seek, and ye shall find; knock, and it shall be opened unto you."[12]

Those who seek knowledge will find it. When we authentically ask experts to guide us, they give willingly of their expertise. To would-be Hunter-Gatherers: Look outward, talk to strangers, and seek mentors to guide you. As you do, you will expand your network and multiply your own expertise.

## CHAPTER SUMMARY

**Hunter-Gatherers** lack the knowledge and expertise they need and are forced into a sense-making mode that causes them to reach out to others for guidance.

**Local Guides** are confident and operate in an environment that they understand, so they stay close to what they know and dole out advice rather than seeking out learning.

## THE MINDSETS AND PRACTICES

|  | ROOKIE SMART MODE<br>Hunter-Gatherers | VETERAN COMFORT ZONE<br>Local Guides |
|---|---|---|
| **Circumstance** | Rookies are new to the terrain, disoriented, and lack the knowledge and expertise they need. | Veterans have experience and knowledge of the terrain, which gives them confidence. |
| **Mindset** | Because they need information and knowledge, Hunter-Gatherers operate in a state of high alert, keenly aware of their surroundings. | Confident in their environment, Local Guides think like an adviser, guiding and directing others. |
| **Practices** | Hunter-Gatherers tend to:<br>1) Scan the environment<br>2) Seek out expertise<br>3) Mobilize ideas and resources | Local Guides tend to:<br>1) Look for data that confirms what they already know<br>2) Entrench within their tribes<br>3) Disseminate their knowledge |
| **Result** | As a result, they learn quickly by tapping into a network of smart, capable, willing collaborators. | As a result, they maintain their existing beliefs. |

## Cultivating Rookie Smarts

You can foster a Hunter-Gatherer mentality by conducting any of the following learning experiments found on pages 94–95 or in Appendix C.

1. **Teleport Yourself**—Rediscover your newcomer, rookie state.

2. **Multiply Your Expertise**—Build an expert network by seeking expert advice.

3. **Reverse the Mentoring**—Ask a junior colleague to mentor you.

4. **Talk to Strangers**—Expand your network and perspective.

5. **Make a Map**—Map your terrain.

6. **Borrow a Job**—Swap jobs for a day.

## CHAPTER 4

# FIREWALKERS: MOVING CAUTIOUSLY BUT QUICKLY

Fear is the freaky troll under the bridge that leads to achievement.

—RICHIE NORTON

It is summer solstice in the Spanish village of San Pedro Manrique, located in the autonomous community of Castile and León, and thousands of visitors have gathered to watch the annual firewalking ritual. At the center of the town square, villagers carefully prepare an open fire pit approximately ten feet long and three feet wide. They comb, level, and stoke the live embers to a peak temperature of 777 degrees Celsius (1,200 degrees Fahrenheit).

Despite the long distances they have traveled, spectators from around the world are not allowed to participate; only villagers are permitted to walk the fire. A band plays and the energy of the crowd swells.

The chosen firewalkers, dressed in traditional white shirts draped with red sashes, have nothing between the soles of their bare feet and the carefully prepared bed of live embers. As they face the strip of fiery coals, an aura of resolve seems to envelop each firewalker before he takes a series of fast and forceful but small steps across them.

Next up is eighty-year-old Alejandro Garcia Palacias, who has crossed the coals fifty-seven times before. His fascination with firewalking began during his childhood. When he was a young boy, he watched the village elders crossing the coals and determined to participate in this rite of passage himself. Like most of the other villagers, Alejandro carries a second person on his back when he crosses the coals, an ostensibly greater feat.

The ancient ritual of firewalking has been practiced for thousands of years, from India to China. In the 1970s, Tolly Burkan introduced this practice to the modern corporate world, attempting to demystify and share the ritual. Building on Burkan's earlier efforts, self-help gurus such as Tony Robbins popularized the practice as a self-realization and team-building event. While these ceremonies might seem like opportunities to conquer fear and transcend physical pain, the popular perception of firewalking as a dramatic demonstration of mind conquering matter is misguided.

In reality, firewalking offers a stunning demonstration of physical laws: Coals do not conduct heat well, so the transmission of heat from the hot center of the coal to the foot is delayed.[1] If you watch closely, you'll notice that those who walk the fire never stop moving; they dance across the coals nimbly and quickly. As a result, their feet do not stay in contact with the surface of the coals long enough to induce a burn. If they slowed down their pace, they would, of course, be severely burned.

Understanding the physics behind walking on fire unlocks one of the keys to those with rookie smarts. They move like firewalkers: both cautious and quick. In this chapter, we'll explore this fundamental question: *How can a lack of experience actually help someone take bold action without getting burned?* We'll also explore a surprising corollary: Is it possible that a rookie's apparently bold actions are not quite as risky as they might seem? Could bold action be less a matter of big moves and more the culmination of a series of swiftly executed small steps, each minimizing risk?

## MARATHONERS VERSUS FIREWALKERS

When people have established a history of positive feedback that accompanies mastery, it becomes very easy (and quite comforting) to project this affirmation into the future. We assume history will repeat itself, and our performance will continue to be stellar.

When this happens, what do we do? Frequently, we simply do more of the same. We proceed in a steady fashion. Isaac Newton's first law of motion provides a helpful illustration. It asserts: Every object in a state of uniform motion tends to remain in that state of motion unless an external force is applied to it. Galileo referred to this phenomenon as inertia. Inertia keeps us going where we've been going and doing what we've been doing.

This more-of-the-same plan of attack produces consistent results in a stable environment where nothing is changing. But when our environment shifts, more-of-the-same can lead to catastrophic failure and unexpected and undesirable outcomes. In the best-case scenario, destabilization forces us out of our state of inertia. But, what if change happens more slowly? What if the clues are subtle and we aren't paying attention? Chris Fry, head of engineering for Twitter, said, "Your mind becomes blind to changes in your environment when you aren't paying attention. When you are walking down the trail for the one hundredth time, you miss things."

As we stop paying attention to details, we become disconnected from reality. It's not just that we don't notice things around us. Sensing our resistance to new ideas or information, the people around us stop sharing the details that might conflict with our preconceived notions.

Brad Skelton, CEO of Depth Industries, a business investment company headquartered in Australia, described it this way: "Experienced people can get distant. They get a skewed sense of their own knowledge and think they know it all. They then become disconnected. It's not that they are off 'playing golf,' they get disconnected little by little. Arrogance starts to emerge and soon everyone is saying 'yes' to them. It happens so subtly, they are oblivious that they've arrived at this place."

Without realizing it, yesterday's masters have become slow moving, stiff, and easily distracted. They go through the motions but are only half there. The feet and the arms are moving, but the brain is dead. Or, at least mostly dead.

While maintaining a steady pace, doing more of the same, experienced professionals may tend to:

1. **Take Big Steps**—They move in extended strides, failing to carefully coordinate their actions with others around them, often bypassing checkpoints with key constituents, stakeholders, and other voices critical to the positive completion of their work.

2. **Move at a Steady, Comfortable Pace**—Veterans are in it for the long haul. They have plotted their course and are maintaining a sustainable pace. Their slow, steady progress means that they can be easily outrun and outmaneuvered by those with greater agility or a heightened sense of urgency.

3. **Assume They Are Still Doing a Great Job**—In this robotic, desensitized state, veterans fail to recognize changing conditions. They move forward, focused on their objective, blithely unaware of feedback that could help them correct course. They end up operating on autopilot unless someone has the courage to break the trance.

Consider how one expert who missed the signals not only veered off track but also hit a dead end.

## Missing the Mark

DATAPROF,[2] a high-growth data processing service bureau, was feeling the pinch. Earnings per share (EPS) was coming in essentially flat (at a penny per share) and the majority stockholder from Asia had replaced the CEO. The new CEO was charged with leading the company through a major turnaround to improve everything from the financials to the company's public face in the marketplace.

As part of the makeover, the board authorized a consolidation of their various office locations and commissioned the build-out of a new corporate headquarters campus in a prestigious business park in Texas. Although expensive, building a new headquarters campus would signal a new direction for the company. It was seen as one of the quickest and surest paths to shore up their damaged image. The task of designing and overseeing the development of the campus fell on the newly hired VP of corporate services and to the incumbent director of facilities, Jack Peterson,[3] who oversaw both the financial and physical administration of the company's facilities. In his early forties, Jack had built a solid career, working previously at a major corporation based on the east coast of the United States. Jack was accomplished, sure of himself, and perhaps even a bit smug. His new boss said, "He knew how to put up buildings and get it done. He projected a sense that 'I've been doing this for a long time, and I know how to do this.'"

With the remit from the board, Jack and his team of managers began doing what Jack knew best. Jack let senior management know that he'd get back to them with a scoping for the project—a critical milestone for a venture measured in the hundreds of millions of dollars. Jack and his staff assembled a team of real estate agents, architects, and developers and began studying the options and crunching the numbers, moving ahead at a steady pace.

Roughly twelve months later, per his prior experience, Jack and his team had scoped out the new campus and prepared to present the renderings and third-party validations to the board. It was a high-stakes presentation and a huge step, as this was the first time the board would see the specs for the new campus. Jack buttoned down his analysis and reviewed the numbers: He'd traveled this path before. He knew where he was going and how to get there.

Assembled in a dark mahogany conference room on the tenth floor of their current high-rise headquarters just north of downtown Dallas, a dozen board members listened to Jack's pitch and reviewed the financials. At first the meeting seemed run-of-the-mill, if not downright dull. Board members were warm to the proposed plan, but their questions turned in a direction Jack had not anticipated. They wanted to know how this property and the requisite investment would enhance DATAPROF's image. Jack was stuck. He knew that the company's image was the driving force behind the new campus, but he hadn't taken this goal much into account when he'd been going through the usual motions with his team. He had approached the project from a facilities and financials perspective, but he hadn't grasped how different this project was from the many others he'd led before: Senior management didn't see this building as just a building. They saw it as a strategic marketing effort, a message Jack had completely missed.

Jack had been plenty confident in himself, but now the CEO and the VPs lacked confidence in him. The VP of corporate services asked Jack to leave the company.

## Moving in Lockstep

The project continued, and the campus was built. But it was built under the leadership of someone who forged a very different path. This time, the VP of corporate services didn't hire another facilities expert; he brought in Bob, a veteran financial manager, with virtually zero experience in facilities.

Bob, a graduate of Southern Methodist University, had been successful as a controller for a large office technology company. Like Jack, Bob was in his forties and had a head of prematurely white hair. He was keenly aware that he knew very little about facilities and probably couldn't tell a steel-constructed building from a tilt-up, but he had important adjacent know-how—he knew how to seek out the views of his stakeholders and operate inside a complex organization.

When Bob began the project, he brought the self-confidence of a successful run at Xerox, but he was anxious in a new organization and in a role that would force him to stretch beyond his comfort zone and to quicken his pace. His new boss gave him the lay of the land with some Texas straight talk: "You don't want the divisions on the outside of the tent peeing all over your project." Acting like a Hunter-Gatherer who leverages the expertise and support of others, Bob knew he would need to bring the other divisional leaders along with him. With the divisional leaders operating as feudal kings of their own empires, this would require both caution and political savvy.

Moving fast, Bob began interviewing the heads of the departments that would occupy the new building. They sat together to review plans and Bob sought feedback. He made sure to touch base with each division head, at least briefly, at least every sixty days, and stayed particularly connected with Marketing, HR, and Investor Relations—the divisions that were sculpting a new corporate image. After several rounds of check-ins, Bob learned that one of the external real estate agents on the project wasn't listening to a number of the divisional leaders inside the company. Bob investigated and had the agent removed immediately from the project. When one divisional leader took issue with features of the new campus, Bob took it with grace and humor. When one stakeholder complained that there would be too much sunlight on his corner of the building, Bob replied, "Well, I can't change where the sun comes up, but let's figure out what we can do." Bob didn't manage the project with top-down scoping; he built the campus from the bottom up, coordinating every step with his stakeholders and taking small but quick actions. Jack's confidence closed him off from productive input; Bob's fast coordination and swift action opened doors. With the full support of the divisional leaders and the board, the campus was completed and became an iconic landmark in the business park and community.

The rookie's reality consists of a glaring, gaping hole between what they've previously done and what they must now do. They don't necessarily lack self-confidence (in fact their natural self-confidence is probably what produced the courage necessary to venture into new territory). What they do lack is *situational* confidence—the easy assurance that you've successfully completed a similar task in the past. Consequently, the rookie feels anxious, uncertain of his footing, and eager to prove himself.

The rookie's anxiety is not of the clinical variety that causes people to shut down; rather it is a productive paranoia, an urge to break out of one's comfort zone, to join a new peer group, to move to the next level of performance. Our study revealed that people in rookie situations were twice as likely to feel pressure to impress their coworkers than in situations in which they were more experienced. They also reported feeling more pressure to impress their boss in these rookie situations. Yet, counterintuitively, employees were more likely to feel a debilitating sense of pressure in situations in which they had more experience. In other words, pressure to perform propels rookies forward while the same sort of pressure impedes progress for veterans.

Columnist David Brooks captured the essence of the rookie's productive paranoia in his August 6, 2013, column in the *New York Times*. He confesses, "I started writing a column for the *Times* about a decade ago, and I endured a tough first few months. That was, in part, because, like anybody starting a new job, I wasn't sure I could pull it off. So, especially in the first few months, I had a self-preoccupied question on my mind: How am I doing? There was no non crazy-making answer to that question. I was always looking for some ultimate validation, which, of course, can never come. But, after a little while, I settled into a routine and my focus shifted from my own performance to the actual subjects I was writing about."

Tomas Chamorro-Premuzic, professor of business psychology at University College London, says that this awareness of our limitations, this realistically lowered sense of self, is actually conducive to success. He states, "After many years of researching and consulting on talent, I've come to the conclusion that self-confidence is only helpful when it's low. Sure, *extremely* low confidence is not helpful: it inhibits performance by inducing fear, worry, and stress, which may drive people to give up sooner or later."[4] He explains that just-low-enough confidence helps people recalibrate and causes them to pay attention to negative feedback, work harder and prepare more thoroughly, and avoid the appearance of arrogance and the delusions that often accompany hubris.[5]

## THE FIREWALKER'S WAY

Anxious to establish themselves as productive members of a peer group, top-performing newcomers propel themselves forward through iterative cycles of experimentation while learning to stay deeply connected to their stakeholders. As an experienced engineering manager at eBay observed, "We have to remember that newcomers are sprinting and you are running a marathon." In their mad dash to advance, the top-performing newcomers tend to take small steps, move quickly, and seek feedback and coaching.

### Practice 1: Take Small, Calculated Steps

The newcomer is operating in the dark, so she minimizes risk by taking small steps. Any frequent traveler knows the feeling of waking up in the middle of the night in a new hotel room and needing to find your way to the bathroom. Your outstretched arms serve as human antennae as you feel your way through the dark. As your arms feel for signs of a bathroom door, your feet take the smallest of steps, lest you give yourself a concussion (as I once did at the Opryland Hotel in Nashville). As you enter the bathroom, you pat down the furniture and fixtures, cautiously trying to orient yourself. By the time you return to bed, your eyes have adjusted and your stride has lengthened.

Rookies use a similar strategy as they seek to close their knowledge gap. They use every available sense to navigate their way through an unfamiliar environment. They maintain close contact with their surroundings to avoid unanticipated obstacles and calibrate their movements in order to mitigate the risk associated with exploring new territory. While rookies often look as if they are performing difficult feats, they aren't big risk takers. Our survey data showed that, compared with veterans, rookies are less likely to take risks. They only act boldly when they don't realize they are acting boldly.

They take risk out of a venture with their small steps and continual feedback loops. Once they realize how clueless they actually are, rookies become risk-mitigating machines. Successful entrepreneurs also practice this sort of risk mitigation. Studies show that the best entrepreneurs are not big risk takers; they remove risk from the equation. University of Chicago economist Frank Knight put it this way: Risk is calculable while uncertainty is just uncertain. Entrepreneurs operate in an uncertain environment, but they do everything possible to minimize risk.[6] Malcolm Gladwell summarized the work of French scholars Michel Villette and Catherine Vuillermot in this way: "The truly successful businessman is anything but a risk-taker. He is a predator, and predators seek to incur the least risk possible while hunting."[7] The best entrepreneurs aren't bolder than the rest of us; they are simply better at calculating a sure thing.

Sometimes what looks like a leap is simply a quick change of direction followed by a series of lightning-fast steps. Consider how Mark Carges took the risk out of a "risky" career move with a deliberate pivot, turning away from a central, standing position, and taking a series of small steps.

Mark earned his professional chops programming; he earned degrees in computer science from the University of California, Berkeley, and New York University and then worked as a programmer and architect at Bell Labs and then BEA Systems. After twenty years of programming and managing programmers (with skills similar to his own), Mark decided he wanted to try his hand at general management. His boss (and CEO) counseled, "You can't just be an engineer, you need to understand the business environment and spend some time in sales. You need to know how to build it *and* sell it." The CEO asked Mark to work for the head of sales in a sales management job, complete with a territory, a set of accounts, and a team of salespeople reporting to him. Mark had spent time in the field and had led several acquisitions, but joining the business side of the team was a different game entirely.

Mark said, "I had worked closely with sales, but working with sales guys is different than being one!" His mind began racing with thoughts like: *Everything I know to do isn't going to work here! It is quarterly driven! They want commissions, and accelerators and going to quota club! What am I going to do?* As a novice leading a team of sales professionals, Mark knew he needed to add value from his position, and he felt pressure to do it fast.

His first step was to get out in the field and talk with customers. Mark focused on the customers in the global accounts program because they were eager to have a relationship with the company and they cared deeply about the thing he knew best—the products they spent lots of money on. Because of his deep technical knowledge he knew which questions to ask, and, because he understood the customers' answers, he could probe and listen intently to their concerns and needs.

Mark realized that he couldn't transform himself overnight and lead by negotiating and closing deals like a seasoned sales leader. But, he still needed to add value quickly. So he started with what he did know—the product roadmap and competitive strengths. It's not that he fell back on old skills but rather that he pointed and pushed his capability into a new space. He used the clout of his new title to secure meetings with the senior executives at the customer company. Once in their offices, he listened to how they wanted to use the technology in their business, and then he worked closely with his sales team to provide solutions that would meet their needs. When he knew their products wouldn't meet the customer's needs, he helped the sales reps see that they were fishing in the wrong pond. Everyone won: Mark and his global account team overachieved their sales targets, the sales team was thrilled to have a leader who knew the products so well, and customers felt good about the solutions they were buying.

Mark's move into a rookie assignment taught him that "A job rotation out of my comfort zone, where I was challenged and had to learn new skills immediately, did more for my career growth than any other "safe" move I have made." And, now as chief technology officer and senior vice president of global products at eBay marketplaces, he continues to challenge his own staff to move into new positions on the team.

Yes, Mark felt out of his league (in a game he had never played) and he felt pressure to put points on the scoreboard. But he didn't actually start firing three-pointers from half-court. He pivoted. He used his current strength (carefully considered) as a pivot point from which he could step in a new direction and drive in closer and make the plays. Pivot, step, and then run.

When we're new and unsure, do we launch wildly from half-court? Do we end up running in circles? The most effective rookies do neither. They start where they are, pivot, and take a series of steps. They start from their position of strength, gain new perspective, and move forward. These movements may start small, but without experience and vulnerable, they are driven to keep pushing toward the goal line and get into a safe zone.

### Practice 2: Deliver Quickly

Mindful of the gap, rookies move quickly to gain ground. In our comparative study, rookies scored 60 percent higher on the timeliness of their deliverables. Rookies may move carefully, but they move fast.

The Comedy & Magic Club in Hermosa Beach, California, has launched the careers of many great comedians. The walls of the club are lined with photos of legends who have performed here in the past: Redd Foxx, George Carlin, Jerry Seinfeld, and Ray Romano are among the mix. The club's stage has been called "the old Yankee stadium of comedy."[8] Every aspiring comedian knows the place, and every comedian wants to play it. For many years, every Sunday night, headliner Jay Leno tested out jokes for the following week's opening monologues on NBC's *The Tonight Show*.

It is late on a Sunday afternoon when Michael Jr. walks through the club's back door. Michael Jr. is an up-and-coming comedian whose sense of humor reflects his deep faith. Throughout his school years, Michael Jr. wrestled with the symptoms of dyslexia. In his struggle to make sense of the world around him, he learned to free-associate and piece together situations based on the clues at his disposal. No doubt this continual state of sense making helped him hone his quick wit.

Michael Jr. has arrived at the invitation of club owner Mike Lacey, who has welcomed him to come down to the club and "chop it up" with a group of experienced comics that Sunday afternoon. From the back door, Michael Jr. walks straight to the greenroom, skipping the Museum of Comedy—a wall of famed photos and trove of comic treasures, like Jerry Seinfeld's Puffy Shirt, all encased in glass. Michael Jr. is just happy to be here. He's all eyes and all ears.

As Michael Jr. enters the greenroom he notices a wall of mirrors on one side of the room and a wall of bricks on the other. Each brick is signed by one of the ridiculously famous comedians who have performed here. In the green room today are three of those ridiculously famous comedians themselves: master funnymen Jay Leno (still hosting *The Tonight Show* at that time), Garry Shandling, and George Wallace, testing the opening monologues Leno wrote for the upcoming week. Although the atmosphere is casual and the other comics make efforts to put him at ease, Michael Jr. is still keenly aware that he is in the presence of what he calls "these soldiers of comedy." He maintains his reserve, holding back, and taking it all in. Observant by nature, Michael Jr. explains, "Like double-dutch jump rope, there's a rhythm to these things. And you need to understand the rhythm before you can jump in. If not, you can make a mess of things."

Leno begins launching into a bit on a news headline: *NFL football player hit in the eye with a referee's penalty flag suffers retina damage and sues league for $200 million.* These champion comedians and writers banter back and forth, searching for a knockout punch line. Some funny stuff has been offered, but nothing has popped. Newcomer Michael Jr. spots an opening in the rhythm. He knows he needs to jump in quickly.

After a short pause, he deadpans, "You know, he's not gonna see the half of it!"

The veteran comedians laugh and then do what professional comic writers do—they give a cool, composed signal of approval: "Yo. That's funny." Mike Lacey invites Michael Jr. to take the stage at the Comedy & Magic Club a week later. Jay Leno tells Michael Jr. that he'd love to have him on his show . . . not in the back room writing jokes, but in the coveted seat next to Leno. Michael Jr. is now a sought-after headliner sharing laughs with audiences around the world.

Sure, Michael Jr. has a quick mind, but most comedians will tell you that, no matter how snappy, most good jokes are developed through a slow, painstaking process. In the greenroom, surrounded by these masters, this greenhorn doesn't have the luxury of time. He can't rely on that same, slow process. He spies a small opening, and jumps at the chance to join a new peer group, to make his mark and deliver the goods. Like the best rookies, he is cautious but quick.

When you are new, do you make steady, slow contributions? Or do you first watch cautiously and then, spotting an opening, jump in with something sizable? Sometimes it is wise to start small before going big.

Ray Lane, former senior executive at IBM, Booz Allen Hamilton, and Oracle, described his learning curve this way: "I was always put in jobs where I was in over my head, so I never had experience to draw on. The knowledge gap forced me to really listen to people, let them teach me, and gather data as fast as I could. But I had this paranoia that I had to show leadership immediately, which forced me to quickly turn these insights into a plan." With each new leadership role, Ray repeated the cycle: get scared, reach out, get data, and move fast. Today, as a venture capitalist and investor, he helps young start-ups operate with this same lean mentality: experiment, get feedback, learn, and iterate your way to market leadership.

Instead of pacing themselves for a long, slow race, rookies tend to operate in bursts, and often at full throttle. But a word of caution is in order. Despite, or perhaps because of, their speed, rookies can quickly get off track. Just because they solve problems quickly doesn't mean that they are good at figuring out which problems are the most impor-tant. Our study showed that veterans were twice as likely to solve the right problem, not just the one presented. Knowing they are highly motivated to move fast, a wise manager will make sure the rookie is pointed in the right direction before the starting gun goes off.

**Practice 3: Seek Feedback and Coaching**

Moving cautiously but quickly in unfamiliar terrain, rookies require constant feedback to know if they are on track. The term *feedback* was coined in 1909 by German inventor and Nobel laureate Karl Ferdinand Braun. Braun first used the term to describe circular action and self-regulating systems in science and later economic markets.[9] As the term found its way into the corporate workplace, the concept was abused and distorted to the extent that, at the mere mention of the word, most expe-rienced professionals tense up and begin to display avoidance strategies. Why the aversion? For many, the idea of feedback conjures associations of evaluation, assessment, negativity, judgment, and even unworthiness.

The Wikipedia definition illustrates the vital role feedback plays in improving performance and accelerating learning: *Feedback is a process in which information about the past or the present influences the same phenom-enon in the present or future.* In other words, feedback is information to help someone calibrate his or her performance and stay on track. When a thermostat is set to 72 degrees Fahrenheit, a feedback process is started. At set intervals, a sensor inside the thermostat measures the air temperature and then adjusts the heating or cooling unit accordingly. If the temperature has fallen below the set point of 72 degrees, the heating unit is activated. If at the next interval the temperature is above 72 degrees (which is likely because the heating unit has been on), the heating unit will be turned off. The actual temperature is rarely at the precise set point, but always approximating 72 degrees. If you want the actual temperature to hit exactly 72 degrees more often (or if you wish to avoid the big swings in temperature), what can you do? You shorten the time between successive rounds of feedback.

Because rookies seek frequent feedback, they regularly receive vital information that helps them quickly learn and calibrate their performance. As they adjust, their adaptability invites the coaching that so naturally follows feedback.

The propulsive power of iterative feedback and coaching on high-performing, rapidly learning rookies is evident in the meteoric career path of Ezekiel Ansah, or "Ziggy," who put on football pads for the first time in 2010 and was rated one of the top defensive players in the nation by 2013.

Ansah left his native Ghana to attend Brigham Young University in 2008. At six feet, six inches, Ansah hoped to play basketball and was convinced he would be the next LeBron James. The BYU basketball coach saw it differently. Ansah was cut from the team the first year he tried out and again in 2009. Disappointed but not defeated, Ansah walked onto the track team and competed for one season in the 100- and 200-meter races and in the triple jump. The track coach saw it differently, too. While Ansah had the speed for track he also had the size for football. So the track coach walked Ansah down the hall and introduced him to Bronco Mendenhall, BYU's head football coach.

Ansah had never before played football. True, he had seen the game from the stands (as one of roughly sixty-three thousand people typically in the stadium for a home game), but he possessed only a vague understanding of the rules. Intrigued by Ansah's enormous athletic potential, Mendenhall granted him a six-week probationary period. During this time, Ansah was to join the team for 6 a.m. weightlifting workouts and team meetings. To Coach Mendenhall's surprise, Ansah (who majored in actuarial statistics) didn't miss a single meeting while maintaining perfect attendance in all of his classes.

At his first practice, Ansah needed help to put on his shoulder pads, couldn't do a three-point lineup stance, and even missed the blue bags when running tackling drills. Undeterred, Ansah, who has been described as "quiet, modest and humble,"[10] sought help from his fellow players and coaches, who rallied around him to teach him the game. Nate Meikle, sideline reporter for the team (and former Cougar wide receiver), approached Ansah during an early-season practice. Meikle, who is five foot nine, 175 pounds and probably looks more like a trainer than a former collegiate athlete, said, "Hi, Ziggy. My name is Nate, and I want you to know that I'm excited to see you play this season." Ansah replied, "Oh, thank you very much. Do you have any advice for me?" Meikle says, "I have met hundreds of football players in my role as sideline reporter and I've said similar things to dozens of players over the years. Ziggy was the only one to ever ask for advice."

As Ansah began learning the game, he was frequently singled out at practice and pushed harder than the other players. He responded by listening, learning, and going to work. In 2010, he got modest playing time on special teams and in 2011 he played nickel pass rusher. By the 2012 spring training, Ansah, at 270 pounds, was playing linebacker and recording key statistics in every series. By midseason 2012, Ansah had so thoroughly mastered the techniques that he was playing every down. Coach Mendenhall observed, "All this is so new to him that he relishes and just kind of takes on every new challenge. While it's new and different, he won't walk away from the challenges, he doesn't see himself above anything, and really has kind of an 'I will work and I'll prove and I'll earn my worth' [attitude] rather than 'I expect anything.'" On another occasion Mendenhall commented, "You want to help him, because he's just so sincere, with this combination of naivety and a genuineness. . . . Anyone who underestimates what he is capable of learning and how fast he can comprehend it and apply it, that would be a grave mistake."[11]

In May 2013, Ansah's family, who had never seen him play football, flew from Ghana to New York for the NFL draft to watch their son join the Detroit Lions as the fifth pick of the first round. Explaining this bold but not surprising move, Detroit Lions general manager Martin Mayhew said, "We had the opportunity to work with him [at the Senior Bowl] and teach him, and we saw the way that he could learn, how quickly he picks things up, and we saw the impact that he had in the game so we felt very comfortable with him."[12]

In his rookie season with the Lions, Ansah, now twenty-four, transformed from a speculative prospect into a legitimate starter. In his third week he was nominated for the Pepsi Rookie of the Week. Head coach Jim Schwartz said, "He learns something new every week. He practices well. His technique continues to improve." Ansah played better as an NFL rookie than almost everyone expected. In the first five games of 2013, he led the Lions' defense with three sacks and two forced fumbles and started three weeks at right end. Ansah's rookie status served him well in several ways. Because he didn't grow up idolizing pro players, he isn't intimidated by them. He just takes down each left tackle as if they are an anonymous target. Veteran defensive end Israel Idonije said, "he doesn't get caught up in all the hype around his opposition. I think that's an advantage." And, although Ansah is highly coachable, former defensive coordinator Gunther Cunningham points out that he's not overcoached and that he thrives "when we just let him play." So, they line him up and turn him loose.[13]

An ankle injury had taken Ansah out of the game for a few weeks, but he finished the season with eight sacks, second highest in the franchise history for a rookie, and was named Mel Farr Rookie of the Year by his teammates.

Ansah's remarkable development from first-time-in-football-pads in 2010 to first-round draft pick in 2013 was fueled by a combination of forces. Yes, he possesses a natural athleticism and a love for this new game. He has also had coaches and teammates who saw his potential and taught him. But what was it that accelerated his sprint up this learning curve? It just might be his humility and coachability. When you let others coach you, you learn fast.

Feedback and coaching are becoming more important in the workplace, both as business cycles spin faster and as a new generation of contributors expect more. Consider this recent research.

- Millennials want "a constant stream of feedback and were in a hurry for success."[14]

- A 2011 poll conducted by MTV found that 75 percent of millennials want a mentor; 80 percent said they want regular feedback from their managers; and 61 percent of millennials say they need "specific directions from their boss to do their best work—a level twice as high as observed among Boomers."[15]

- A study published in the *Journal of Consumer Research* suggests that rookies seek and respond to positive feedback, whereas veterans seek and respond to negative feedback. Why is this? Alina Tugend of the *New York Times* explains: "One reason is that as people gain expertise, feedback serves a different purpose. When people are just beginning a venture, they may not have much confidence, and they need encouragement. But experts' commitment is more secure than novices and their focus is on their progress."[16]

Due to a combination of factors, experienced, successful professionals are often deprived of feedback. They've been successful, and others assume their internal navigation system will keep them on course. These veterans fall into the pattern extolled in the old adage "It's better to give than to receive." However, while the veterans are busy giving feedback, the rookies are seeking it. They're learning and building valuable connections. Smart managers need to make sure rookies have a regular stream of feedback and information to help them calibrate their performance and the connection points to stay on track. And, if experienced managers are truly smart, they will ensure that they, too, are receiving the same sorts of feedback to help them optimize their own performance.

Because rookies lack confidence, they operate cautiously but they also operate quickly, seeking to close the knowledge gap. Through feedback, they rapidly convert information into intelligence. This anxious, cautious, and quick approach does more than just benefit the rookies' learning and performance. Their mindset and skill set are perfectly suited for the lean and agile movements that are sweeping businesses, especially across manufacturing and technology organizations.

## BUILDING ROOKIE SMARTS

You don't need to walk on coals to develop a Firewalker's mindset. You simply need to move closer to the heat in whatever venture you are pursuing and begin to take well-considered risks. In innovation circles, there's much ado made of the phrase "fail fast." Taken at face value, this mantra seems counterproductive. However, the real goal isn't failure. The real purpose is to learn from your mistakes. So, get close to the heat. And, if you fail fast, make sure you learn faster. Try either of these two experiments to make failure safe and secure your learning.

1. **Risk and Iterate—*Remove risk as a blocker by defining a space for experimentation.*** Define two categories of work: 1) those tasks where success has to be ensured and 2) those where failure can be recovered from. This second realm becomes your playground—a safe space for you, your team, or newcomers to

struggle and potentially fail without harming your stakeholders or their business. Within the playground, identify a project
where you or your colleagues can take a risk and then in a
series of small, calculated steps, iterate until the solution hits
the mark.

2. **Get Your Hands Dirty—*Get close to the action.*** Getting closer to
the action can help you stay connected with the needs of your
customers, stakeholders, or employees. In the world of mining,
someone who is "at the coal face" is in the part of the mine
where they are actually digging and extracting the coal. As you
might imagine, at the coal face, you get your hands (and your
face) dirty. When you bypass layers of management (with its
share of sycophants, yes men, and plodders) and get to where
the coal is being extracted, you can get the information and
feedback you need to stay on track.

## THROUGH THE FIRE AND FLAMES

Thomas Dewar, Scottish baron, whiskey distiller, and world traveler,
observed, "There are two kinds of pedestrians . . . the quick and the
dead." His words capture the reality of walking through Hanoi, the
bustling capital city of Vietnam. With 2.6 million people and 4.5 million motorcycles flowing through the city every day, traffic is a torrent
of trucks, cars, motorbikes, and rickshaws. Heavy on traffic, Hanoi
is noticeably light on traffic lights (and those that do exist often seem
optional). Driving is technically done on the right side of the road, but
periodically, aberrant motorcyclists will cut through opposing traffic.
Crosswalks do exist, but they seem to be little more than suggestions:
locations where the odds of making it across alive are slightly higher
than elsewhere.

On the first day of our family vacation, the six of us stood on one
shore of a river of traffic raging through a four-lane road in central

Hanoi that we needed to cross. With no traffic lights to be seen, we assumed that the best strategy was to wait for a break in the flow. Our guide Hoang, a native of Hanoi, gently corrected us. He told us that no break in the traffic would be forthcoming, but he assured us that, nonetheless, it was possible to cross the roadway. Hoang instructed us to first watch—not only to make sure we saw what was coming, but also in the hope that the drivers might see us, too. Then he told us, "Just step out into traffic. Move quickly, but consistently. The traffic will go around you. And, do not stop. That will get you hit."

My teenage son seemed delighted with this system and was eager to lead the way. Suppressing all my parental instincts, I watched my son step confidently into the crossfire of oncoming traffic. Despite my fears, with each step he took, the speeding vehicles diverted around him. The sea of traffic parted, and he made it safely to the other side.

At their best, rookies make similar moves. Possessed of a productive anxiety to establish themselves as players and peers, they first scope out their situation. Then, avoiding bold, blind moves, rookies reduce risk by taking small, calculated steps while keeping their eyes wide open.

As newcomers facing a daunting challenge, we can feel the heat. We may wonder if we'll get burned or even consumed. But what at first looks impossible can be accomplished with a rookie tactic: Be cautious but be quick. And keep moving.

## CHAPTER SUMMARY

**Firewalkers** lack confidence and operate cautiously but quickly, seeking feedback to calibrate their performance and close the gap.

**Marathoners** feel capable and confident and operate at a steady pace, often forgetting to check in with stakeholders along the way.

## THE MINDSETS AND PRACTICES

|  | ROOKIE SMART MODE<br>Firewalkers | VETERAN COMFORT ZONE<br>Marathoners |
|---|---|---|
| Circumstance | Rookies lack situational confidence. | Veterans have proved themselves and have received accolades and validation. |
| Mindset | Because they are eager to prove themselves in a given situation, Firewalkers operate with a sense of urgency and with a cautious but quick mentality. | Because they are confident, Marathoners tend to pace themselves and have a "steady as she goes" mentality. |
| Practices | Firewalkers tend to:<br>1) Take small, calculated steps<br>2) Deliver quickly<br>3) Seek feedback and coaching | Marathoners tend to:<br>1) Take big steps<br>2) Move at a steady, comfortable pace<br>3) Assume they are still doing a great job |
| Result | As a result, they stay on track with their stakeholders. | As a result, they can veer off track and do their own thing. |

**Cultivating Rookie Smarts**

You can foster a Firewalker mentality by conducting any of the following learning experiments found on pages 118–119 or in Appendix C.

1. **Risk and Iterate**—Remove risk as a blocker by defining a space for experimentation.

2. **Get Your Hands Dirty**—Get close to the action.

## CHAPTER 5

# PIONEERS: FORGING AHEAD

The more you go to your limits, the more
your limits will expand.

—ROBIN SHARMA

The great Mississippi River—flowing south to the Gulf of Mexico a thousand miles west of the eastern seaboard of the United States—was the edge of civilization in the early 1800s. To the east of the river lay civilized lands; to the west: nothing, from the European perspective, a vast blank space on the map. Into this uncharted territory strode the pioneers and the frontiersmen. Some of these rugged individuals sought to stake a claim in the homestead free-for-all. Others prospected for treasure and riches—or trekked into the void in pursuit of religious freedom. The first, and perhaps the greatest, frontiersmen, Meriwether Lewis and William Clark, journeyed west on high commission from the U.S. government.

In 1803, after orchestrating the Louisiana Purchase, Thomas Jefferson was eager to discover a water route linking the Missouri and

Columbia Rivers, thus establishing a continuous passage from the Atlantic to the Pacific. Jefferson chose thirty-year-old Lewis, a highly intelligent man with a military background and wilderness survival skills, to lead the expedition. Although Lewis had been Jefferson's personal secretary and a member of the Washington elite, he traded in his pen and paper for rifle and powder and set about organizing the expedition. His first order of business was to recruit skilled draftsman and frontiersman William Clark to serve as co-captain.[1] By 1804, Lewis and Clark had assembled their team of thirty men and began their two-and-a-half-year expedition.

The expedition paddled their boats one thousand miles up the Mississippi to Camp Wood, just outside St. Louis, Missouri. From there they embarked on their journey into uncharted waters. They continued paddling or portaging their boats another thousand miles up the Missouri River until they reached the Continental Divide. Every day brought novel challenges and new discoveries. As historian Stephen Ambrose described, "Every time they went around a bend in the river, they had a surprise. Every time they crossed a mountain pass, they didn't know what they would see on the other side."[2]

To travel beyond the known boundaries, the Lewis-Clark expedition pushed through day after day of discomfort. When they finally reached the Bitterroot Mountains, a seemingly impenetrable mountain range in what is now northern Idaho, their stamina had been exhausted. Although they were pushing the limits of their ability, strength, and supplies, they knew they would need to cross these mountains if they were ever to reach the Pacific Ocean. And so, braced for a few more days of rough travel, they made their way through the steep mountain pass. What started as a daunting task turned nearly impossible when their scout lost the trail midway through the pass. The expedition wandered aimlessly for days through the difficult and treacherous mountains. They ate one of their horses just to survive. On day five, they awoke covered in snow. Wet, cold, and out of food, they began to eat their candles and wondered where, or if, they would find their next meal. On day eleven, they stumbled out of the Bitterroots and, with the help of the Nez Percé tribe, made their way down the Columbia River and to the Pacific Ocean. After wintering in modern-day Oregon, the expedition returned east, bringing vital information about the land.

As American travel writer William Least Heat-Moon captured, "Lewis and Clark went as students. They came back as teachers."[3] On their expedition, Lewis and Clark climbed more than just mountains; they climbed steep learning curves. They lived lean and hungry lives on a journey rife with conflict and discomfort. They built a pioneer mentality by continually pushing through and climbing up.

In this chapter, we'll explore several questions: Why does a lack of experience drive some people through a discomfort zone and up a learning curve toward new frontiers? Why do others settle where it is comfortable? Finally, we'll explore the constitution of those individuals who seem to thrive on the outer fringes.

## SETTLERS VERSUS PIONEERS

Like pioneers, rookies build paths through new territory every day whereas veterans tend to stay where it is comfortable and settle in. It's understandable why this happens. The more we do something the easier it gets. We acquire the tools to do the job, we learn, we build infrastructure. But the ease that comes from repetition and familiarity can be dangerous. As the going gets easier, we get comfortable and settle back in our easy chair, and soon we are working on Easy Street. When we need something, we grab for what's in reach, so we don't have to move from our comfort zone. Lebanese poet Kahlil Gibran captured this temptation in his exquisite book *The Prophet*: "The lust for comfort, that stealthy thing that enters the house a guest, and then becomes a host, and then a master."

In our study of more- and less-experienced employees, managers characterized veterans as twice as likely to seek certainty and to default to past behavior. For too many wizened workplace veterans, work becomes the equivalent of ordering a hamburger at every new restaurant we try. Once comfortable and consuming the fruits of previous labor, we can slip into a mode of behavior where we:

1. **Rely on What's Available**—When we are holding "a bird in the hand," we are less concerned with the two birds in the bush. So we cling to what we have, what works, and what is safe. I am reminded of this tendency every time I see the alert come up on my computer screen that says, "Software update available." I contemplate the risk of destabilizing my otherwise stable computing environment and the loss of productivity. I opt for "Not now" while wondering if there is a "not ever" option. I can get stuck in this cycle for months until program incompatibility forces me to upgrade.

2. **Follow Protocol**—With knowledge and experience come established practices, so we default to what we've done before. Existing players are often bound by existing infrastructure, processes or contracts that are already in place, while newcomers (and start-ups) have the luxury of developing the "right" processes from scratch. One corporate manager described the tension he feels daily between the possibilities that he sees versus the protocols that he follows: "Experienced people can see that things aren't optimal or could be improved. But they also see how hard it would be to change so they just accept what they've got and keep doing what they're doing. Eventually it just becomes 'the way it is around here.'"

3. **Stay in a Comfort Zone**—When you've built a comfortable environment, it can be hard to venture out into the cold. When a superstar sales manager for a rapidly growing company was promoted from his New York City metropolitan area to a broader regional sales executive role, he kept running the same plays

that had worked for him in New York. He walked the halls and worked through his local network. And, while he had a vast territory, he managed the business from the comfort of his New York office. He barely made his numbers, but never grew the business. The head of HR for the otherwise fast-growing company said, "His leadership just isn't scalable."

If Settlers operate with a silver spoon in their mouths, Pioneers make do with a shovel in their hands. Living on the outpost, they find a way to feed themselves. Those who forge ahead build what doesn't exist, and occasionally dig their way out of peril. To build something new, they must be willing to explore, to learn, to fail, and to improvise. Above all else, they must be willing to work.

Many of us know the headline: Starting with a $5,000 investment Sara Blakely built the billion-dollar Spanx undergarment empire. But this story of a modern entrepreneur addressing a very modern problem is a tale straight from the frontier. It is a testament to building, improvising, and working with the mind and grit of a true pioneer.

In 1996 Blakely was selling fax machines, making $40,000 per year, when she saw an opportunity right behind her. Unable to find the right underwear to wear with a pair of white pants, Blakely crafted her own solution. She recounts, "I cut the feet out of control top pantyhose. And realized it was better than anything I can buy on the market as far as smoothing. [But] it rolled up my leg all night under my pants. So I went home that night and said, 'I have to figure out [how] to keep this below the knee.'"[4]

Spotting an unmet need in the market, Blakely set out to build a product. She said, "I went to craft stores and found little bands and things that I thought could maybe go on the end of it. I researched yarns . . . and we went through hundreds of prototypes before we came up with the original Spanx."[5]

But Blakely knew absolutely nothing about manufacturing women's clothing or running a business. She read several marketing books and then designed a logo on a friend's computer. When it came time to trademark the Spanx name, she bought another book and did it herself. The first two years, Blakely recalled, she was involved in every aspect of manufacturing and selling the product, and reached out to countless lawyers and manufacturers to try to get her idea off the ground. All but one turned her down because of her lack of backing and experience. Instead of hiring experienced business managers, she hired people who also had no experience in their functional area, including the head of product development and public relations.

Blakely and her team of rookies worked tirelessly from her apartment, avoiding costly office space or other marketing and business tools until the product had taken off. Even then the team continued to improve. They figured out how to mass-produce the product *after* landing a major deal with seven Neiman Marcus stores. They quickly built a website after Blakely was invited to appear on *The Oprah Winfrey Show*. Blakely was working in uncharted territory, planning one step at a time.[6]

The company and Spanx brand are currently valued at over $1 billion. They sell hundreds of shapewear products for both men and women in more than sixty-two countries. In the years since the commercial success of Spanx, dozens of imitation products have been brought to market. Not only did Blakely create a company, she pioneered an entire industry.

Spanx is a tale of relentless resourcefulness. Ironically, what began as a quest for comfort pushed Blakely into an uncomfortable place, a business frontier where necessities had to be built from scratch and where progress was forged by overcoming setbacks and obstacles. Reflecting on the journey Blakely said that "failure is not an outcome, but involves a lack of trying—not stretching yourself far enough out of your comfort zone and attempting to be more than you were the day before."[7]

Are you working in your comfort zone, or have you stepped out into uncharted territory? Are you hungry enough to work this relentlessly?

## THE PIONEER WAY

Like those who brave the frontier, rookies are willing to tolerate discomfort and evince a relentless drive to tame the wilderness and survive. Their lack of experience places them on the fringe, where they are driven to meet basic needs and build a solid foundation. As Daniel Pink outlined in his book *Drive*, making progress in one's work is one of the most powerful and natural forms of motivation.[8] Because rookies are in an uncharted territory and an often uncomfortable zone, they are driven and work tirelessly to make forward progress. In our research, we've found that those who are new to a situation or type of work tend to build new tools and structures, improvise, and work relentlessly.

### Practice 1: Build New Tools and Structures

The pioneer often lives a subsistence lifestyle, scavenging for the resources needed to stay alive. He gathers or grows what he can eat now. The logic is "see a bear, shoot a bear." If the pioneer is fortunate, he will have a little left to trade for other goods, like cloth or tools, that he can use to make or build other basic necessities.

Consider one global company that operates with a pioneer mentality. It performs best when operating in uncharted territory, tackling problems outside its area of expertise. Fredrik Schuller, vice president at global consulting firm BTS (profiled in chapter 3), explained the BTS business philosophy by saying, "Our clients often ask us to do projects they know we have never done before. We feel comfortable taking them on because we know we will figure it out." This rookie spirit is embedded in the core of this Nordic company.

BTS was born of necessity. Working as a strategy consultant in Stockholm, Sweden, Henrik Ekelund saw how companies struggled to execute strategy, and he began using business simulations to sharpen their strategic thinking. Soon his clients were asking for customized simulations and were willing to pay more for something that truly solved their problem. Henrik and other leaders at BTS grew confident contracting for work they didn't know how to do because they had built a shared capacity for solving new, complex problems. In other words, they knew they could tackle new problems because they had years of experience being inexperienced—and being successful.

What is the secret of BTS's success? Part of the answer lies in the company's work process, where they collaborate closely with their clients and take on the problem in full, committing to a solution. They work in small steps, improvising until the business simulation is built to suit the need. The other factor is their people strategy, which reflects the twin values of freedom and responsibility. Jessica Parisi, senior vice president of BTS in the western United States, explains: "When you give people freedom, they rise to the occasion. But, with freedom comes responsibility and accountability." Instead of sheltering their junior staff, the senior partners expose them. They proudly place their inexperienced but bright and courageous junior staff on the front line, where they gain direct contact with the clients (including senior and C-level executives) and exposure to the harsh realities of the problem they've committed to solve. Meanwhile, the senior partners stay alert, scouting for potential problems and serving as a safety net for their junior staff who are out on the tightrope (see chapter 9 for how BTS creates this safety net). Each successful project strengthens their belief that they (and their clients) are at their best when solving new problems.

The "impossible deals" struck by BTS succeed because the company simply *has to* succeed. Henrik reflected on the last thirty years building BTS: "There is a certain passion and hard work when you are doing something for the first time." This small Swedish firm now operates globally, serving 26 of the world's 100 largest companies and more than a third of the Fortune 100, because they were willing to venture out and work on the front line with their clients. On the frontier, you build it because you need it.

How does working in "survival mode" focus your energy and attention? Is it possible that when we work to survive, we sow the seeds needed to actually thrive? And, is it possible that we do our best work in this hungry state? Perhaps passion is a by-product of working hard and the most intense form of learning—subsistence learning. We learn because we have to. Out in the field, in the moment, we must improvise and adapt to ever-changing conditions in order to survive.

## Practice 2: Improvise

"When you don't have resources, you get resourceful," said K. R. Sridhar, CEO of Bloom Energy and former rocket scientist for NASA. Without traditional resources, you learn to think and act like MacGyver, the secret agent of the eponymous TV series who could solve the most complex problems with everyday materials, some duct tape and his trusty Swiss Army knife. Authors Radjou, Prabhu, and Ahuja capture this MacGyveresque resourcefulness in their book *Jugaad Innovation*, which describes a fast and frugal approach to innovation based on the Hindi-Urdu term *jugaad*, meaning, "a creative or innovative idea providing a quick, alternative way to solve a problem."[9] Their central argument is that operating with scant resources increases inventiveness. C. Page Moreau of the University of Colorado has also studied the factors contributing to creative thinking and solutions. He has found that, given adequate time, constraints on resources actually encourage creative thinking. He explains: "We propose that, when certain constraints are active during a creative task, more creative processes will be employed."[10]

In our research, we found that those new to a task were twice as likely to believe that they didn't have the resources or skills they needed. So they have to get scrappy and make do with the resources they can scrounge up. Additionally, managers of newcomers rated rookies 44 percent higher than their veteran counterparts in "working without arrogance" and 40 percent higher in "subordinating personal needs." Rookies work without excessive ego, they improvise, and they just keep moving. They are improvisers and imperfectionists.

Modern pioneer Jane Chen has developed truly novel solutions to long-existing problems by embracing limits and maximizing constraints. In 2007 Jane was enrolled in the "Entrepreneurial Design for Extreme Affordability" course at the Stanford Graduate School of Business. The assignment for the course was to design a low-cost infant incubator to meet the needs of the developing world. Instead of trying to find a solution under this already significant price constraint (existing incubators cost $20,000), Jane and her team looked at the situation and decided that they needed even more constraints. Jane realized that the vast majority of premature births in developing nations occur in rural areas where there is limited access to a hospital. So, Jane decided that not only did her team need to develop a low-cost incubator, but they also needed to develop one that could function outside of a hospital, work without electricity, was easily transportable, required little to no training to use, and was sanitizable.

Piling on constraint after constraint didn't shut down Jane's project—it allowed her to develop a truly innovative incubator that is the first of its kind. The incubator she developed, called the Embrace Incubator, resembles a sleeping bag. It wraps around the underweight infant and keeps her warm through a pouch containing phase-change material that retains heat for four hours and can be recharged in boiling water in a matter of minutes. The entire incubator can be sanitized in boiling water, is compact and portable, is extremely intuitive, and costs $25.[11]

When faced with constraints, we improvise. We get creative. Improvisation can lead to discovery and land us in new places.

### Practice 3: Work Relentlessly

What drives someone to forge ahead rather than retreat to a place of comfort and safety? Are they simply the most motivated? Or perhaps they are those who are most constrained? As Paulo Coelho wrote in *The Alchemist*, describing the crossing of the great Sahara, "Once you get into the desert, there's no going back . . . and when you can't go back, you have to worry only about the best way of moving forward."[12] Perhaps the most motivated are those who lack another choice. A scuba diver exploring a sunken shipwreck dove into the vessel and followed a dive mate through an interior passageway. When his regulator hose got stuck in the wreckage approximately two-thirds of the way through the passage, he faced an urgent choice: Retreat back or move forward? Unable to negotiate backward through the dark, narrow passageway, his only choice was to find a way to untangle himself and continue forward. Like the diver, we can venture far enough onto the frontier that forging ahead is the only choice. For example, when the boss has already hired a backfill for our former job, we have no choice but to push forward.

Our research highlighted several conditions that cause newcomers, facing large gaps in their knowledge and capability, to move forward with urgency, working relentlessly along the way.

1. **Basic needs are not yet met.** When we are on the bottom rung of the ladder, and when that rung is mostly underwater, we are propelled to climb.

2. **New player.** When we are the new guys on a team, we are highly motivated to establish ourselves as players. Our survey of managers revealed that rookies are 12 percent more likely than veterans to persist in the face of failure. Roger Hill of the University of Georgia found that workers with less than two years of full-time experience had significantly higher work ethics than workers with two to eight years of experience.[13]

3. **Public scrutiny.** When all eyes are on us, retreat can equal failure. In our survey of professionals, we found that rookies were 40 percent more likely than veterans to work harder and put in longer hours in response to pressure or scrutiny. Veterans, on

the other hand, were 30 percent more likely to feel a debilitating or significant pressure not to fail.

Consider how Mark Zuckerberg forged his way from reckless hacker to serious CEO of the social media juggernaut Facebook. When Zuckerberg ventured out of his Harvard dorm room into the wilds of Silicon Valley in 2005, he faced intense public scrutiny. Not only did he lack business acumen, but many saw him as a socially awkward nerd who was not to be trusted with your personal data (or your friends). Others saw him as an eccentric genius, a boy CEO not capable of running a real company, even on Silicon Valley's relaxed standards. Either way, all eyes were on him.[14]

This young programmer didn't just work tirelessly on the product; he went to work on himself. He hired an executive coach and systematically studied the leaders that he admired. He began holding all-hands meetings to rally his growing troops. He focused on recruiting to bring in the brightest talent and created a unique and enabling culture. He wore a tie every day during 2009 to signal his seriousness about the company (and to shed some of his "hoodie" image). He continues to hire extremely capable leaders who share his vision for Facebook and bring skills that complement his own.

In building Facebook, Zuckerberg closed perhaps the most important business gap—his own capability as a CEO. He dug in, but not with the all-nighter, stereotypical of the programmer mentality. He worked iteratively and relentlessly over years until he was fit to lead.

## BUILDING ROOKIE SMARTS

Faced with the choice between a scrappy, relentless rookie and the more urbane sophistication of the experienced professional, why would a manager choose the former? While the experienced person has arrived, the rookie is arriving. They are striving. And, as a result, they are often more willing to do the hard work and endure difficult work conditions and challenges. Under the most difficult conditions, limits expand. Everything is possible for lack of another choice.

Consider what explorer Hernán Cortés did when he landed in Veracruz on the eastern shore of Mexico in 1519. He feared that those men who were still loyal to the governor of Cuba would rise against him in mutiny. So, on the pretense that the vessels were no longer seaworthy, Cortés ordered the ships to be scuttled. With the ships sunk and the option to retreat removed, Cortés led the march two hundred miles inland to conquer the legendary city of Tenochtitlan.[15]

"Burn the boats" was how Francisco Cervantes de Salazar captured this moment in his 1546 *Dialogue of the Dignity of Man*. With retreat no longer an option, one must forge forward. To build a pioneer mindset, push yourself into your discomfort zone. To ensure you don't retreat, burn the boats.

1. **Disqualify Yourself—*Move into your discomfort zone by taking on a job you aren't qualified for.*** Is it possible that our best work and greatest career successes come when we are working in a role that is daunting and quite uncomfortable? Perhaps it is time for you to take a job for which you aren't fully qualified. Instead of playing to your strengths, you might consider pivoting from strength, stepping out of your comfort zone into a zone of learning. When you step out, you might feel a pull to step back to the place where you feel capable, even safe. If so, take a lesson from Cortés and burn the boats so your only option is to move through the discomfort. Try any of the following:

   • **Take a job in a new domain**—If you've been running a consumer products marketing team at work, perhaps you need to venture over to the enterprise product division and learn how to lead in this new market.

- **Take on a broader role**—Maybe it's time to take your divisional program to the next level and champion the initiative across the entire company.

- **Take on a stretch challenge**—Take on a challenge that is a size or two too big.

2. **Become a Half Expert—** *See how fast you can get halfway up the learning curve.* While becoming an expert may be a long, arduous process (requiring up to ten thousand hours of deliberate practice in some fields),[16] one can quickly learn the basics and the latest developments through deliberate inquiry. Interview experts and ask them to teach you the essentials of their field or their expertise. Then ask them to tell you about the latest discoveries, debates, and dilemmas. To get started, try studying the field of expertise from the perspective of an actor or journalist doing research. For example, ask yourself: If I were an actor playing an astrophysicist on a TV series, what would I need to know and understand to get into character? If I were interviewing a social media maven, what would I need to know to be able to hold an intelligent conversation?

    Don't just learn enough to be dangerous. Learn enough to stay out of danger. Learn enough to know the right questions to ask. Then find the right people to ask and let the true experts answer them.

3. **Staple Yourself to a Problem—** *Attach yourself to a complex problem and let it drag you to a new space.* Geoffrey Moore, author, speaker, and business adviser, explained to me how he keeps his thinking and his work fresh. Geoffrey counters the temptation to come into a company, speak about what he knows, and then leave, by stapling himself to his client's problem. Geoffrey commits to a challenge and then lets it drag him into unknown territory. In

these unfamiliar places, his current models, theories, and perfunctory answers don't suffice. He must now improvise, think, rethink, and co-create with his clients. He must not only teach, he must learn. Geoffrey said, "I don't let go of the problem. I hold my breath knowing I will be dragged underwater. But, when I let this happen, it is a brand-new game every day."

Try stapling yourself to a problem. Let it drag you underwater and to a new place. You will not only arrive at new solutions; you too will become renewed.

## THE LUNATIC FRINGE AND THE OPEN FRONTIER

"Where there is an open mind, there will always be a frontier," said Charles Kettering.

Our continents may be settled, but the human mind needs to be continually pushed to its outer limits. People need uncharted territory.

For some, a sense of adventure or activism drives them to the fringe. Others go kicking and screaming. Some require a push. Those willing to leave the comfort zone of their expertise have the opportunity to climb a learning curve, forge new ground, and reap the promise of growth. As leadership blogger Dan Rockwell observed, "You grow on the fringes where comfort meets discomfort."

When we go to the edge of our limits, our limits expand. When we step into our discomfort zones, we might find that we have a much bigger comfort zone than we previously thought.

As the civilized world continues to expand, our frontiers are shrinking. Uncharted territory is mapped and becomes easily accessible (even from the comfort of laptops) and part of the establishment. The developing world becomes the developed world. However, with ventures of the mind, there should be no permanent settlements—only temporary camps. As Nelson Mandela illustrated with his life as well as his words, "After climbing a great hill, one only finds that there are many more hills to climb."

Perhaps it is time to disqualify yourself, and take a job you aren't fully qualified for. Trade in the silver spoon for a shovel and venture out into the open frontier. Take a look around and ask, What needs to be built? What needs to be done? Then start building something. Get scrappy. Persist until it's done. Explore, don't settle. While you might find that the learning curve is steep and a bit exhausting, the journey will prove exhilarating.

## CHAPTER SUMMARY

**Pioneers** are traversing uncharted and often uncomfortable territory, so they work to survive, improvising and working tirelessly to provide for basic needs.

**Settlers** are in established territory and have access to more resources, so they tend to follow protocols and do what is more comfortable.

## THE MINDSETS AND PRACTICES

|  | **ROOKIE SMART MODE**<br>Pioneers | **VETERAN COMFORT ZONE**<br>Settlers |
|---|---|---|
| **Circumstance** | Rookies are in uncharted territory and lack the resources that they need. | Veterans are working within the establishment and have their basic needs met. |
| **Mindset** | Because they need to forge through the unknown, Pioneers work tirelessly with a hungry, slightly desperate mentality. | Because their needs are met, Settlers are oriented to maintain comfort and create ease. |
| **Practices** | Pioneers tend to:<br>1) Build new tools and structures<br>2) Improvise<br>3) Work relentlessly | Settlers tend to:<br>1) Rely on what's available<br>2) Follow protocol<br>3) Stay in the comfort zone |
| **Result** | As a result, they push boundaries, take responsibility, and are creators of new value. | As a result, they use the resources that are readily available and become consumers, not builders. |

## Cultivating Rookie Smarts

You can foster a Pioneer mentality by conducting any of the following learning experiments found on pages 135–137 or in Appendix C.

1. **Disqualify Yourself**—Move into your discomfort zone by taking on a job you aren't qualified for.

2. **Become a Half Expert**—See how fast you can get halfway up the learning curve.

3. **Staple Yourself to a Problem**—Attach yourself to a complex problem and let it drag you to a new space.

# PART TWO

# CULTIVATING ROOKIE SMARTS

## CHAPTER 6

# THE PERPETUAL ROOKIE

It's what you learn after you know it all
that counts.

—JOHN WOODEN

"I had no clue how to do this, but somehow this turned out to be an advantage. . . ." That's how Bob Hurley recounted how he built Hurley International into an action sports powerhouse. Wielding a Skil 100 planer, a power hand tool used to shape surfboards, he described how it had all begun back in the late 1970s.

At the time, he was a shop kid working at a surf shop at Sixth Street and the Pacific Coast Highway in Huntington Beach, California—aka surf capital, USA. Not much good behind the counter, Hurley begged the store manager to let him work in the back, shaping the surfboards. A young husband and father with sun bleached blond hair, Hurley needed the work, and he delivered the boards on time—a rarity in the surf world. Soon some of the top surfers were competing on Bob's boards. Aaron Pai, one of Bob's surf buddies, bought Huntington Surf and Sport and offered Bob $2,400 to build eight boards branded under his own name. And so Hurley Surfboards was launched. Bob opened a shop of his own, and he never forgot Pai's initial leap of faith. Indeed, throughout his career, Bob Hurley would extend the same sort of trust and confidence to others that Pai had extended to him.

When Hurley decided to sell board shorts in his shop, he set his sights on Billabong's hot, new, long, punk-style shorts. Clueless about how to become a Billabong distributor, Hurley and his shop manager wrote dozens of letters to owner Gordon Merchant. After months of unanswered letters, Merchant showed up on Hurley's doorstep one day and agreed to let the persistent kid represent and manufacture for Billabong. Hurley grew sales from $7,500 to $300,000 and then $700,000 annually, until one day he found himself with $3 million worth of orders but no cash to purchase the raw materials.

Declined for a $200,000 line of credit by every banker he contacted, Hurley finally turned to Sam Simon, the eighty-five-year-old banker to the Los Angeles garment industry. Hurley told Simon his story straight up, admitting that he had neither the collateral to back the loan nor a formal contract with Billabong. Simon bypassed his bank's loan committee, which was sure to reject the loan, and handed Hurley the cash with a simple handshake. The cash infusion allowed the young company to continue to grow and form their own brand, deeply rooted in the dreams of the youth surf and skate culture. Today Hurley is an important part of Nike's vibrant action sports business.

While Hurley's early days were replete with rookie moves and naïve maneuvers, Bob has still not lost his rookie smarts. When Bob and I met at Hurley headquarters in Costa Mesa, California, it took fifteen minutes to get from the reception area to his office because, like a kid at play, he stopped to high-five employees, show off their killer new product line, and tell the designers how stoked he was about their latest work. In his office, Hurley unabashedly showed off his collection of the most fabulous Hurley products, punk rock memorabilia, and toys.

While he expresses no fear of failure, he admits to having a real fear of mediocrity: "I constantly worry that as we get bigger, we will stagnate." This aversion to being average keeps him and the company pushing the boundaries of what's possible.

Despite his innate sense of enthusiasm and opportunity, this perpetual rookie does admit that he has tough days when he can't find his sense of wonder and feels dead in the water. On those days, he remembers a chance encounter he had with Wayne "Rabbit" Bartholomew, the world champion surfer from Australia, in the 1970s. Bob explains that, back in the day, Huntington Beach had a clear pecking order, with tight cliques and skill levels that didn't mix. The top athletes surfed together in the prime waves, while the new kids and foreigners were relegated to the smaller swells. Hurley was just on the fringe of that inner circle of top surfers. One day, Hurley lost his board and swam toward the pier, chasing it down. On the other side of the pier Hurley spied Rabbit, surfing with a group of young kids—teenagers and twenty-somethings. Hurley paddled over to this celebrity surfer. "Whoa, Rabbit, you're a legend, dude," he said. "Looks pretty tight in there. Come surf with us," he added, as he motioned toward the bigger waves and professional surfers. Rabbit thanked him. "That's kind of ya, mate, but I need to be here with the kids. This is where I get my energy. They teach me." The Aussie champ then went back to play where the waves were inferior, but where the energy was infectious and the learning curve was still something to be conquered.

Like Rabbit, Hurley finds his inspiration from the young and the young at heart. When Hurley is stuck, he grabs his surfboard, heads to the beach, and rides the waves—not with the pros (some of whom are Hurley sponsored) but with the kids, the newcomers, the unknowns. They amaze him. Some days surfing does the trick; on other days, he simply walks down the hall to toss around ideas and consider wild possibilities with the rookies in his company.

Hurley possesses a special brand of rookie smarts—he is a perpetual rookie. Perpetual rookies are leaders who, despite years of experience and success, maintain a rookie mindset. They stay amazed—curious, humble, and fun loving. Instead of clinging to a false sense of mastery, they live and work perpetually on the steep side of the learning curve. These leaders aren't just rookies by circumstance; they are rookies by choice and through deliberate practice. It is a choice that is available to each of us.

## TAPPING THE WELLSPRING

Why do some people retain their rookie smarts? How are they able to avoid the pitfalls that snare so many successful professionals? To understand how perpetual rookies maintain a youthful approach to their work, let's get to know a few of these fascinating leaders—from athletes to artists to thought leaders to journalists to entrepreneurs.

Magic Johnson may have authored the greatest rookie upset in the 1980 NBA finals, but this remarkable performance wasn't his only brilliant act. While he was still playing with the Los Angeles Lakers, Johnson began thinking of life after basketball. He wondered why so many athletes failed at business, so he sought advice and created a network of experts. He began reading business magazines and absorbed everything he could about the world of business, going out of his way to meet with executives while on road trips.[1] After leaving the world of professional basketball, he started and continues to run several successful businesses and numerous charities and is now a joint owner of the Lakers and the Los Angeles Dodgers. When Magic led the bid to buy the Dodgers in March 2012, some worried that he had only played baseball once as a kid and didn't know anything about the sport. His response: "Did I play baseball? No. Do I love baseball? Yes." Magic then learned the game and brought his playful enthusiasm and characteristic "showtime" magic to the franchise.

At the other end of the spectrum is Annie Leibovitz, perhaps the most acclaimed and prolific photographer of our time. She has redefined the celebrity portrait and given us iconic images such as entwined

John Lennon and Yoko Ono, a pregnant Demi Moore, and Arnold Schwarzenegger astride a white polo horse. Unlike most famous photographers, however, Leibovitz doesn't have a large portrait studio. She prefers to operate unhindered by the constraints of a designated space. Not only does Leibovitz operate with the mentality of the Backpacker; she dresses the part. Clad in her signature hiking boots on the day of the shoot, she's the one wading through the water and sloshing through the mud to ensure every detail is right.

In 2007, when Disney approached her to capture a series of epic fairy-tale moments, Leibovitz was surprised. The combination of Disney's storybook magic and her own raw, edgy aesthetic seemed incongruous, but soon she discovered common ground in a shared love for great storytelling. Nevertheless, this was uncharted territory, as Leibovitz described the challenge: "It was an uncomfortable path. I didn't know what I was doing. I was definitely flying without a net." She began by ensuring that every A-list celebrity cast for the shoot was hungry for the role. The subject of the first shoot was Cinderella, featuring Scarlett Johansson. Like most of the other celebrities who took part, Johansson considered the chance to portray such an iconic image the role of a lifetime. Leibovitz studied dozens of versions of the Cinderella story to find the story's moment of maximum tension. On the day of the shoot, she obsessed over every detail. The result? A stunning portrait that captures both hope and despair as Cinderella descends the stairs at the stroke of midnight.[2] Gordon Bowen, a longtime collaborator and friend to Leibovitz, said, "We think that the most famous photographer in the world would have it down. But Annie approaches every job as if it is her first."

In the realm of business thought leadership, Peter Drucker was a prolific writer and a professor and management consultant who studied the ways human beings organize themselves and interact in the workplace, much like an ecologist would study the biological world. If you visit the Drucker Institute at Claremont Graduate University you can see a vast display of his forty published books, arranged in chronological order. One-third of the way through is *The Unseen Revolution*, which he wrote at age sixty-five. The other two-thirds of his creative work came *after* that, during a time many people consider retirement age. Drucker always eschewed the idea of being a guru, suggesting that people use the word only because *charlatan* is too long to fit into a headline. Colleagues at the Drucker Institute submit that this great thinker's work was "driven by an insatiable curiosity about the world around him—and a deep desire to make that world a better place, which allowed Drucker to continue to write long after most others would have put away their pens."[3]

Like Drucker, Helen Thomas, the trail-blazing political reporter who died in 2013, enjoyed a long career, one marked by numerous firsts: She was the first woman assigned to cover the White House, the first female officer of the National Press Club, and the first female member and president of the White House Correspondents Association.[4] Known for being "outspoken, blunt, demanding, forceful, and unrelenting," Thomas made many a president squirm, never ceasing to ask the hard-hitting, uncomfortable questions. She worked for seventy years, through eleven presidential administrations, celebrating her eighty-ninth birthday in the White House press room with President Barack Obama. It was said that Thomas worked with keen curiosity, an unquenchable drive, celebrated constancy, and stamina.[5] While Thomas's role required gravitas, she also had a keen enjoyment of her profession. Thomas said, "I love my work, and I think that I was so lucky to pick a profession where it's a joy to go to work every day," and "I think I'll work all my life. When you're having fun, why stop having fun?"

Described by many as one of the greatest entrepreneurs of our era, the perpetually boyish Elon Musk has founded or cofounded a handful of successful new ventures, including electronic payments giant PayPal, solar power systems provider SolarCity, SpaceX, which routinely launches rockets into space for NASA, and Tesla Motors, the maker of high-performance electric cars. Musk is the quintessential autodidact: He read the entire *Encyclopaedia Britannica* when he was eight or nine years old, taught himself computer programming at twelve, left his home in South Africa at fifteen, and put himself through the University of Pennsylvania. With degrees in physics and business, he has also taught himself aerospace, electrical, and automotive engineering. One of the reasons Musk is a serial entrepreneur is that he is an obsessed serial learner.

Perhaps the most stunning revelation about all of these leaders is not that they have maintained their rookie smarts; rather, their rookie mindset is the very source of their continued brilliance. Despite their varied innate talents and skills, all of these leaders share a set of traits that continuously replenish their rookie smarts: an insatiable curiosity, a humility that makes them lifelong students, and a playful but intentional approach to achieving their goals.

Let's begin at the source—the rookie's voracious hunger to discover and learn.

## Curious

Curiosity, or the strong desire to know or learn something, is more than just casual interest; it is a thirst for knowledge and understanding and a hunger to seek out novel experiences. Curiosity grows from a deep-seated belief that what you don't know is more interesting than what you do know. It might be expressed in a litany of probing or penetrating questions or an irresistible urge to disassemble a piece of electronic equipment to see how it works.

Those with curious minds want to learn from the people around them: They want to understand. They seek and explore. They are oriented outward, focused on other people, and interested in others' ideas and concerns. Psychologists distinguish between two types of curiosity. *Specific* curiosity causes you to actively seek knowledge. This leads to greater expertise and better recall of information. *Diversive* curiosity results in actively seeking out varied sources of novelty and challenge. It keeps one open to new possibilities by allowing us to reframe problems and explore unconventional paths and ultimately leads to better job performance.[6] Both types of curiosity shift people into rookie mode: seeking out ideas, and staying hungry and open. Moreover, curiosity underpins diligence and grit: Studies have found that people are willing to work harder to find answers when they are curious.[7]

Although the biology of curiosity remains mostly unknown, most researchers agree that curiosity is an innate, basic emotion that can be nevertheless easily extinguished by habit, routine, and other life experiences. Once lost, how do we rediscover our innate curiosity? By breaking habits and thrusting ourselves into new and unfamiliar circumstances where our assumptions are challenged and our senses can be overloaded.

Those who maintain or reengage their curiosity can also have a powerful effect on the organizations they are a part of. Their wonderings open up new possibilities. Their openness doesn't create weakness; it builds strength.

When Moied Wahid, a senior engineering manager at PayPal, was exposed to our research on rookie smarts, he gave his team a challenge: Forget what you know and think like you are doing this for the first time. Moied led the way. Instead of dispensing his view and giving out pointed feedback, he began asking questions and exploring new paths, often just asking, "Why is that?" or "Is there a way we can improve this?" His curiosity would spark curiosity in his engineers, who would then work ten times harder. These engineers would beam as they brought back their new discoveries and solutions to him. "There are so many things that I don't know, and I need my team to speak their mind," said Moied. This technology manager turned perpetual rookie continued, "I love it when people disagree with me because it keeps me thinking harder. My best day at work is when I'm proven wrong or when I learn something new."

Clinical psychologist Henry Cloud said, "Certainty is one of the weakest positions in life. Curiosity is one of the most powerful. Certainty prohibits learning, curiosity fuels change."[8]

## Humble

The perpetual rookies I studied were able to fend off hubris and retain humility, despite repeated success and mastery. While *Webster's Dictionary* defines humility as "the quality or state of not thinking you are better than other people," I find the Hindu perspective, as taught by Indian philosopher and statesman Sarvepalli Radhakrishnan, to be more instructive. Radhakrishnan suggests that humility is the non-judgmental state of mind from which we are best able to learn, contemplate, and understand everyone and everything else. Truly the first step to learning is accepting that we don't know everything. When we recognize our own limitations, we seek guidance and remain open to correction. Humility, without regard for expertise or position, allows for the development of coachability and teachability.

Unfortunately, hubris is the common cold of the smart and the successful, striking politicians, professional athletes, school principals, and corporate executives alike. In the business world, it can be particularly deadly, bringing down both established and start-up companies. As tech executive and blogger Frederic Kerrest wrote, "It lulls them into cockiness, complacency and a sense of invincibility and causes them to lose sight of what matters most—making customers successful."[9] When we see ourselves as bigger, stronger, and more capable than we really are, we turn inward and rely solely on our own strength, when, ironically, our earlier successes were likely a result of our turning outward, accepting the help and counsel of much-needed guides and mentors. Hubris is the great stumbling block to progress.

While I've seen many organizations and careers destroyed by hubris, I have also witnessed how a simple act of humility can transform an entire organization. I was working for a technology company during a time of rapid growth, massive change, and upheaval in the industry. My team was charged with ensuring that the company's senior managers understood and had the skills to execute the business's growth strategy. Ours was a highly visible program, and I worked closely with the three top executives: the president, the chief financial officer, and the chief technology officer. The senior executives would articulate the company's strategy to the program participants; my team and I would build execution skills.

The first run of the program went well, but the participants claimed that they didn't understand the strategy. We made a few adjustments. In the second run of the program, the participants' negative feedback was even stronger. By the third run, the participants were nearly hostile—recommending the program be halted until the senior executives could more clearly articulate the strategy. We were all frustrated yet eager to get it right.

As was customary after each program, I met with the three executives and shared the participant feedback. They were unusually quiet. Assuming they didn't understand the participants' perspective, I reiterated the problem. Jeff Henley, the CFO (and my boss's boss), became agitated and blurted out, "Liz, you don't need to beat us up. We know we need to fix this. The problem is that we don't know how to do it." He motioned to his two colleagues, both senior executives whom I held in great esteem, and explained matter-of-factly, "We've never run a twenty-five-billion-dollar company before, so this is new to us." The president and the CTO nodded in concurrence. I went slack-jawed. It had never occurred to me that these veteran executives were learning along with everyone else. Jeff continued, "If you could help us learn how to do this, that would be useful." I was deeply touched by his admission and this moment of humility turned the tide. I arranged for a renowned strategy professor who had been teaching strategy to our junior executives to come teach the senior executives (and me), and we shifted from teaching to learning. We re-architected the strategy, held the next program, and knocked it out of the park. It was a toss-up as to who was happier: the participants who received a clear, compelling growth strategy, or the senior executives who grew themselves.

In fast times, everyone is winging it—even the leaders at the top. But amazing things can happen when we admit that we don't know.

## Playful

If mastery requires deliberate practice, being a perpetual rookie requires purposeful play.

Many corporations have introduced measures to increase a sense of playfulness and informality at work: Ping-Pong tables in the lunchroom, beanbag chairs in the gaming room, and random dancing breaks. It's a good start, but my research shows that perpetual rookies inject a spirit of fun into everything they do, not just into the time they take "off" from work. For them, *all* work is play.

Paul Erdös, one of the twentieth century's greatest mathematicians and one of the most prolific, with more than 1,500 papers to his name, exemplifies this spirit of playful engagement. The founder of the field of discrete mathematics (the foundation of computer science), Erdös posed and solved some of the thorniest of problems in number theory.[10] Erdös had a burning love for his work and was affectionately called "the boy who loved math" by Deborah Heiligman and LeUyen Pham. Erdös regularly invited people to come "play" with him and was known for arriving at the home of potential collaborators and announcing, "My brain is open."

What happens when our work becomes play? What happens when we inject pleasure, fun, and humor into the daily grind? In his book *The Levity Effect*, management consultant Adrian Gostick discusses the role of humor in workplace performance. He draws upon multiple workplace studies to conclude that humor strengthens relationships, reduces stress, and increases empathy. Leaders who operate with a sense of humor create an environment where people can contribute at their fullest and those who work in a fun environment have greater productivity, interpersonal effectiveness, and call in sick less often.[11] In the classroom, when professors used levity in their lectures, students scored 15 percent higher on exams.[12] When our work is play, time flies and we stick with it. We forgive mistakes, improvise, and learn. We invite others to join the fun. This levity effect lightens our load as we climb an arduous learning curve.

## Deliberate

While play is imperative, lifetime rookie smarts isn't all fun and games. The first three characteristics of the perpetual rookie—curiosity, humility, and playfulness—are decidedly childlike in nature, but the last is not. Perpetual rookies are also deliberate; they approach their work with a great deal of intentionality. By deliberate, I don't mean focused, grueling, repetitive, and self-monitored. I mean that these perpetual rookies are likely to be mindful of what they are doing and how they will do it. They don't jump in impulsively or erratically; instead they deliberately adopt an open mindset, much like Twitter and Square co-founder Jack Dorsey, who said, "I'm not a serial entrepreneur. I'm not a serial anything." For perpetual rookies, each time is their first; each challenge is unique.

Imagine how tempting it can be for a skilled, experienced physician, familiar with the standard diagnostic differentials and treatment options, to quickly jump to a diagnosis. Dr. Hollander, who has practiced internal medicine for fourteen years, is one of those doctors who, despite her mastery, does not let her mind automatically race to the obvious conclusions. When she encounters a complex condition, she doesn't offer a snap judgment; instead she intentionally goes into rookie mode, taking a couple of days to contemplate, read relevant articles and books, or just sleep on it. She is remarkably accurate with her diagnoses. She believes it is not because of her expertise, but because of her restraint and her deliberative approach, which has provided dozens of patients with early warning on cancerous conditions. Ironically, it takes a methodical self-awareness to avoid getting trapped by the current methods and practices of our professions.

What do we find at the nexus of curious, humble, playful, and deliberate? The first three traits come together to produce an openness to the world and a fresh way of thinking. Add to this mix deliberateness and you find someone not only able to think fresh, but someone who is willing to hit the refresh button, much like we do when our personal computers get bogged down or even corrupted. Perpetual rookies stay fresh by clearing the cache and wiping the slate.

But it takes more than just an occasional refresh. Perpetual rookies are skilled at toggling between states of mind, between their veteran savvy and their rookie smarts, like the Marvel comics superhero who lives an ordinary life (for example, as Clark Kent) but is vigilantly watching for a situation that warrants the superpowers of his alter ego (for example, Superman). The real skill of the perpetual rookie is knowing when to play the role of veteran and when to don the rookie cloak. In times of tumult and transition the best leaders know when it is time to stop, unlearn, and relearn.

## FINDING YOUR INNER ROOKIE

Like so many other successful leaders, you may still have the heart of a rookie, but you now find yourself playing the role of the seasoned veteran. Is it possible to rekindle your rookie smarts? What do you do if you've lost your rookie edge? Consider how creative genius Andrew Stanton rediscovered his rookie mojo.

Andrew Stanton had been part of the Pixar brain trust for years. He collaborated as a screenwriter and co-director with John Lasseter on a string of mega-hits: *Toy Story*, *A Bug's Life*, *Toy Story 2*, *Monsters, Inc.* But when Stanton got a chance to sit in the director's chair with *Finding Nemo*, he became consumed by the fear that this movie would be Pixar's first failure. He told *New Yorker* writer Tad Friend, "I just felt, I suck, I suck, I suck, and they're going to replace me." Things came to a head over the Fourth of July. While he was celebrating at his parents' house, Stanton finally admitted to himself that he had lost his naïveté and sense of wonder, and he determined to get it back. Friend describes the mission statement that grew out of Stanton's realization and determination:

"Try to get fired," he wrote, as a corrective. "Don't be concerned about box office, release dates, audience appeal, Pixar history, stock prices, approval from others." He added, "You have a gift for looking at the world with a child-like wonder. . . . You lose that and you lose it all." After this reckoning, he began to ask colleagues for help, and the main thread of the film, Marlin's quest for Nemo, finally came together: Kids thought it was hilarious, and adults found it almost unbearably poignant.[13]

Stanton relearned how to be a rookie. He learned that he could embrace his inexperience *and* still be the director. When he admitted that he was stuck, others rose up to help him, just as they'd done, he now remembered, when John Lasseter had admitted he needed help. Stanton's epiphany wasn't a reinvention of himself; it was simply a restoration of a mindset. While finding Nemo, Stanton rediscovered his own sense of wonder.

For those who need to rekindle your once-bright rookie smarts, try one of these experiments:

1. **Try to Get Fired.** *Instead of playing it safe, just play.* Don't over-think or second-guess yourself. Just do what feels right. If you are spending too much energy trying to win, try once again working the way you did when you had nothing to lose. Like Andrew Stanton, you might find that when you push the limits, you will end up doing what is natural, and what you once did easily. If the thought of trying to get yourself fired is too terrify-ing to face, play a game of make-believe: Ask yourself, "What would I do if I wasn't afraid of losing my job?" Write it down and then go build organizational support for these ideas. With this safety net in place, when you walk out onto that high wire, you are far more likely to get inspired than fired.

2. **Throw Away Your Notes.** *Toss out your best practices and de-velop new practices.* The late management thinker C. K. Pra-halad was repeatedly ranked as the world's top business professor by the Thinkers50 website. At his memorial in 2010, his wife,

Gayatri, revealed that C.K. threw away his teaching notes every semester. When she responded with alarm the first time she saw his precious teaching notes in the rubbish bin, he replied, "My students deserve my best, fresh thinking every time." It is no wonder students at the University of Michigan's Ross School of Business lined the halls trying to listen in to his perpetually oversubscribed classes, creating a fire hazard. Try shredding your crib notes, stump speeches, and the other templates that have you stuck in a rut. As you do, you will offer fresh thinking to others while also renewing your mind.

3. **Surf with the Amateurs—*Spend time with the amateurs and the young at heart*.** Instead of working with your peer group of experienced professionals, spend time with the newcomers. Watch how they work and play: Learn from them. When Sergio Marchionne, fifty-nine-year-old Italian chairman and CEO of Chrysler Group, was turning around the failing automaker, he vacated the chairman's office on the top floor and moved his office next to the design and engineering teams and spent time on the shop floor. He got rid of many senior management positions, combed through the organization, and found twenty-six young leaders who would report directly to him.[14] They kept him close to the action and energized as he reinvigorated the whole company. If you are stuck at the top, go talk to those at the bottom of the organization or those new to the game. How might their ideas shape you and their energy renew you?

Rekindling our rookie smarts requires conscious effort, but it doesn't have to be hard work. It might be as simple as returning to our wonder years when we were curious, unpretentious, and playful. Could this be as easy as slowing down, stepping off the path, and learning to see something with new eyes?

## LEARNING TO SEE

What happens when we learn to see the world through a child's eyes? I was given this gift of sight a number of years ago, schooled by a three-year-old and a dozen flapping fish.

At the time, I was working in a demanding management job and raising three young children, ages seven, five, and three. My boss, John, was also a father to a young son, so he knew the joys and challenges of being a working parent. Sensing early signs of burnout in me, John "sentenced" me to three weeks of play. "Go use up your vacation balance. I don't want to see you for three weeks." My husband and I decided to serve out this sentence at the Sheraton in Maui. For the first few days of vacation, I was in my normal mom mode of "hurry and worry" (as in, get ready for this, finish that, hurry or we'll be late).

By the sixth day of the vacation, I had finally begun to allow myself to slow down the pace. The morning started the same way the others had: Get the kids up, dressed, fed, and slathered in sunscreen, so we could go play. My husband left the hotel room with our two oldest children in tow and headed to the outdoor breakfast spot that overlooked the pool and the beach. Christian, our three-year-old, and I were to catch up. As I cajoled our overactive toddler out the door, I remembered something John had shared with me months earlier. John, who practiced meditation, had been trying to take more time to just *be* with his son, letting his young son lead the way and set the pace. I was intrigued by the idea but had tucked it away for a time when there would be a pause in the chaos of parenting three young children. Today seemed like a good time to let Christian set the pace and the agenda for play. Instead of being the leader, I would follow his lead.

Christian meandered slowly along the path that led from the hotel lobby to the breakfast area, noticing every curiosity and would-be treasure he might gather along the way. We moved at a painfully slow pace. When I saw the koi fish pond ahead, my "hurry and worry" mode kicked in, and I hoped he wouldn't notice the fish and instead would skip across the little bridge to the breakfast hut, so we could catch up with the rest of the clan. Of course, he stopped to inspect the brightly colored fish. Following his lead, I stopped, commented on the "pretty fish," then gently reminded him that Daddy and the girls were already eating breakfast and would be playing in the pool soon. He was undeterred. Finally, I surrendered completely, squatted down, and started watching the koi fish with him.

At first I feigned interest. I had seen koi fish many times before. I had even seen them at the ancient temples in Kyoto, Japan, and at Larry Ellison's Japanese villa; I had seen koi fish. But as I watched Christian, I began to notice things I hadn't truly *seen* before—unique patterns, colors, and even shapes. I was now on my knees, eye level with my toddler, seeing what he was seeing. We made a hopeless attempt to count each fish in the pond. After a few minutes, Christian laid himself down on the walkway that crossed the fish pond so he could run his hands through the water and feel their scales. He was shrieking with delight as the fish lunged up to nibble his finger. I joined in and now we were both belly down, blocking a good portion of the pathway, with me sheepishly apologizing to other guests as they navigated around us. A good fifteen or twenty minutes, and a lot of people, went by.

Through the eyes of a child, I began to see differently. These fish weren't just overgrown goldfish; they were interesting and magnificent. Instead of hurrying up for prescheduled play, I finally slowed down and just *played*. That's when I saw koi fish for the first time.

What does your work look like through the eyes of a child? How could a stretch target be recast as an interesting puzzle or a chance to "level up" at a favorite game? How could a crisis or an emergency task force be reimagined as a pickup ball game with your mates? Could a brainstorming session become a game of make-believe?

We often ask children what they want to be when they grow up. Most quickly rattle off a long list: doctor, astronaut, teacher, pro athlete, racecar driver, or sometimes even princess. If you ask college students, they are likely to fake an answer. If you ask working professionals, many will admit they haven't a clue. But perpetual rookies have a different mindset. When they grow up they want to be a kid—permanently young of heart and mind. And they work deliberately and daily toward this aspiration.

When we look at the world through the eyes of a child, we awaken our natural curiosity, adopt a simple humility, revel in the chance to play, and, at times, behave willfully. When we make the deliberate choice to bring this perspective to our work, we renew our inner rookie. Instead of leaving work to go play, our work *becomes* play. Instead of leaving work to attend training, our office becomes the classroom.

The Buddha said, "It is better to travel well than to arrive." A Zen master knows that when it comes to knowledge, the joy is in the mastering, not in being a master. It isn't always an easy journey, but the sting of learning can be transformed into joyful relearning. The perpetual rookie knows that the real joy is climbing the learning curve, not standing on the top. When they reach the apex, they start looking for a new curve to climb, the same way a surfer is always on the lookout for the next big wave. And, if they get stuck? They just do what Rabbit the Aussie champion surfer did: Walk farther down the beach and go surf with the amateurs.

## CHAPTER SUMMARY

**The Perpetual Rookie** is a professional or leader who, despite years of experience and success, maintains a rookie mindset. They stay amazed—curious, humble, and fun loving.

### Perpetual Rookie Traits

**Curious**—A strong desire to know something, a thirst for knowledge and understanding, and a hunger to seek out novel experiences.

**Humble**—A belief that we are not elevated over others and a state of mind in which we are teachable and able to understand and learn from everyone around us.

**Playful**—A belief that our work is play, not just bringing play into our work environment.

**Deliberate**—Approaching one's work with high levels of intentionality, being mindful of what we are doing and why we are doing it.

### Rekindling Rookie Smarts

If you've lost some of your rookie edge, play around with the following learning experiments found on pages 156–157 or in Appendix C.

1. **Try to Get Fired**—Instead of playing it safe, just play.

2. **Throw Away Your Notes**—Toss out your best practices and develop new practices.

3. **Surf with the Amateurs**—Get inspired by the young and young at heart.

CHAPTER 7

# ROOKIE REVIVAL

The illiterate of the 21st century will not
be those who cannot read and write, but
those who cannot learn, unlearn, and
relearn.[1]

—ALVIN TOFFLER

Candido Camero was about to take the stage at Dizzy Gillespie's jazz club at Lincoln Center in New York City. The occasion was a celebration of his ninety-first birthday. One of the great improvisational jazz percussionists of the 1950s, Candido had played with most of the greats, including Dizzy Gillespie. Tonight he would be playing with students from the Manhattan School of Music.

Candido stood offstage, steadied by two loyal friends. As an announcer called his name, Candido shuffled toward the stage, taking small, deliberate (and seemingly painful) steps. His pace slowed as he took his position at the conga drums. He repositioned the microphone carefully; several fingers on his worn, dark hands had been banded together with rings of medical tape. Finally, he welcomed the audience and apologized for being slow, conceding that arthritis had made it hard for him to walk. Then, with a twinkle in his eye, he added, "I may be ninety-one, but when I play the drums, I feel twenty."

Candido began slowly and established the rhythm. Then he quickened the pace until his hands became a blur of white tape. No longer hesitant, he played with gusto, giving the audience a glimpse of what it must have been like all those years ago when Candido and Gillespie had burned up the room. Candido's performance that night wasn't just a jazz jamboree; it was a revival—a return to his earlier, rookie days.

As Candido's performance shows, rookie smarts need not be the exclusive domain of the young or naïve. In this chapter, we'll focus on two distinct approaches that can help even the most established players get into the groove again. One approach involves a shift in attitude; the other requires a change in circumstances. In both cases, the first step is to examine the *how* of cultivating rookie smarts, and the second is to decide *how fast*. A revival usually doesn't transpire with one performance; it grows out of a series of small steps and carefully calibrated moves that allow one to build momentum and respond as new patterns emerge—just as ninety-one-year-old Candido did in his performance with a much younger ensemble.

## JAZZING IT UP AGAIN

Every revival begins with an awakening, an increased level of focus and awareness. Immanuel Kant, German philosopher of the Enlightenment, claimed that he "woke from his dogmatic slumber" by reading the skeptical philosophical works of David Hume.[2] Once roused from our dogmatic slumber, we begin to see the world and our place in it with greater clarity and a sense of wonder. Rabbi Abraham Joshua Heschel described this awakening as "radical amazement": a way of getting up in the morning and looking at the world in a way that takes nothing for granted.[3]

But what does it take to rouse us from the comforts of convention, from the boredom and complacency—and downright unhappiness—that so many professionals experience? According to one Gallup poll, 70 percent of American workers claim to either hate their jobs or to be completely disengaged from them. Another poll found that 63 percent of American workers report having high levels of stress at work, with extreme fatigue and feelings of being out of control.[4] Is it really too much work that leads to stress? Or is it a toxic combination of too much busywork and too little challenging work that is to blame?

In my research, we surveyed approximately one thousand people from across a variety of industries, asking them to indicate the current level of challenge in their jobs and their current levels of satisfaction. We found a strong correlation between "challenge level" at work and "satisfaction level" at work. In other words, as the challenge level goes up, so does satisfaction.[5] Unfortunately, job satisfaction plummets for those shielded and walled off from real challenge. If this dynamic sounds at all familiar, you're not alone.

What are the signs that you have hit a wall and come to a standstill? You may have lost that "jumping out of an airplane" feeling of exhilaration that comes with new adventures. Perhaps you have slipped into the "been there, done that" mode where you whip out pat answers for the recurring problems you encounter weekly. Or maybe you lack energy and, despite being constantly busy, you're bored. For those who have lingered far too long on a plateau, you might even find that your boredom has turned into negativity. You can't imagine how this could have happened. Fortunately, you don't have to stay stuck in the grind.

Taking on more work can be exhausting, and yet, ironically, the antidote to this strain of burnout isn't *less* work. The cure for burnout is *harder* work. When we take on new challenges that require us to stretch ourselves, we become exhilarated and we rededicate ourselves to learning. A leader who had worked with Steve Jobs at NeXT Computer, Apple, and Pixar reflected on his career working in a perpetual zone of discomfort in this way: "When we can't find the pattern, the job is fascinating." Panera Bread CEO Ron Shaich agrees: "If you are learning, you'll never need to recharge."[6]

## 10 SIGNS YOU ARE
## READY FOR A NEW CHALLENGE

❑ Things are running smoothly.

❑ You are consistently getting positive feedback.

❑ Your brain doesn't have to work hard to be successful.

❑ You don't prepare for meetings because you already know the answers.

❑ You've stopped learning something new every day.

❑ You are busy but bored.

❑ You're taking longer showers in the morning and you take your time getting to work.

❑ It makes you tired to think you could be doing the same job a year from now.

❑ You've become increasingly negative and can't identify why.

❑ You're spending a lot of time trying to fix other people's problems.

*If you are experiencing one or two of these signs, you are ready to renew your rookie smarts. If you have three or more, you are also ready for a new challenge!*

The escape from a mountain of work is not *through*, but *up*—up the learning curve, that is. It is in these moments, when we start working our intellectual "muscles" again, that we feel the most engaged. Our muscles may burn, but, ironically, we don't burn out; we feel recharged and ready for more. All the more reason why the Backpacker mentality—light and unencumbered—is so freeing.

Easier said than done, of course, as novelist David Foster Wallace articulated so vividly in this admission: "Everything I've ever let go of has claw marks on it." Why do we cling so tightly to our knowledge and expertise? The reasons have less to do with fear than with utility. The process of unlearning isn't like packing up boxes of unused clothing or meaningless relics to take to the thrift store; rather, it is like giving away things we still use and the hard-earned treasures and precious pieces of our identity—the very things that have served us so well in the past.

Perhaps no story better illustrates the process of unlearning than the one Jim Collins tells. If you've read any of Jim Collins's widely influential management books, you will have discovered that he researches and writes with fanatical discipline. But Jim's expertise isn't limited to the field of business; he is also an avid and accomplished rock climber who approaches this pursuit with the same level of discipline and tenacity. In his mid-forties after twenty-five years of climbing, he could see that he had reached a plateau (literally!), so he retained a coach to help him grow as a climber.

Jim had learned to climb in the era of slanted or sheer vertical terrain, where a fall left you banged up and broken (if you survived at all). But today's top climbers traverse routes with a very different terrain. Much of the climbing now is done under overhangs, so the consequences of falling are minimal. When a climber falls, the bolt catches the rope when it comes tight, and he swings through the air with nothing much to hit—that is, assuming his anchors hold. The climber mostly suffers a bruised ego. To master this more challenging terrain, Jim would need to forget much of what he knew. Jim describes this journey in a chapter he wrote for the book *Upward Bound*.[7]

> The most important lessons from my climbing coaches—Nick and Heather Sagar—lay not in what I needed to learn, but in what I first needed to unlearn. . . . When Nick and Heather first began working with me, my years of experience on scary, vertical climbing taught me to fear falling and ingrained in me a careful, deliberate style that ensured survival. This conservative manner impeded my ability to ascend harder modern climbs, which require big dynamic moves constantly on the edge of failure. To climb a modern route at your absolute limit requires dozens of falls before you succeed—otherwise, well, it's not at your limit.

Jim's coach warned him, "We need to make you a worse climber for a while, so you can become a better climber." Jim had always climbed with precision and discipline, being sure of every step, but his deeply ingrained caution would hinder him on the new terrain he wished to climb. Jim began his relearning process by learning how to fall. It all started with a petrifying, but not painful, assignment from his coach: While in lead position, take a thousand falls over the next year. Jim started with baby falls, and then worked up to the bigger falls, eventually coming to enjoy them. He was awkward at first, fell often, and dropped down a few climbing grades while he learned to climb again.

Jim said, "My climbing did indeed worsen for a while. But then the new techniques started to click, and I felt the excitement of progress, of becoming expert again—only with a whole new style and mind-set. I was in my mid-forties, feeling a passion for climbing that I haven't felt since my teenage years. Rather than being depressed by 'stepping backwards in order to step forward,' I feel renewed energy." Through the ups and downs of the learning process, Jim concluded that the only way to attain a higher level of mastery was to let go of his expertise and adopt a beginner's mindset. To climb higher, this expert had to first let go. He let go of habits, strengths, and even his sense of stability and caution.

When we've hit a professional wall, are we able to let go of what we know and get comfortable being a beginner again? Are we willing to labor through a valley of incompetence? Many experts will continue at their current level—performing well enough but perhaps not reaching the heights they are capable of or that they have always imagined achieving. Those who are willing to let go and relearn, however, will most assuredly climb higher—and they'll find a lot more satisfaction in the effort than those who play it safe.

## LEARNING TO RELEARN

Bill Hybels, senior pastor of Willow Creek Community Church in South Barrington, Illinois, has observed, "We don't tend to drift into better behavior."[8] Indeed, it takes deliberate and conscious choice to improve and to shift into new modes of thinking and more mindful ways of operating. Initially, making the shift may force us to operate in a lower gear, to slow down, but ultimately such shifts give us the wherewithal to ascend even steeper learning curves.

Here are several strategies for planning your own climb on new terrains. First, change your mindset: Shift from the certainty of leadership to the uncertainty of *learnership*. Second, change your venue: Place yourself in a situation that demands rookie thinking and behavior. Finally, pace yourself.

## 1. Shift from Leader to Learner

Psychologists use the term "confirmation bias" to capture the tendency of people to favor information that supports their preexisting beliefs or hypotheses. One reason we are susceptible to confirmation bias is that once we are deemed experts, once we are in a position of power, the costs of being wrong can feel dangerously high. When faced with conflicting data, we weigh the impact of weakening our own position against the odds of being wrong. We gauge the trade-offs, often unaware of our own mental calculations. Many leaders succumb to the pressure to show conviction, be consistent, and stay the course. The very trait that makes them seem so desirable—their reliability and steadiness—can cause their organizations to cling to faulty decisions or untested assumptions. Another reason we accept information that supports our preexisting beliefs is that doing so often appears to be the shortest, most direct route between where we are and where we'd like to be.

What missteps are we making because we are convinced we are right? Or because we are in a hurry? Or believe that because we are the leader, we know the way? The times when we feel most sure of ourselves and least vulnerable are the times when we (and our teams) are, in reality, most vulnerable to disruption and defeat. To defeat the blinders of confirmation bias, we need to shift our sights: Instead of looking down from our position of leadership, we need to begin looking outward and upward.

Here's how one leader took his whole team back to their beginner roots to prepare for the performance of a lifetime.

It was January 2013, and the San Francisco 49ers had just won the divisional playoffs and advanced to the National Football Conference Championship game, where they would face off against the Atlanta Falcons, hoping to secure a spot in Super Bowl XLVII. Jim Harbaugh was only in his second year as the head coach and rookie quarterback Colin Kaepernick had been given the starting position just eight games previously. The team was stocked with many NFL veterans and nine Pro Bowl players, but they had missed making it to the Super Bowl by one game the previous year. Harbaugh and his coaching staff needed the team hungry and focused for the playoff game the following week. Instead of relying on the usual prep (practice, game films, physical therapy, etc.), Harbaugh kicked it up a notch. He enlisted the help of the team's media relations staff and the back office crew to help with this special assignment.

When the players returned to the locker room after practice, each found a laminated poster above his locker. It wasn't a team picture or a high-gloss mock-up of the coveted Super Bowl ring. The poster above each player's locker bore his own high school photograph, the name of his school, his ranking, and his stats. Sports columnist Monte Poole observed, "In a flash, Harbaugh had taken his players, adults and mostly wealthy, back to a time when they were boys playing for free, perhaps dreaming of that faraway day when it might pay off. Maybe they'd be in the NFL, perhaps with an opportunity to play in the Super Bowl."

Can you imagine the conversation in the locker room as the players were teleported back to the days when they first played the game? Could they remember what it was like to play when they were eager and uncomplicated? Those were the days without agents, contract negotiations, or press conferences, when their biggest fans were likely to be their parents. They remembered what it was like to play hungry. They remembered what it was like to have something to prove.

The players understood Harbaugh's message: The road from high school ball to the NFL was a hard grind. As a defensive tackle said, "[Harbaugh] wants you to grind the same way you did in high school."[9] This trip back to their youth was an invitation to take the field the upcoming Sunday the same way they did when they were all rookies— with nothing to lose and everything to gain.

The following Sunday afternoon, after trailing by seventeen points, the Niners pulled out a 28–24 win over the Atlanta Falcons, advancing to the Super Bowl (for the Harbaugh vs. Harbaugh brother competition). Transporting his team back in time, this leader helped the whole team recover their rookie state of mind.

Here are some strategies practiced by leaders from a variety of settings, making the shift from leader to learner.

**Keep an "I Don't Know" List.** Shane Atchison, CEO of POSSIBLE, a creative agency, maintains a list of "seven things I don't know." He says, "Every so often, I sit down and write out a list of things I don't know and need to understand. This is easily the most important part of my toolkit. Why? Because the list forces me to get out of my own bubble and take a critical look at what's going on around me. It's a bit like the old saying, if you don't admit you have a problem, you'll never find a solution. A list like this can also help you get out of your ego. . . . It reminds you that Einstein was brilliant, you're not, and there are important things you need to work on."[10]

**Announce Your Ignorance.** Instead of pretending you know what you are doing, let people know that you're clueless . . . but learning. A naval officer recounted a watershed moment he experienced on an aircraft carrier. Cliff Bean, then a lieutenant commander in the navy, was one of those "golden boys" who was admired by all his colleagues and fellow officers. He had recently assumed a new role as a cryptologic resource coordinator as part of a carrier strike group staff embarked in an aircraft carrier. In one of his first meetings with his fellow cryptologists, he made an announcement: "Hi. My name is Cliff and I don't know what I'm doing." The sigh of relief in the room was audible. This proactive confession prompted other officers to admit that they felt like they had been imposters, faking expertise they didn't actually yet have. Cliff's vulnerability was a powerful display of real leadership.

**Dump Your Assumptions.** When leaders and their teams operate under false assumptions, they waste enormous amounts of money and manpower, and their efforts are not productive. Worse yet, erroneous assumptions can blind us to the changes swirling around us. To combat this type of waste, Pastor Stephen Blandino periodically conducts an assumptions audit to surface and prosecute the core logic of his leadership team.[11] You can adopt this practice by making a list of your team's core beliefs. Review them one at a time to see if current evidence supports them. Next look for evidence to the contrary. If there are any assumptions you need to let go of, strike them out and replace them with a new set of beliefs—or just new hypotheses to test or wonder about. For example, you might find that a deeply held assumption that "working together in a central office increases productivity" may no longer be true.

**Reverse the Mentoring.** USAA is a financial services company with a focused mission and strong values that help keep the organization consistently focused on serving the financial need of the military and their families. So, to open up the intake valves and expand their vision, the executive team identifies junior employees to become mentors to more senior executives. The executive team opens their strategic planning meetings to a broad range of management to advocate their view of the future. USAA has established a regular pattern of bringing in outside voices, for the sole purpose of stretching the team's thinking. At the United Arab Emirates' Jumeirah Group, the vice president of strategy/excellence used the "Reverse the Mentoring" experiment (see page 94) and asked a young UAE national who had recently joined her team to mentor her. They established one-hour weekly meetings where the young mentor came impeccably prepared and radiated enthusiasm as she taught the executive how to understand and operate in the local culture.

To reap the full benefit of reverse mentoring, take it beyond the realm of social media and unfamiliar technologies and cultures: Ask junior colleagues to give you their insights on how to lead. The quality of their insights may amaze you.

**Borrow a Job.** When the technical documentation team at Salesforce.com wanted to reignite rookie smarts on their team, they conducted the "Borrow a Job" experiment (see page 95). Sue Warnke, the director of documentation tools, swapped jobs with Jean-Paul Connock, a technical writer on her staff. Jean-Paul organized her morning work: Make updates to twelve pages of a technical guide. It sounded simple, but Sue would need to use a complex system that enabled these changes to ripple across a myriad of other similar documents. After four hours, she had updated just four of the twelve pages. Having experienced the challenges of her team firsthand, she quickly became a better advocate for them, elevating a fix to this system to the top of the priority list and securing significant funding to make it happen. Sue was scared going into this experiment but came out of it more appreciative of her team's work; she also got to experience the thrill of doing the kind of work that had originally attracted her to this field and was so integral to the team's success.

While Sue was in learner mode, Jean-Paul was playing understudy for the role of leader. In one meeting, he listened intently as managers discussed ways to spread their finite resources over a seemingly infinite amount of work. In Firewalker mode, he was cautious at first, but then spoke up by suggesting a more efficient way to allocate the technical writers' time that would produce better results and a much happier team. The managers listened, learned, and implemented his proposal. Despite having a great relationship with his own manager, Jean-Paul had wondered if the manager role involved a lot of behind-the-scenes criticism of their teams' work. As he crossed into the realm of management, he found the opposite. He concluded, "Wow, managers are far more reasonable than I thought. They aren't judges. They are coaches helping us solve problems." Attending these management meetings helped key decision makers visualize him in a leadership role, and just three months later, Jean-Paul was asked to step into a formal management position. This experiment in job swapping was so successful that the team has since made it a recurring event; word has spread to other teams who have also incorporated job swapping as a means for building empathy, churning up new insights, and keeping their teams fresh.

**Ask Naïve Questions.** To shift into learner mode, try the "Ask Naïve Questions" experiment from chapter 2 (see page 67). Peel back what you know, and ask the questions that get to the core of the issue. Biz-Group, a Dubai-based training and consulting company, enlisted the help of Nicola Tyler to facilitate a strategy work session. When Nicola presented an agenda of seven simple questions, founder and CEO Hazel Jackson balked: She thought the agenda looked too simple to uncover the real issues. Soon Hazel realized that these naïve questions were actually just what was needed. In previous sessions, Hazel had noticed that many team members seemed inhibited and unclear of the boundaries of what could and couldn't be discussed, and consequently, held back and sat quietly. "The naïve questions eliminated all of these behaviors," Hazel said. "It removed jargon and fear of saying the wrong thing, and leveled the playing field and enabled free dialogue and thinking. Because the questions were naïve and jargon free, so were the responses." Like Biz-Group, you can develop a Backpacker mentality by asking the fundamental questions that elicit fresh ideas from all the members of your team.

The best leaders are learners. They know when it is time to lead and to be certain and when it is time to shift into learning mode. They can temporarily shed the burden of leadership and feel a renewed joy in followership. Their ability to reassume their rookie state of mind sets the tone for the rest of the organization. One of the telltale signs that you have shifted from leader to learner is that you have more questions than answers. Once you have shifted into the mode of learnership, you are ready to accelerate (if not force) the learning process by stepping into unfamiliar territory.

## 2. Step into a Discomfort Zone

Popular psychology would have us believe that self-improvement is a function of positive thinking and sheer will, but research doesn't support those claims. A large study in 2007 by Richard Wiseman (no relation) showed that 88 percent of those who set New Year's resolutions failed within one year, despite the fact that 52 percent of the study's participants were confident of success at the beginning of the year. He found that those who failed to keep their resolutions had relied heavily on their own willpower, and failed to make their goals both explicit and public.[12] Additional research suggests that we humans have only a finite amount of willpower.[13] For example, when we exercise willpower in one aspect of our lives, such as dieting or a fitness regimen, we have little left over for other areas, such as professional or intellectual development. When we pump ourselves up, it is all too easy to fall flat. We begin with a burst of enthusiasm, confident in the strength of our own will to succeed, but if our environment hasn't changed and we are exposed to the same triggers that led to our undesired behavior in the past (for example, same job, same people, same bait), it is simply too easy to retreat into familiar habits and behaviors.

Generally we don't learn because we *want* to; we learn because we *need* to. The Center for Creative Leadership analyzed thirty years' worth of data in their Lessons of Experience report and found that the optimal formula for workplace learning is a 70-20-10 blend of challenging assignments, developmental relationships, and coursework and training. This ratio emphasizes the critical role of challenges in the learning process—challenges place us in a position of ignorance. We don't know what we are doing, we are stretched beyond our known limits, and so we learn because we must.[14]

While many corporate training and development programs are anchored in aspiration-based learning, the reality is that we respond better to desperation-based learning. We learn more completely and quickly when we desperately need the skills and knowledge we are trying to learn. We learn to fund-raise when we sign up to be the school auction chair. We develop leadership skills when we need to move a group toward action or implement a big project that requires the support of others. Formal development programs can never replace these powerful boots-on-the-ground situations, but they can reinforce and amplify this critical desperation-based learning and growth. Situational motivation is much more powerful than self-motivation. In other words, what we need is less aspiration and more desperation. Instead of trying to "will" back our naïveté and openness to new ideas, we simply need to put ourselves back in situations where we will be nothing more than a bona fide rookie.

When we leave our comfort zones, we become more likely to encounter what cognitive scientists call "expectation failure." These are situations when we expect one thing to happen but are surprised when something else takes place. When things work as we expect them to, we begin to assemble mental scripts that explain the world around us. These scripts help us predict the outcomes of our actions while at the same time limiting our thinking. The more scripts you know, the less likely your expectations will fail to be met. But there's a downside to increased predictability. It is easy to become boxed in by our scripted understanding of the world around us: Our curiosity dulls a bit more each time our scripts successfully predict the future. But when we are in an unfamiliar situation and things don't work the way we expect them to, our scripts fail. Without a way to explain events, we are motivated to seek and find new explanations—we are motivated to learn.[15] We learn when our expectations are violated.

How can we recapture this powerful combination of circumstances: out of our comfort zone, in a high stakes situation, facing expectation failure? Let's take a look at some professionals and leaders who have successfully re-created these circumstances in their work.

**Take a Job You Aren't Qualified For.** Gabriela Maselli, a psychologist with a counseling background, works for Grupo Entero, a rapidly growing Guatemalan conglomerate. After working in an HR role, Maselli was hired into the innovation department as a commercial coach by Malte Holm, the innovation director. Maselli learned quickly, and just as quickly Malte elevated her to a position where she would be coaching senior executives. With her limited understanding of finance terminology, Gabriela didn't even know the right questions to ask in a discussion of costs and profitability. Realizing she was out of her league, she quickly arranged biweekly training sessions with one of the company's financial gurus. In the Pioneer mode, she poured through the book he gave her, completed homework assignments, weekly tests, and even passed a final exam he created for her. Malte watched Gabriela step up into this oversized role and commented, "When we get challenges in front of us, we do things we never thought we could." Take the "Disqualify Yourself" experiment on page 135. Push yourself into the discomfort zone by signing up for a job the way a wise parent shops for shoes for preschoolers . . . one size too big. Like oversize shoes, the new role will be initially uncomfortable, but you'll grow into it. If you are in a leadership role, you can supersize a role for someone on your staff. Size it just one (or maybe two) sizes too big, remind them to engage their rookie smarts, and they will grow into it.

**Move to the Edge of the Frontier.** Don Kraft had run many learning and development functions inside major corporations. But a trip to Southeast Asia pushed him out of his comfort zone and prompted him to establish the Windhorse Foundation to provide health and educational support to communities in need in Southeast Asia. Don described the process of establishing and running a foundation while he continued working in his corporate job. "I knew nothing about nonprofits or fund-raising, not even how to conduct a board meeting. It was extremely challenging, but I read books and reached out to advisers and learned along the way." For a corporate education professional, starting a nonprofit wasn't entirely new terrain; he just pushed himself to the outer edge of his capabilities. You don't need to make a radical career change to reconnect with your inner rookie; just increase the size of the skill gap and you'll find yourself on a frontier.

Forget New Year's resolutions. Forget motivational posters and multipage development plans. Just take one responsible, well-considered step out of your comfort zone. Sign up to do something new, hard (but not impossible), and visible. You won't need to muster motivation; you'll be driven by desperation. This is the way of the rookie.

### 3. Take Small Steps

What happens when we size our challenge wrong? What happens when we overreach and the gap between what we are capable of and what is required of us is simply too big?

Several years ago, and for no good reason other than I had turned forty, I registered for an Olympic distance triathlon. I'm a good runner, a decent cyclist, but the one-mile swim would be challenging—a half mile out into the ocean along the Santa Cruz, California, pier and back. My only real swimming credential is that I like water sports and, having snorkeled in many an ocean, I can float pretty well.

To prepare for my midlife triathlon, I outlined a balanced training routine, placing some extra emphasis on swimming, my weakest sport. I trained in a large pool at an athletic club, starting with a dozen laps and then working my way up to a full mile, roughly thirty minutes in the water. With the triathlon just three weeks away, I figured I should practice swimming in the ocean. After all, the cold ocean would surely be harder than the comfortable pool. An upcoming weekend with friends in the coastal city of Capitola, California, seemed like the perfect opportunity.

The morning I planned to do my open water swim, a Capitola resident warned me about the red tide—an overabundance of blooming,
and potentially toxic, algae that had turned the seawater red and cloudy.
Determined to complete my swim, I assured him I wasn't afraid of a few
toxic shrimp and some murky water, zipped on a borrowed wet suit that
was two sizes too big, and briefed my husband, who would watch from
the shore: "I'm going to swim about a fourth of a mile [roughly seven
minutes] south down the coast and then back up. If I am waving my
hands, that means I am drowning, not saying hello, so send rescue." In
my oversize wet suit, I thrashed out past the breaking waves to smoother
water, put my head down, and began swimming. Unable to see a thing
in the coffee-colored water, I recoiled for a minute, but tried again with
the same result. Yet a third time, I slowed my breathing, summoned
inner strength, submerged my head, and took a series of strokes.

With no swim lanes and no big black line on the bottom of the
pool, I was directionless. I pulled my head up after a minute or so to get
my bearings and came face-to-face with a seal. I tried to assure myself
that seals are harmless and continued swimming, and yet I couldn't
stop thinking about the seal: Where there are seals, there are surely
sharks, I thought. I tried thinking of Ellen DeGeneres as Dory the fish
chanting, "Just keep swimming, just keep swimming. . . ." But even
Dory couldn't counter my outsize odds: alone and disoriented; tangled
in a baggy wet suit; in a dark, creepy, toxic ocean. Beaten, I swam back
to shore, head up, Tarzan-style, on the lookout for dorsal fins.

"That didn't go well," I announced somewhat unnecessarily to my
friends and family. After watching me swim in circles for ten minutes,
they needed no such briefing. "There's no way I can do this ocean
swim. I'll have to drop out," I said, defeated.

Several days later, I recounted my story to a friend and colleague, Dr.
Jacques Bradwejn, a psychiatrist and dean of the University of Ottawa
Faculty of Medicine. After listening, he noted, "You overreached and
tried to do too much at once." He then explained how psychiatrists
treat phobias. They don't lock a snake-phobic in a pit of serpents and

tell them to "get over it." They take small steps. The patient first looks at a photo of a snake, then, later, they touch a plastic snake, then they watch a snake through glass. Only after taking a series of increasingly more challenging practice runs do they work up to touching and holding the thing they were once terrified of. Jacques then instructed me to do the same things: First, go buy a wet suit that fits you. Second, try it out in a pool. Then go swim in a protected area where you are close to land. Once you do this, then you are ready for the open ocean again, but go with a buddy and not during red tide.

I bought the wet suit, tested it in a pool, and did a few practice swims in San Francisco's aquatic park. I then asked my friend Greg Madsen, a management adviser and avid surfer, if he would swim the Santa Cruz pier with me. If nothing else, I assured him, he'd have a good laugh. We met up three days before the race. Greg brought his surfboard and paddled out ahead of me, so I could follow his path. He taught me how to keep a straight line by sighting against the pier. Soon he was next to me instead of in front. After he coached me through the really difficult, choppy water at the end of the pier, he dropped back, letting me swim in front for the last half mile back to shore. He called out occasionally. We clocked in at thirty-one minutes: Not too bad. I just hoped I could do as well solo.

Three days later, I dove into the breaking waves and swam the course alone (albeit in a school of frenzied swimmers). I looked at my watch as I came into shore, high-stepping over the kelp, I had finished in only twenty-six minutes—a full five minutes faster than my trial swim.

Jacques and Greg didn't just help me swim that ocean mile; they taught me an essential professional lesson: If it's hard, break it into small steps.

But what happens when the gap really is too big? When we overreach or swim out too far from shore? When Cathleen Black, the former president of Hearst Magazines and a respected leader, was appointed chancellor of New York City schools, she faced an enormous task and steep learning curve. It was a big bet with big risk. Black had at least three major gaps to close: She was new to the industry, dealing with new and diverse stakeholder groups, and working in the new arena of municipal government. Mayor Michael Bloomberg asked for her resignation after just ninety-five days.[16] The gap was just too big.

When the gap is too big, we break. We may simply give up or we may even be forced out. Those who master the learning curve, on the other hand, have sized the gap just right by taking on challenges that are uncomfortable, but not impossible to achieve.

When Chris Fry wanted to introduce a new leadership mindset in his engineering organization, he had high hopes but set a small goal. He said, "I want my whole organization to get just one degree better at this." He gathered his management team for a leadership development program. Chris focused the team on his magic number—one. They started with a single experiment: changing a policy that would allow talent to flow more freely across their team. After seeing results, they made adjustments. Their experiment became a pilot and then a program. That program is now in use across an entire division.

As we take small steps, we build our capacity to climb up steeper, higher paths. Chris learned this lesson from his mother, who used to say, "You want your kids to fall from the small trees, so when they get to the tall branches, they know how to climb." Any of the experiments listed in Appendix C is a practical starting point for sharpening your rookie smarts. You don't even need to know where the experiment will lead. Just start.

## FROM REVIVAL TO RITUAL

Many of us find ourselves in a dogmatic slumber, rigidly adhering to beliefs or stuck in the ruts of experience. While it may require a great awakening for us to break out of old patterns of thought and action, this revival will be sustained through the replacement of our old habits and actions with new rituals—not routines to get stuck in, but rituals to keep us continually fresh. This process parallels the treatment of those who suffer from heart failure: An immediate electrical shock delivered to the chest wall or urgent coronary angioplasty may initially revive the patient, but continued vitality is ensured only by a sustained lifestyle change.

Leaders who operate as perpetual rookies form habits and rituals that help them remain vital rather than waiting for a career-changing revival. French film director François Truffaut began his career in film by reading a book on filmmaking that he bought at a local bookstore. As he progressed as a filmmaker—he made twenty-five films before his untimely death at fifty-two—he maintained a ritual that helped him remember what it was like to make that very first film. He walked back to the same bookstore, purchased a new copy of the original book on filmmaking, and read it all over again.[17]

John Donahoe, CEO of eBay, takes a "think day" in the office every quarter. This is part of his commitment to be a leader who never stops learning. He says that after these think days (as well as after the two-week break he takes from the Internet each year), he can see things through a more creative lens. He emerges with new insights and greater clarity.[18] When one sales leader at Apple finds himself in a rut, he puts away his beloved electronic devices and pulls out paper and pencil to scope out new possibilities—an act that takes him back to his rookie roots. Another Internet CEO has two different and rather unconventional rituals. When he feels stuck, he takes a long walk in a single direction and doesn't let himself turn back home until he has had a legitimately new idea. Some walks have been . . . quite long. When he is really stuck, this same CEO goes into his closet, shuts the door, strips down to the bare essentials, and just thinks. The physical act of removing his clothes and shutting out distractions helps him strip away the assumptions that he's built up that might be holding his company back. Whether you physically return to your roots, take a think day, or strip down to the essentials, how will you revive your rookie smarts? What will be your routine for shedding experience and regenerating a fresh outlook?

## RENEWAL RITUALS

Develop habits to help you maintain and revive your rookie smarts when you get stuck.

**Periodically:**

- Broaden your perspective by running the *Talk to Strangers* experiment
- Get a ground-level view by running the *Get Your Hands Dirty* experiment
- Do a one-day job swap by running the *Borrow a Job* experiment
- Take a think day
- Dedicate a week to reading
- Take a multi-day break from the Internet
- Attend a conference outside your industry

**When you are stuck:**

- Run the *Teleport Yourself* experiment, recalling how you worked when you were new to a hard piece of work
- Run the *Ask the Naïve Questions* experiment
- Use a different medium. If you work on a keyboard, pull out a pencil or a pack of markers.
- Take a walk. Don't turn around until you have a new idea.
- Meditate for ten minutes
- Go talk to a rookie

A caveat is in order: Aspiring perpetual rookies must continually guard against routines. The very rituals that rejuvenate us, at some point become the habits that bind us. In your pursuit of renewal, break routines, change rituals, and be skeptical of dogma. Maintaining our rookie smarts is like maintaining a house or your good health—it is never done.

## TAKE THE BAND ON THE RUN

When the Beatles disbanded in 1969, Paul McCartney wasn't yet ready to hang up his guitar; he wanted a second act. In the final years of the Beatles, the celebrity lifestyle had become oppressive. Shouting from the fans during concerts was so loud that the band couldn't hear themselves singing. These men were musicians and artists, but McCartney recalled feeling like a puppet onstage. But where does a musician go after the Beatles? What learning curves are there left to climb?

McCartney decided he wanted to do it all again, only differently. Instead of relying on his superstardom to launch a new band, he let it go and just let it be. He formed a new band: Paul McCartney and Wings, with his wife, Linda, and two musicians who had played guitar and drums for his earlier recordings. He said, "We decided to do it from the ground up, rather than do a supergroup. We knew nothing and we had to learn it all again. We had to learn how to be a band." He admitted that it was a grind in the early days. They started playing gigs at local colleges. The band loaded into a van (kids, dogs, and all) without a gig or even a hotel booked. They would arrive uninvited at a college campus, find the student union, and ask if they could play the next day. Sure, the band members told the powers-that-be that they had Paul McCartney with them, but no one believed them—that is, until McCartney took the stage the next day, reborn as an artist and without all the trappings of superstardom. Paul McCartney and Wings had five number-one albums and only one fewer number-one singles in the United States than John Lennon, George Harrison, and Ringo Starr combined in their post-Beatle careers.[19]

Too many professionals, and entire organizations, stagnate because they can't let go. They can't let go of a strategy that seems to be working. They can't let go of expertise or expectations that might give them an advantage in the next gig. Sometimes we need to let go of what we know so we can be surprised by what we don't know. Perpetual rookies—those who want to remain at the forefront of their field of endeavor—must learn to unlearn, relearn, and keep moving. Alain de Botton said, "Anyone who isn't embarrassed by who they were last year probably isn't learning enough."

Are you learning at the speed of work? When you stay on an accelerated path of learning, you can keep up. But, even if you've been traveling on cruise control and have drifted off course, you can still jump back on the learning curve and revive your rookie smarts. Get back on the highway, just like the former Beatle and his band on the run.

## CHAPTER SUMMARY

Rookie smarts is not the exclusive domain of the young, the inexperienced, or the naïve. Even the most experienced and successful professionals can renew themselves and find their rookie groove again.

### Revival Strategies

1. **Shift from Leader to Learner**—The best leaders are learners and create an environment of inquiry and discovery. Instead of looking down from a position of leadership or expertise, they look outward and become a learner. Try any of the following:

   - Keep an "I don't know" list
   - Announce your ignorance
   - Dump your assumptions
   - Reverse the mentoring
   - Borrow a job
   - Ask naïve questions

2. **Step into a Discomfort Zone**—Generally we don't learn because we want to; we learn because we need to. When we move out of our comfort zone, we are placed into rookie mode and are forced to climb up a learning curve. Try any of the following:

   - Take a job you aren't qualified for
   - Move to the edge of the frontier

3. **Take Small Steps**—When we overreach and create a knowledge or skill gap that is too big, we can break. We can size the gap just right by taking on challenges that are uncomfortable but not impossible.

**4. Create Rituals for Renewal**—We can break out of old habits and actions with new rituals—not routines to get stuck in, but rituals to keep us continually fresh. See the *Renewal Rituals* sidebar chart.

# CHAPTER 8

# THE ROOKIE ORGANIZATION

Stay Hungry; Stay Foolish.

—STEVE JOBS

In the 1940s, Converse produced the most popular basketball sneaker in the nation, the Chuck Taylor, and they also made the most sneakers for every sport. By the 1960s, 90 percent of college basketball players wore Converse and the brand had cornered 80 percent of the overall consumer market for sneakers.[1] Not wanting to mess with success, Converse continued doing what had made it so successful in the past. By the 1980s, however, Converse began to lose considerable market share as a slew of hotshot new companies introduced higher-quality athletic shoes to the market. Still Converse remained mired in the past: As Magic Johnson observed in 1992, "Converse is stuck in the sixties and seventies." Less than a decade later, the company filed for bankruptcy.

In 2003, Nike purchased the company, eager to spur a resurgence of this once-iconic brand. Building on Converse's rich history, Nike executives initially attempted to reestablish a (ahem) foothold in the realm of athletic footwear only to be blocked by other competitors. Meanwhile, Converse's legendary Chuck Taylor was fast becoming the go-to sneaker for artists, skaters, pop stars, and youthful, creative thinkers. The brand reminiscent of yesteryear had been given new life by the youth market and other tastemakers. Recognizing this trend, Jim Calhoun, who joined Converse as president and CEO in 2011, pivoted the company away from its roots in high-performance basketball and toward a new opportunity: youth culture. To achieve this, Calhoun recognized that Converse would need to become more like their customers—creative, quick, and willing to experiment.

The design and innovation team played a key role in making this shift. The team was led by Peter Hudson, who is known for challenging his team by creating high expectations and stretch challenges. Peter quickly coopted Bryan Cioffi to his management team, naming him director of innovation. Together they challenged the team to speed up the design process by adopting a "design by making" approach (both Bryan and this new design approach are described in chapter 2). The new process unsettled many of the established players, and many felt stuck and unclear how to move forward.

Peter, perhaps even without realizing it, began infusing the team with a fresh injection of rookie smarts. For example, Peter hired Eric, a Dutch artist whose fresh designs had been posted online. Peter gave Eric two basic sneaker silhouettes and a simple brief: What could these look like in the future? Eric began experimenting and immediately produced several samples that blew Peter away. Peter gave Eric even more creative space and asked, "What else do you have for us?" His next designs were even more amazing. Eric provided an injection of what Peter called "unadulterated, smoking-hot rookie talent." As the other designers saw the results of this new approach, their rigidity and resistance began to melt away.

Meanwhile, Bryan identified underutilized junior employees and gave them greater responsibility and voice. Angela, who had been in a smaller role on another team, was given the chance to become an inno-vation developer. Bryan told her, "You have my trust. Just go for it, I've got you covered." Immediately, Angela started asking questions, and within two days, she began making changes, working directly with the factories to innovate in order to shave weeks off the production sched-ule. Bryan also gave a new, future-leaning research role to Jordan, who not only solved every challenge Bryan tossed his way, but also incited collaboration and cross-pollination throughout the design team as he sought help wherever he could find it. Converse's decision to reposition these two individuals as rookie talent within the organization had a ripple effect: By necessity, they were learning fast, but so was everyone else as the pace quickened.

Even as the rest of the team was getting unstuck, Dan, the team's most experienced developer, remained at a standstill. For years, Dan had been the guy that Nike sent in to make sure the elite athletes' shoes fit perfectly. Several professional athletes referred to Dan as the "Nike SEAL" (referencing the navy's special operations force) because he would suddenly appear in the locker room, perfect the athletes' shoes, and disappear. But now this master craftsman had to unlearn the pur-suit of perfection and learn to make fast, imperfect prototypes. Dan was uncomfortable with the idea of this quick, scrappy work, and he strug-gled. Dan said, "I just couldn't get past the idea that I was an expert at performance. I wanted to show the other designers how to do it right."

Finally, Peter sat down with Dan and said, "Dan, I need you to change." He continued: "We need your expertise, but I need you to use it differently." Dan explained that he was a lot more comfortable rounding a track than pivoting and taking off in a different direction. He admitted that he didn't know how to make this 90-degree turn but he was willing to try. Peter counseled Dan, "Take a leadership role and help the others produce great designs *fast*." This was just the direction Dan needed.

Dan realized that to do great design fast, the other designers would need a simple pattern to work from. So Dan rounded up the best pattern-making experts at Nike and asked them to help him build a one-seam flat pattern for a perfect Chuck Taylor upper. With this newly designed, simple form in hand, Dan gathered his colleagues and explained, "This is the fence. As long as you stay within this yard, you can play however you want." After enabling his colleagues, Dan joined in the fun of rapid prototyping—designing and making sneakers in a single day. His contributions included a hand-stitched low top of gorgeous Italian leather and a featherweight Chuck Taylor made out of a puffer-jacket nylon. He and the whole team were now exploring.

Several months later, while visiting Nike headquarters with Peter, Dan and Bryan were playing around with some new concepts in the design kitchen. As Dan experimented with new designs for the rubber sidewalls, Bryan playfully texted over pictures to Peter, who was across the campus in executive meetings. Peter ratcheted up the game, asking if they could make it transparent or reflective. They could. Peter, who was about to enter an important strategy meeting, asked if they could put these new experimental sidewalls on a sample sneaker they had ready to show at the meeting. It was risky—they only had one sneaker and they had worked for a month on it. The new, nimble Dan jumped in saying, "It can be done." He then went to the grinding wheel, destroyed their perfect (and only) sample, rebuilt it in five minutes, and ran it across campus and into the meeting. This master craftsman had mastered the art of speed.

This "make it fast" movement has continued to grow and spread across the company, allowing Converse to respond quickly to changes in the market and to produce on-trend products. An informal crew of urban youth and artsy trendsetters may have rediscovered the Converse brand, but it was an organized band of bold executives, veteran designers, and unabashed newbies who called upon their rookie smarts not only to revive the brand, but also to give it an entirely new life.

In this final chapter, we'll explore how great leaders and entire organizations can tap into rookie smarts—at all ages and in all stages of the organization's life cycle. We'll consider the leadership and talent management practices that enable companies to best leverage their rookie talent while creating practices and a culture that keep the whole organization, including the most experienced employees, fresh and invigorated. It's the combination of pure rookies and perpetual rookies that separates organizations that climb higher from those that rest on their laurels.

We'll begin with the leadership that rookies need to perform at their best.

## LEADING ROOKIE TALENT

Rookies are more capable than most people imagine. A manager at eBay remarked, "I had thought that people who were new to the work were empty and I needed to fill them up. But they come whole and full, just like any other collaboration." Still, rookies need leadership and guidance. In fact, rookies tend to operate at their best working under vigilant, mindful leaders—leaders who give them freedom to explore new possibilities coupled with enough responsibility to propel them up a learning curve. Rookies need managers who know when to rein them in and when to unleash them, and they need to be placed in an environment conducive to learning and insight. Indeed, it is the same kind of leadership I identified in my previous book, *Multipliers*, that rookies need most.

Effective leadership is less like holding a leash and more like holding the strings of a kite. The leader steadies the string, providing just enough tension to guide the talent as it soars.

When you offer rookies your best leadership, they will in turn work at their best. Here are three ways vigilant leaders can maximize the contributions of their rookie talent:

## 1. Freedom with Direction

When we asked managers to describe the key to managing rookie talent, their most common answer was "give them space to fail." Rookies work fast, but sometimes they run in the wrong direction and get to the wrong answer quickly. Too often a wide-open terrain can leave them wandering aimlessly. Sean Heritage, while serving as a commanding officer in the U.S. Navy, said, "Rookies tend to be all thrust and no vector." They're full of energy and willing to do the work, but they need to be pointed in the right direction. As Dan at Converse found out, when a team has a unified pattern to build from or a broad set of parameters to work within, they are freed to explore.

To provide clear direction, do the obvious—clarify what needs to be accomplished and why it's important. Set the guardrails and criteria for completeness of solution. But remember to also direct them to the experts who can provide guidance. You can help activate the Hunter-Gatherer mode by providing a set of contacts, making introductions, and even challenging them to consult with at least five experts. Once you've given clear guidance on what, why, and who, let them figure out how.

To provide sufficient freedom, try the "Risk and Iterate" experiment on page 118. By identifying the type of work from which failure can be recovered, you define a safe space for experimentation. Then offer the assurance Converse's Bryan Cioffi gave his newest team member: "If you totally blow it, I've got you covered."

## 2. A Constructive Challenge

Offer stretch goals, but don't overwhelm rookies. Sure, when the learning gap is too big, people can break down. Conversely, when the challenge is too small, people never embark. When someone is in a rookie assignment, err on the side of making the first challenge doable—make it a constructive "micro-challenge," one with enough tension to create movement and with just the right mix of relevance, difficulty, and opportunity for recognition. For more junior staff, carve off a project that can be completed within two weeks, so the rookie gets immediate feedback and recognition. When leaders offer a right-size challenge, people contribute quickly, build confidence, and are readied for bigger challenges.

When establishing the degree of stretch, leaders must also consider what is at stake and reconcile the tension between letting people learn and protecting others from their potential mistakes. While I was teaching a leadership seminar at a hospital for the Yale Medical School, several physician-leaders who oversee residency programs voiced an intriguing frustration. While they wanted to give the resident physicians space and freedom to do their best work, the life-and-death nature of their work forced them to micromanage and bark orders. They insisted that there was no room for learning when someone is flatlining on the operating table. I agreed and asked, "What percentage of your time is spent in these situations?" They suggested it was probably 3–5 percent of their time. I acknowledged their dilemma, but suggested that the other 95 percent of their time might warrant a different leadership approach. Several months later, I had a similar conversation at the U.S. Navy Postgraduate School with a group of officers who commanded military ships. They estimated that, at best, 2–3 percent of their time dealt with life-or-death moments. Yes, these critical situations aren't rookie moments. But the other 95–97 percent of the time just might be.

Along with a micro-challenge, rookies need micro-feedback—a steady stream of information to help them correct course and stay on track. The best feedback comes in small doses and quick bursts. It is typically delivered in drive-by fashion rather than in formal meetings. The newer someone is to a task, the more feedback they need and the more they need you to recognize and amplify what they are doing right—what's on track.

### 3. A Tightrope with a Safety Net

When people are working above their current skill level, with real responsibility and visibility, they are essentially walking on a tightrope. It is inevitable that they will wobble and perhaps even fall off at some point. Veteran leaders and mentors must not only place the rookie up on the tightrope; they must also be there to catch them when they fall.

BTS, the global consulting firm profiled in chapters 3 and 5, developed a highly effective system for launching and securing rookie talent on high-stakes projects. Vice president and partner Dan Parisi (husband of Jessica Parisi, mentioned in chapter 5) said, "Our job is to move people from left to right, up a learning curve. When there's a steep learning curve, you need to build a safety net under it." On every project, one person, such as the account manager, is the designated safety net. When veteran consultants or project managers assume this role, it is their job to launch the junior talent and be their safety net. When they see a struggling team member, they intervene without usurping control, and then put the rookie back on the tightrope.

How can managers intervene without usurping control and avoid the resentment that can come from public recognition of the protégé's false steps? No one likes falling off the tightrope, landing on her back, and needing to be "saved" by the boss. Here's how BTS uses safety nets to launch people, not deflate them: First, they've figured out that the best safety nets aren't managers, but rather senior colleagues and project managers (who oversee the client engagements rather than directly manage staff). Second, they've popularized the term "safety net" across the company. Instead of being seen as a punishment, the safety net is seen as a service, a benefit to which a more junior colleague is entitled and can ask for. Third, the senior partners and project managers are given a very large span of control (essentially running a three-ring circus), which means they have just enough time to offer meaningful coaching and mentoring, but not enough time to micromanage their junior talent. Lastly, when someone is a complete rookie, the rope may be set low and the net set high. But, as rookies gain experience and have success, the manager can raise the rope and lower the net without rookies even knowing the parameters have changed.

Of course, managers do not have sole responsibility for launching rookie talent. The rookie holds an equal, if not greater obligation. (See sidebar on "Obligations of the Rookie.") Rookies need to be willing to work outside their comfort zones, ask for help, and learn quickly. They also need to let their management know when they are ready for a stretch assignment. Despite these expectations for rookies, managers don't need to wait for someone to declare their readiness. Sometimes people just need a push.

---

### OBLIGATIONS OF THE ROOKIE

Respond to a rookie opportunity by embracing your neophyte status, operating in the four rookie smart modes, and by emulating the traits of perpetual rookies. Specifically:

- Don't underestimate your own abilities
- Be willing to take a constructive challenge
- Step out of your comfort zone
- If the challenge is legitimately too big, resize it
- Announce your ignorance; tell people you are a rookie
- Seek out experts
- Seek feedback
- Work lean and agile
- Be humble, curious, and playful; don't take yourself too seriously!
- Be deliberate; have a plan
- Be open, flexible
- Be willing to lead, even if from the back of the pack

## BUILDING POWERFUL TEAMS

Not only are rookies capable of doing amazing work themselves; they are frequently the critical spark that ignites a team of veterans. Often the combination of rookies working in tandem with veterans is what produces truly spectacular results. How would you configure a team or a partnership to maximize both rookie smarts and veteran savvy? In studying how the sagacious managers combine the best of what rookies and veterans have to offer, I identified four configurations that have the potential to produce stellar results.

**The Ground and the Spark.** In this power duo, the veteran typically brings clarity, gravitas of purpose, and a ground to reality. The rookie brings new energy and determination. For example, in the 2013 movie *Captain Phillips*, Academy Award winner Tom Hanks plays the steady, resourceful captain of a cargo ship seized by Somali pirates. He brings a focus to this role, shaped no doubt by years of experience and diligent practice. Opposite Hanks is Barkhad Abdi, a first-time actor playing Muse, the lead pirate. When Abdi answered Hollywood's casting call for Somali natives, he was working as a limo driver in Minnesota. In contrast to Hanks's calm clarity, Abdi brings nervous energy and an alertness that "stole the film," according to Matt Lauer of the *Today* show.[2]

Per director Paul Greengrass's instructions, the two actors did not meet each other until the day on-set when Abdi's character, Muse, bursts through the doors of the ship's bridge and seizes control of the ship from the captain. Onscreen, you can sense Abdi's nervous energy: He knows that he needs to give his debut everything he's got.[3] Opposite the legendary Tom Hanks, this rookie actor improvises what may be the best line of the movie. Glaring at the captain, he declares, "Look at me. I'm the captain now!" The one-two punch of veteran chops, combined with the raw genius of a rookie, resulted in a masterful performance and award-winning film.

**The Talent Scout and the New Talent.** In this power duo, the rookie brings novel ideas and an innovative approach, while the veteran sees and champions the promise and potential in their work. In 1980, seven years after the close of the Vietnam War, the Vietnam Veterans Memorial Fund commissioned a war memorial to serve as a symbol of national recognition and reconciliation. They held a public competition, requesting a design that would be contemplative, harmonize with its surroundings, feature the names of those who had died in the conflict or were still missing, and make no political statement. A jury of eight internationally recognized artists and designers was tasked with choosing the final design. The jury of experts narrowed the initial 1,421 entries to 232 and then down to 39. On the day of the final selection, each juror wandered through the massive hall reviewing the finalists' poster boards. They made their selections by removing the boards and bringing their choices into the conference room where they would debate and make a final selection.

One juror, Harry Weese, a renowned architect from Chicago, arrived late. While his colleagues gathered in the conference room and began reviewing the final selections, he was still roaming the hall viewing the entries they had passed over. Weese was struck by the elegance of submission #1026. It was a simple illustration of two walls, connected in a V-shape, to be made of polished black granite containing 57,661 names inscribed in chronological order of their loss. The polished granite would reflect the images of those viewing the memorial, connecting the present with the past. Weese took submission #1026 off the wall and into the meeting room. For the next two hours, he articulated why the simplicity of this unconventional design, which broke from the norms of Egyptian or Roman-Greco architecture, was brilliant and met the criteria perfectly. The rest of the jurors came to see the promise of this design and unanimously selected it as their final choice.

Entry #1026 belonged to Maya Lin, at the time a twenty-one-year-old undergraduate student of architecture at Yale University. The memorial was completed in October 1982 and continues to be a powerful place of personal reflection and private reckoning. The simple black walls seem to erupt from the earth, symbolizing a great gash in the social fabric of the country and conveying the gravity of the loss of these servicemen and women.[4] Not only was Lin's memorial ranked as one of the top ten favorite pieces of American architecture, but it also became the prototype for American war memorials, influencing architecture for three decades.[5] Newcomer Lin had vision, but her vision did not become a reality until a veteran architect recognized its brilliance and championed its promise. Lin went on to design more than thirty influential memorials and major public art installations and to serve on the jury in 2003 for the World Trade Center Site Memorial Competition. This designer who said, "Art should be an act of every individual willing to say something new and that which is not quite familiar," was awarded the U.S. National Medal of Arts in 2009.[6]

All too often rookie talent goes unnoticed, remains buried inside an organization, or is cast aside. Those with experience and expertise have the insight and the clout—and the responsibility—to identify and elevate new talent, popularize fresh thinking, and challenge convention.

**The Adviser and the Entrepreneur.** One of the most powerful talent configurations in technology and innovation-driven organizations is the partnership between the rookie entrepreneur and the veteran business adviser. The rookie brings new ideas and technologies that have the potential to disrupt an entire industry. Venture capitalists, typically accomplished technologists and experienced business operators, provide both funding to accelerate the growth of these young companies as well as critical guidance to the rookie founders as they navigate the business world. The veterans typically open up their business networks, creating rich terrain for rookies in Hunter-Gatherer mode. The rookie gets connected to a stable of experts to guide them and to a deep talent pool from which to recruit new employees. Veteran business leaders provide critical advice and words of caution, which is especially important because rookie entrepreneurs will inevitably find themselves in Firewalker mode.

Like other venture firms, Andreessen Horowitz pairs brilliant entrepreneurs who want to change the world with expert advisers who can guide them. But this hot new venture firm takes the philosophy a step further. Instead of assuming that their founders (who are often product geniuses but inexperienced leaders) will eventually be replaced with experienced CEOs, Andreessen Horowitz favors going the distance with the founder, helping him or her grow and succeed in their leadership role as the company grows. Currently two thirds of CEOs of their portfolio companies are first-time CEOs. The Andreessen Horowitz team thinks through what each founder is not likely to have experience with and then gathers a network of experts, putting the founder/CEO at that network's hub. But the learning doesn't just flow from the experts to the novice CEO. One of the core values of Andreessen Horowitz is a deep respect for the entrepreneur, which means the experts and mentors learn as much as they teach.

To generate a big impact, pair someone who wants to change the world with someone who already knows how the world works.

**A Hetero-Genius Team.** When a team is heterogeneous, composed of people of dissimilar backgrounds and experience levels, working together can be harder, but it can also produce better outcomes, especially where creative, cutting-edge thinking is needed.[7] Stanford University professor Bob Sutton notes, "At places where intense innovation happens, they often combine people who know too little and people who know too much."[8] The tension between massive knowledge and fresh thinking can spark a fundamental breakthrough. Some of this advantage is generated as rookies act as knife sharpeners for veterans; the rookie's lack of knowledge forces the veteran into teaching mode, which surfaces assumptions that can then be examined and challenged by all. When the distinct talents of both the veteran and the rookie are appreciated, the tension between their disparate contributions sparks collective brilliance. When either is dismissed, the tension dissipates into frictional loss.

What is the right balance of rookie smarts and veteran savvy on a team? My research suggests that an even balance isn't nearly as effective as more extreme ratios. When rookies and veterans are evenly matched, veterans naturally dominate and suffocate the rookie voice. Jerl Purcell, executive engineer at Cummins Inc., a global power leader, balances project teams in his organization with 10–20 percent experienced people and the remaining staff with less than three years of experience. Nestlé, the Swiss food and beverage company, takes a job enrichment approach that requires their managers in certain functions to configure teams as follows: 5 percent experts, 85 percent with 1–3 years of experience, and the remaining 10 percent new college graduates.

Managers can also swing to the opposite extreme with good effect, placing a small number of rookies on a team but giving them permission to offer fresh perspectives and contrary views. Sometimes a single naïve question is all it takes to shift the direction of a team's thinking. For example, when renowned physicist Paul Davies, sixty-five, was invited to meet with leaders at the National Cancer Institute, he wasn't sure he could add value—he barely knew of the NCI and joked that his only qualification was being unencumbered by any prior knowledge of oncology. This newcomer began asking NCI leaders the basic questions, simply trying to understand their universe. His questions surfaced assumptions and sparked new thinking, which has led to $120 million in funding for twelve physics-oncology centers. Davies was invited to serve as the organization's principal investigator and is still doing what he does best: asking the disruptive questions.[9]

The naïve question allows a complex situation to be defined into digestible pieces, surfaces assumptions, and establishes a level playing field so the entire team can contribute. The careful infusion of rookie thinking can trigger the beginnings of a wave of rookie smarts washing across an entire organization.

## THE RE-LEARNING ORGANIZATION

Once a team or a company has lost its rookie edge, can it be recaptured? Can an entire company learn to think and act like a rookie once more? If so, how do corporate or institutional leaders break out of intellectual inertia and reawaken that hunger and curiosity in people and organizations that have reached a comfortable place?

Business history is replete with organizations that have revived their nearly extinguished rookie smarts. IBM came back from low growth and a stifling corporate culture to regain their position as a leader in business software and IT services.[10] Apple Computer, nearly relegated to the heap of irrelevant technology companies, came back under Steve Jobs's second act to become the most valuable company on the planet.[11] While these revivals often involve the introduction of new products, the transformation is enabled by an infusion of new, different thinking across the organization.

The following are three strategies for leading a learning revival in your organization.

## 1. Rethink Talent Management

Susan Burnett is a savvy talent management leader, having worked as the head of talent management for a diverse set of global companies: Hewlett-Packard, Gap, Deloitte, and Yahoo. Upon reviewing our research behind rookie smarts, Susan declared, "This calls into question almost all of our human resource management practices of the last twenty years." Then she began listing the dubious practices: hiring based on experience, succession based on experience, the identification and development of high-potential employees, and executive development, annual performance reviews, etc. The list went on.

Susan's observation begs the question: Are the experience-based HR policies that have been so pervasive in past decades fit for the future of our workplaces? Some of these practices appear to have faulty logic at their foundation. For example, many of the practices assume that an employee skill level and experience are predictors of success. How might these practices change in an environment where success is much more dependent on employees' ability to learn rapidly? Many talent development programs were built on the assumption that experienced people should be the teachers and mentors. But in today's fast-paced world of work, would more learning occur across an organization if those at the top were encouraged to listen while those at the bottom were given forums for sharing their insights and observations?

Better understanding of the intense learning and contribution that can occur when people are in rookie mode allows us to rethink and refocus our talent management strategies. While there are numerous ways to keep an entire company agile and in a state of constructive challenge, I offer the following as a starter set of talent management practices for the rookie smart organization.

**Hiring.** Instead of hiring for experience, hire for learning agility. While there are numerous instruments that test for learning agility, the four traits of perpetual rookies are a good guide—curious, humble, playful, and deliberate. These traits both produce and predict the endurance of rookie smarts.

The rookie smart modes we've focused on are those sets of behaviors that rookies frequently display: They are what rookies *do*. The perpetual rookie traits are fundamental characteristics that underpin both the mindsets and modes of rookies: They describe how someone *is*. Traits are much harder to inculcate than behaviors. For example, it is easy to coach someone to seek out experts (in Hunter-Gatherer mode), but it is hard to teach someone to be humble. Hence, hire people who already possess the traits of perpetual rookies and then coach them to operate in the rookie smart modes—especially if they've hit a comfort zone.

Smart people can overcome a lack of experience, but it is very difficult to do so if they lack the essential traits. When you hire people who are curious, humble, playful, and deliberate, you will realize a much higher return on your coaching investment than if you simply hire people who display rookie smart behaviors.

## Rookie Traits, Mindsets, and Practices

| Perpetual Rookie | Rookie Smarts | |
|---|---|---|
| **Traits**<br>*How you are...* | **Mindsets**<br>*How you think...* | **Practices**<br>*What you do...* |
| Curious | Backpacker | Explore |
| Humble | Hunter-Gatherer | Seek experts |
| Playful | Firewalker | Move quickly |
| Deliberate | Pioneer | Build & improvise |

The Los Altos (Calif.) School District, under the leadership of Jeff Baier, has introduced new hiring criteria for teachers. They have established a specific set of qualities beyond a teacher's technical skills, which include: open-minded, adaptive, growth-minded,[12] sense of humor, and joyfulness. The district is finding that their new teachers are better able to innovate and adapt in the perpetually shifting field of education. A number of these traits are key components in Google's hiring criteria. According to Google's human resources chief, Laszlo Bock, the least important hiring criteria is expertise. But at the top of the list are 1) learning ability, 2) leadership (specifically the ability to flow between leadership and followership), and 3) intellectual humility.[13] Bock explained their hiring strategy (which often favors generalists over experts), "There's so much coming at us so fast, and it creates an extraordinary cognitive burden. We need people who are smart and learn fast and humble enough that they don't have to carry the load of knowing it all themselves."

Venture capitalist and blogger Tomasz Tunguz wrote, "I asked two heads of engineering to identify the most important characteristics in new hires. Both responded, 'humility.' For one startup ascertaining humility is so important, it is the first filter in the interview process."[14]

**Job Design and Succession Planning.** Too often well-meaning managers shield their employees from change and disruption, essentially placing a DO NOT DISTURB sign on the employee's door. While employees may seem temporarily relieved, could it be that they are actually unhappy when they are cloistered and comfortable? When is it time to disturb someone, wake them up, and lead them into a discomfort zone?

My second wave of research focused on just these questions: When are employees ready to be challenged and how much of a challenge can they actually handle? We asked approximately one thousand individuals to indicate how long it took them to 1) figure out their current role, 2) be ready for their next big challenge, 3) be ready for a new role, and 4) begin to feel stale in their current role. In general, we found that after receiving a challenging assignment, people:

- Have figured out their role within three months[15]

- Are ready for the next big challenge within just three months[16]

- Are ready for a new role within one year[17]

- Begin to feel stale within two years[18]

When we analyzed the data by job role we found that individual contributors are the first to feel stale and the first to be ready to tackle a new challenge.[19] Middle managers, on the other hand, report being ready for an entirely new job or role the soonest.[20]

Given that the majority of employees are ready for a new challenge every three months and ready for a new role at one year, what can you do to prevent your workforce from getting stale? Most organizations can't play a perpetual game of musical chairs, moving employees into new roles every twelve months. But here are some other strategies to keep your talent in the rookie zone.

1. **Design one rookie component into each job.** While the majority of a role may play to the employee's strengths and utilize their current skills, ensure that everyone has at least one aspect of their job where they must close a significant knowledge or skill gap.

2. **Offer lateral (as well as promotional) assignments**. Financial services firm Vanguard routinely moves their management talent between diverse roles. A job swap between purchasing and IT isn't unusual. The current CIO is a deep techie but had just come from managing a high-net-worth-client group. He replaced the CIO who is now running the retail investment group. The previous CIO is now working as the firm's chief investment officer. Why the shuffle? It allows leadership to keep the thinking fresh and ensure that management has a panoramic view of the business.

3. **Make management changes mandatory.** Chevron Corporation generally expects members of their upstream global workforce to move to a new assignment every four years. If someone has been overseeing upstream asset management in the San Joaquin Valley in California, he or she might next be running oil operations in Kazakhstan. Nestlé, the Swiss food company, takes a similar approach. When senior managers approach three years in tenure (or even before) they must hit the refresh button and move into a different role. This not only keeps the managers fresh and challenged; it breathes new life into the organizations they lead.

4. **Redefine the succession planning criteria.** As you review candidates in the succession planning process, factor in each candidate's learning agility—are they curious, humble, playful, and deliberate? Look at their job history to see if they have a track record of success in rookie assignments. If you are considering someone for a job that is more than one size too big, look through his career history to see if he has been successful in other equally oversize jobs. This might be the best predictor of the ability to handle a stretch assignment.

**Learning and Development**. Most learning and development professionals understand the power of desperation-based learning: They too have been rookies with little choice but to climb the learning curve. So, why are most formal training programs designed the other way around, in an attempt to inspire comfortable people to get off the couch and go charge an unseen hill? Many organizations have slipped into the cycle approach to development, conducting training consistently at regular intervals (for example, quarterly management classes, annual management meetings, annual development plans). But we don't learn because the calendar says it is time to; we learn when we need to.

Precious resources are wasted on talent that doesn't yet have an appetite for development. Nowhere is this more obvious, and more costly, than in one-on-one coaching—the highest investment companies tend to make in their management teams and star performers. Several years ago I participated in an important coaching initiative for a large, global enterprise. They gathered ten top leadership coaches to work with their top twenty executives (each coach working with two executives). At the end of the initiative, the coaches met to reflect on the outcomes and learning. This was a group of masterful leadership experts, so I was blown away as I listened to them discuss a surprisingly high number of tepid or failed coaching engagements (I too had one). Many of the leaders we worked with only engaged in the process superficially and continued to lead the way they always had, having apparently gained nothing from their company's massive investment in their development. In a moment of clarity, I could see that our results had little to do with the skill or actions of the coaches and almost everything to do with the coachee's situation and his hunger (or lack thereof) for improvement. The window for learning wasn't open.

In my ongoing coaching with executives and in consulting with other executive coaches, I've noticed only a few scenarios where the learning window is likely to be open, the client ready to learn new skills and approaches. I have found that people in the workplace are most open to learning when they are:

- Brand-new to their role

- Facing a daunting challenge

- Coming out of a painful failure or loss

- Returning from an epiphany outside their normal terrain

- At a loss for how to get to the next level in their career

What is common across all these experiences? In each scenario, individuals are working without a script; they've encountered an unprecedented situation. Their expectations have been violated, and their existing scripts and frameworks have failed to work. They are stunned and feeling desperate. In other words, they are in rookie mode. Rookie assignments create learning windows; hence they make good targets for your training and development investments.

How might you reframe your learning and development efforts to take advantage of these natural learning windows? Here are several strategies to help you target your investment.

1. **Executive coaching.** Before you commission coaching, assess the situation to determine if the executive has an open learning window. Think twice before proceeding with mass coaching efforts—that is, simultaneously providing individual coaching for all the leaders on a team—or "gifting" coaching to someone who isn't out shopping for help.

2. **Mentoring.** Instead of matching mentors and mentees by job title or years of service, match people by skills—the skills the mentor has that the mentee needs right now. Intel has redefined mentoring to fit their competitive environment and uses an intranct to do this matchmaking across state lines and national boundaries. This targeted mentoring enables new practices to spread across the company quickly.[21]

3. **Onboarding**. Instead of filling up "empty" newcomers with company information, treat them as "full" and ready to contribute. eBay revamped their onboarding process for recent college graduates to send a strong message: Don't hold back, but do jump in, share your ideas, and make an immediate contribution. In their first few months of work, the 2013 recruits on average submitted 25 percent more ideas for patents than the rest of the company and had more ideas that led to formal patent submissions.

4. **Training programs**. Instead of teaching competencies, use training programs as a forum to solve real, high-stakes problems (not case studies or simple action learning). When program participants are given a daunting challenge "above their pay grade," a chance to contribute to something important, and the accountability to deliver a solution immediately, they learn quickly and perform immediately.

## 2. Give Rookies a Voice

Rookies exist all across a company, but many are underutilized, written off as novices and considered too inexperienced to contribute. They stand ready, but need to be put onstage and given a speaking role. How might you amplify the rookie voice inside your organization?

The best, most unique insights from rookies tend to come in the first six months of their tenure in an organization or role. So, mine their insights before they become absorbed into the system. When Moied Wahid, a senior manager at PayPal/eBay, hired Matt Castagnolo right out of college, both Moied and Matt took the message from the onboarding program to heart: Encourage the recent college graduate to contribute immediately. Moied invited Matt to the design review meeting for a new set of products that is typically attended only by more experienced, senior engineers. When Moied presented a user interface for a new product that had been vetted and praised by numerous team members, Matt spoke up: "It's awful—it looks like it's from 1995." After a moment of stunned silence, the room erupted into laughter. Moied began asking the others for more feedback. It turns out they thought it was pretty awful, too; they had just been reluctant to speak up. Had Moied waited six months for Matt to get his bearings before including him in such meetings, Matt might have learned to remain silent, as well.

Give your rookies greater voice by putting them to work on your most vexing problems. Instead of handing over seemingly intractable problems to your most experienced players and asking them to "get out of the box," consider turning to those who haven't yet found the box. You can invite rookies into your debates and onto your task forces. In these forums, senior leaders can define the questions and then turn the rookies loose. You might be surprised how quickly they find the answers.

Rookies, especially those at lower levels in the organization, can also play a vital role in the strategic planning process. In times of transformation and strategic change, the best insights may come from the people working at sea level rather than those in the C-level jobs (for example, CEO, CFO). Those at the bottom of the ladder and on the fringes of the organization typically have the best perspective on what is happening outside the company and on the competitive landscape. When you include rookies and junior staff in the strategic planning process, new knowledge tends to bubble up, in contrast to the usual sequence of events—that is, allowing the same old ideas to trickle down.

## 3. Lead with the Veteran Executives

If you want to spark a rookie revival across your entire organization, start at the top by giving your senior leaders more rookie experiences themselves. Instead of having them lead the way with shallow words, they will be forced to *live* the way. Our research showed that the highest-performing rookies were experienced executives operating in new domains. Such assignments leverage existing veteran savvy while igniting rookie smarts.

Often senior leaders need a push into a rookie assignment. Jumeirah, the Dubai-based luxury hotel corporation, established a set of task forces as part of a quality initiative; they chartered each task force with preparing a submission for an award. But instead of asking their C-level officers to lead the task force in their own domains, they mixed it up by asking the execs to lead groups they knew little about. The executives were initially resistant and uncomfortable leading outside their respective areas of expertise, especially with an award at stake. In the end, however, the process not only yielded an unprecedented number of awards for Jumeirah, but it also developed a set of executives who were grateful to have gained new knowledge and insights by learning as well as just leading.

Senior leaders also need to be given explicit permission to be rookies themselves: to be uncertain, to learn, and to be vulnerable. When senior leaders embrace rookie assignments, it sets the tone for the rest of the organization. Not only do they enjoy heightened learning and fresh insights themselves, but they also inspire junior colleagues and, having just sat in the rookie chair, they are now less likely to squelch the contributions of the rookies in the organizations they lead. Give your leaders permission to be learners. Their rookie-mindedness will leave behind footprints for the next generation of leaders.

Greg Pal, a vice president of marketing for Nuance Communications, was in New York on business and went for a run in Central Park with a few colleagues. One colleague, Mary Ann, had never run more than four miles before. That morning, she ended up running seven miles and still managed to have a spring in her step at the end. In reflecting on Mary Ann's excitement at having just blown away what she previously thought possible, Greg asked his team, "What if we could all start off each day accomplishing something that we've never done before?"

What happens across a team or an organization when people are continually surprising themselves on the upside? When we build from success to success, high expectations become contagious. Leaders no longer need to play the role of cheerleader, pumping optimism into the air. Instead optimism becomes deeply rooted, grounded in past successes, and, because it is shared, it pushes the organization toward the future. In this state of optimistic growth, people move faster and eliminate wasted effort. On the learning curve, they are more likely to be the market disrupters rather than the disrupted.

The rookie smart organizations, those that stay relevant and competitive, will not just be learning organizations; they will be *re-learning* organizations—organizations with the ability and determination to learn, shed assumptions, and relearn as the world around them changes. Unfortunately the "learned" organizations, those that rest on their accumulated knowledge, will be prepared for a reality that will soon cease to exist.

## PROSPERING AS A ROOKIE NATION

Nowhere is this trajectory from high growth to prosperity to decline more apparent than in the rise and fall of nations. Like a high-growth company, the climb to national greatness can be seen as an outgrowth of hunger and resourcefulness while the fall follows naturally from a toxic cocktail of hubris, lethargy, and disenfranchisement. But, could there be subtler, more insidious forces at play? Could we fall because the path has become routine and mundane? Do nations fail from boredom and ease?

In *The Decline and Fall of the Roman Empire*, Edward Gibbon wrote, "The ascent to greatness, however steep and dangerous, may entertain an active spirit with the consciousness and exercise of its own power: but the possession of a throne could never yet afford a lasting satisfaction to an ambitious mind." While the developing nation's climb to prosperity is challenging, living in a developed nation is, in some respects, too easy.

## Falling Out of the Lead

What happens when a nation prospers, wealth and resources are abundant, and life is no longer hard? What disadvantages arise when people, especially those at the top of the economic ladder, no longer face hardship and challenge? Does it come as a surprise that an entitlement mentality creeps in when there are no rocky roads to travel and no rugged mountains to climb?[22] Without a worthwhile outlet, the hungry, challenging, and quick spirit of the underdog is instead channeled into infighting and small-minded politics. As opportunities for economic and overt career growth disappear, polarization and the blame game become pastimes and outlets for previously productive energy.

What of the youth, the next generation of leaders? While many are forging tough paths and making a difference, others are engaged in passive entertainment-advocacy that requires little more than reposting or liking the website of a noble cause. Columnist and media critic Tom Shales said, "Maybe the decline is just taking a really long time, like the Roman Empire's did. The Romans had gladiators and Christian-hungry lions and that sort of thing. We have MTV." The absence of hard work for young people can corrode their discipline, sense of responsibility, and self-worth.[23] One of the greatest challenges for developed nations may be the lack of challenge.

Meanwhile, in the developing world the extreme poverty rate has decreased from 52 percent in 1980, to 34 percent in 1999, to 21 percent in 2010, and it continues to fall each day.[24] As more and more people move beyond the need to fight for day-to-day survival, they will turn their energy to other pursuits. They now have the tools to participate in the global economy and are hungry and hardworking. Their behaviors and mindsets epitomize the rookie mode: unburdened by preconceived notions and eager to learn, whether from world-class experts via MOOCs (massive open online courses) or from improvising and innovating on shoestring budgets. For those who work in the developed world, you shouldn't be too surprised when these smart, hungry newcomers eat your lunch. Those in this rookie uprising offer promise. As Charles de Montesquieu, the French political philosopher, said, "It is always the adventurers who do great things, not the sovereigns of great empires."

With all of the challenges that accompany success, is the decline of established nations a foregone conclusion, or can old dogs learn new tricks? Can a great, established nation struggling with complacency and decline engender underdog thinking in its people once again?

## Staying in the Game

While both the reasons and inevitability of national decline are subject to debate, one thing is clear: We need less empire building and more community building. We need our leaders to consider the implications of economic and social policy and focus on the continued evolution of our educational models and investment levels. In addition to addressing these policy issues, we must also ask ourselves where we will find the leadership we need in both the business and social sector. In each of these arenas, my questions far outnumber my answers. Thus I will simply offer a few insights in the two areas where I have a particularly keen interest: education and leadership.

**Reimagine Education.** Children may only represent 20–30 percent of our population but they represent 100 percent of our future.[25] In my earlier career managing corporate education, I participated on a number of advisory boards for local universities. Like other industry education leaders, I was asked what the university should be teaching students to ready them for the workforce. I was expected to rattle off a list of technical skills and the latest programming languages. Rather, my answer was simply this: "Teach them to think rigorously and build a strong foundation. We can do the rest." Sure, newcomers to companies (or just those new at a particular job) bring valuable knowledge and skills, but their greatest value comes in what they will learn while working. We need educational systems that produce graduates who are hungry learners, who know how to think, to question, to find answers, and to sort the wheat from the chaff as they do.

Currently, our schools appear to do more damage than good to a student's creativity: As education levels go up, curiosity levels actually go down.[26] Formal education should be neither a kill zone for curiosity nor a petri dish for hubris. It is no secret that most education systems are good at helping students master knowledge but are anemic when it comes to teaching them to integrate, apply, and generate new thinking. Fortunately, a myriad of innovations are coming together to transform our education process to deliver deeper learning. Technology-enabled classrooms (and homes) create the conditions for independent exploration and discovery, enabling learning to be so individualized that all education becomes special education. MOOCs amplify access, giving those students with high-bandwidth Internet connections access to the world's leading experts. Forward-thinking schools and teachers can now flip their classrooms and use the most precious resource—teachers and classroom time—for the most valuable learning. Classrooms cease being factories where students are stuffed with information; instead classrooms become labs where student teams concoct new solutions, integrating what they know with what they learn from their peers. Meanwhile, in the United States there are local, state, and national efforts to ensure educational standards reflect the new realities and help schools prepare students to participate fully in the global economy.

Our educational systems are changing in positive ways, but are they changing fast enough and deeply enough? The hardest part of revitalizing education won't be formulating new practices; it will be the letting go of the old ones. Educational leaders can't be expected to innovate and explore new models of learning while carrying the weight of an outdated education model on their backs. We can't move forward until we let go of yesterday's measurement practices, such as testing models that incentivize rote memorization (and cheating by both students and faculty alike). We need to rethink how we introduce new teachers into the system and question the assumption that new teachers should be trained and evaluated by the veteran teachers. We need to allow our veteran teachers to be rookies themselves and learn as much as they are teaching. We need to celebrate good ideas and effective teaching, no matter the source (veteran or rookie).

We desperately need the input of all of our children, not just those who have parents who can provide them with access to the best-quality educational opportunities. And we might just need to slay one of the higher education's most sacred cows—legacy admissions that give children of alumni greater access to elite institutions. Too much of our education reform has us rounding a track, hanging on to old practices, when we need the courage to pivot, and face the future.

Salman Khan, whose eponymous academy has enabled many aspects of the current education revolution, said, "What really matters is whether the world will have an empowered, productive, fulfilled population in the generations to come, one that fully taps into its potential and can meaningfully uphold the responsibilities of real democracy."[27] The youth uprisings, revolutions, and aspiring democracies that we are seeing across the world will falter unless there is a simultaneous awakening and uprising of intelligence.

**Invite Rookies to Lead.** There is a growing trend among elite global organizations (which often play the dual role of wise owl and watchdog) to elevate the voice of young leaders. The World Economic Forum has long held the Forum of Young Global Leaders, a unique, multi-stakeholder community of more than nine hundred exceptional young leaders under the age of forty. These leaders gather to collaborate, learn, and take collective action to make the world a better place. In 2011, the World Economic Forum formed an additional community of leaders—Global Shapers. This network of individuals (twenty to thirty years of age) demonstrates a great potential for future leadership. They represent the voice of youth at World Economic Forum events and channel their energy toward building a more peaceful and inclusive world.[28] The United Nations is also increasing the presence of young people throughout its organization, and has established a youth assembly to bring youth to the UN and the UN to more youth. The Elders, founded in 2007 by Nelson Mandela, is a group of independent global leaders working together for peace and human rights. In 2012, the group added four Youngers to enrich their debate.

In their book *Why Nations Fail*, MIT and Harvard economists Daron Acemoglu and James Robinson argue that historically, when the ruling elites have pulled up the ladder and kept newcomers from getting a foothold, their economies have suffocated and died.[29] To maintain healthy economies and vibrant social structures, incumbent leaders need to lower the ladder to include young, diverse, and atypical leaders in the conversation. Organizations in business and across the social sector would do well to create their version of the New Crew or the Global Shapers. These rookie leaders have the power to see new possibilities and break logjams. When the U.S. government was suffering from deep polarization of the political parties and faced a dire shutdown in the fall of 2013, who was it that broke through? A coalition of bipartisan female (and mostly freshman) senators committed to working across boundaries and ideological differences. To break through the echo chamber in the establishment we need to make new, diverse voices heard.

We need to build a rising generation of leaders who aren't afraid to tackle the world's toughest challenges. We need leaders who know how to mobilize a diverse set of experts and use all the intelligence and human capability inside our organizations. But as surely as we need rookie leaders, we also need our veteran leaders for their wisdom and their savvy. Like an a capella choir or a high-performing heterogeneous team in the workplace, we need to harmonize both voices. Indeed, those who seek to change the world need those who know how the world works.

## FINDING COMFORT IN THE DISCOMFORT ZONE

Every great discovery begins when pioneering individuals leave the known world behind. Lewis and Clark had to leave Camp Wood in St. Louis before they could chart the American West. Roald Amundsen and company had to leave the safety of the ships at the Bay of Whales on the Great Ice Barrier before they could plant the first flag at the South Pole. The same holds true in our workplaces and our professional lives. Leaving the known world behind is not a comfortable process. We cling to the comfort of our expertise. We go kicking and screaming into the dark night of the unknown. A colleague I admire for his ability to thrive amid the ambiguity of stretch assignments once confessed, "Every rookie experience I had I hated at first. None of them did I really want to be in." Fortunately, he was surrounded by wise leaders who gave him a reassuring pat on the shoulder *and* a push. And he was smart enough to let go and embrace what was, at first, uncomfortable.

New discoveries are not made by staying at home. New territories are not found by taking the freeway. To make new discoveries, we have to leave the well-worn paths. We might need to go off-road for a bumpy thrill ride or take a seat in the "splash zone" where the signs indicate "If you sit here, you will get wet." Stepping into a zone of discomfort can feel unnerving. We feel growing pains. Yet, when we venture out, we discover that our comfort zone expands. Why? Because we are programmed for progress. Viktor Frankl captured this sentiment when he wrote, "What man actually needs is not some tension-less state but rather the striving and struggling for some goal worthy of him."[30] Among our most human of needs is the need to overcome and advance—the pilgrims's progress.

Strangely enough, this steep climb, with its scramble and struggle, is our happy place. It is while striving that we feel joyful and most alive. Stanley Marcus Jr. said, "The stimulation of learning is more rejuvenating than any mythical fountain of youth." Over and over again, when I have asked managers and professionals to "teleport" themselves mentally back to a time when they were tackling a hard, important piece of work for the very first time, this is what I've heard: *I want to be a rookie again. I love the feeling.* Why do we feel joyful when we know so little? Can we really be at our best when we don't know what we're doing? The research my colleagues and I have done shows that we are actually at our best when we are in the process of mastering something challenging, not when we've finally achieved mastery. Why? Because in the process of learning new things and overcoming challenges, we engage our creative energies. It is in the climbing that we feel on top of the world.

Too many people are stuck trying to climb career ladders when they would be much happier climbing up new learning curves. A friend of mine felt stuck in his midlevel corporate job, pigeonholed and underutilized. He wanted to signal to his manager that he was ready for a bigger challenge, so he prepared a pitch (complete with a slide show) and titled it "Put me in, Coach!" Like him, many employees today are busy, but bored. What looks like apathy is actually the exhaustion of being underutilized. Not fully engaged, they stand ready to do more, but need to be put into the game. If you or your company shows signs of stagnation, it might just be an indication that you are ready to make a rookie move. Maybe someone on your team is ready for a challenge two sizes too big. Maybe that someone is *you.*

Rookie smarts isn't an age or an experience level; it is state of mind—one that is available to those willing to unlearn and relearn. It is also a choice. As the world of work speeds up, we can either slow down and get left behind, or we can quicken our step and keep up. It is a choice between the dull ache of stagnation and the short-lived discomfort of unlearning what has worked for us in the past, and then relearning what we need to know now.

Robert Noyce, cofounder of Intel, said, "Don't be encumbered by history. Go off and do something wonderful." Leaders, don't limit yourself or your team to what you already know how to do. Make a rookie move. Move into the discomfort zone. Walk back to the bookstore where you bought your first trade book. Surf with the amateurs. Find your rookie mind. Wonder what is possible. Then go off and do something wonderful.

As the playing field is leveled and the pace of play quickens, the learned and the proud will be left behind. In the new world of work, the game will go to the learners.

## CHAPTER SUMMARY

Leaders and organizations can tap into their rookie smarts at all ages and at all stages in the organization's life cycle.

### Leading Rookie Talent

For individuals in rookie assignments to be most successful, they need leaders who operate as Multipliers and provide:

1. **Freedom with direction**—Provide space but set clear direction by clarifying what needs to be accomplished and why and then direct them to experts who can guide them.

2. **A constructive challenge**—Offer a stretch goal, but don't overwhelm them. Right-size the challenge so they contribute quickly and build confidence.

3. **A tightrope and a safety net**—Give them a challenge that puts them on a tightrope, but make sure someone is there to catch them if they fall.

### Building Powerful Teams

Create partnerships and teams that combine the best of what rookies offer with the savvy of the veteran. Some powerful configurations include:

1. **The ground and the spark**—The veteran brings clarity and gravitas while the rookie brings energy and determination.

2. **The talent scout and the new talent**—The veteran sees the potential and promise of the novel ideas of the rookie.

3. **The adviser and the entrepreneur**—The veteran knows how the world works and guides the entrepreneur who wants to change the world.

4. **A hetero-genius team**—When the disparate contributions of experience and naïveté are appreciated, the combination sparks collective brilliance.

## Revitalizing a Rookie-Smart Company

1. **Rethink talent management**—Adjust your talent management practices to keep the entire organization agile and in a state of constructive challenge.

   - *Hiring*—Hire for traits shared by perpetual rookies, such as curiosity, humility, playfulness, and deliberateness.

   - *Job design and succession planning*—Design jobs so that each job has a rookie component, rotate talent to keep it fresh, and, when considering a candidate for promotion, look for a history of success in rookie assignments.

   - *Learning and development*—Target your development investments when people are in rookie assignments and are most open to learning.

2. **Give rookies a voice**—Elevate the voice of newcomers in your strategic planning and decision making, especially during their first six months.

3. **Lead with veteran executives**—Give your executives permission to be rookies again themselves. They will set the tone for learning for the whole organization.

# ACKNOWLEDGMENTS

There are a number of people who formed a brain trust that enabled this book. The first is Hollis Heimbouch of HarperBusiness. This book began with one of my random rants—I was meeting with Hollis (who published *Multipliers*) and was musing about something I'd always wondered about—*When is not knowing more valuable than knowing?* Hollis listened carefully and said, "That right there is your next book." Hollis saw the promise in this book well before I did and then patiently poked and prodded me until I was ready to work on it. She not only helped germinate the idea, she collaborated with me throughout the process, offering insights, pushing me harder, and so wisely wielding her scalpel. Hollis is deeply insightful and collaborative. Every author should be so fortunate to work with an editor and publisher like Hollis.

Hilary Benedick, my research assistant, was my constant companion through the research and writing, despite being three thousand miles away. She scoured for research, analyzed heaps of data, and served as a thoughtful sounding board. And she did it all while attending Columbia University full-time and applying to law school. She is wicked smart, as persistent as a bloodhound, as meticulous as a sushi chef, and a pleasure to work with in every way. When I grow up I want to be like Hilary.

Jesse Boyett Anderson was not just an editor but was a Multiplier to me. Jesse's edits made everything better—sometimes it was fixing an awkward sentence or finding just the right word. Her most important contribution, like that of great leaders, might have been showing genuine delight when I did something really well. She kept me from going astray and helped me run faster down the right path.

My research team also contributed mightily to the development of the ideas in the book. They conducted interviews, reviewed early versions of the manuscript, and pushed on the ideas. My heartfelt appreciation goes to: Elise Caruso Foster, who conducted interviews and helped think through the research data structure; Deepa Krishnan Dhaliwal, who conducted interviews and helped me flesh out the core concept early on; Nadia Laurinci, who conducted interviews and offered critical insights; Alex Peterson, who managed all the case studies; AJ Secrist, who crunched and helped me interpret the core data; and of course Hilary Benedick.

Along the way, the following people offered important insights and resources: Anais Saint-Jude and Greg Haake at Stanford University for the Latin translations; Adam Grant at the Wharton School who pointed me to key academic research papers; David Burkus at Oral Roberts University for the research on expertise; Marc Jedel at Apple for the 49er locker-room story; Deb Giffin, Jocelyn Kung, John Hall, Heidi Brandow, and Rob Delange for their guidance on learning windows in coaching; and the numerous people who responded to surveys and polls and offered insights via social media.

My thanks also goes out to my colleagues at the Wiseman Group who taught early seminars to help refine the ideas in the book and gain insights from employees. We were aided by these early adopters who helped us better understand the ideas in action inside their companies: Rajani Ramanathan and Cheryl Porro at Salesforce.com, Ilana Tandowski at eBay, Alison Parrin and Lisa Gevelber at Google.

There was a phenomenal and diverse set of people who reviewed various versions of the manuscript and offered thoughtful critiques and much-appreciated encouragement. Each is someone I hold in high regard: Lois Allen, Heidi Brandow, Bryan Cioffi, Sarah Dijani, Elise Caruso Foster, Chad Foster, Alyssa Gallagher, Hazel Jackson, Judy Jung, Deepa Krishnan Dhaliwal, Nate Miekels, Greg Pal, Fredrik Schuller, Rick Segal, and Mark Schwartz.

I was fortunate to work with a capable and collaborative team at HarperCollins (and beyond) who breathed life into the book: Eric Meyers who shepherded this project from editorial to distribution; Tom Pitoniak, our eagle-eyed copy editor; Kris Tobiasson, the interior designer; Milan Bozic, the exterior designer; Stuart Sharpe for the cover graphics; and Heather Drucker and Stephanie Cooper in marketing. Once the book came to life, Mark Fortier lent his genius spreading the word. This entire process was made possible by Shannon Marven at Dupree-Miller, who is not only an agent but also a friend.

On a personal level, I continue to be grateful to a set of bosses who took a chance on me years ago when I was young and very inexperienced. Thank you to Bob Shaver and Elisabeth Otero for giving me a big opportunity and then to Phil Wilson, Jeff Henley, and Ray Lane for continuing to push me outside of my comfort zone. Larry Ellison, thank you for creating a culture that gave oversize jobs to underqualified people like me. These experiences sparked my inquiry and eventually led to this book.

Fast-forwarding to the present, I am deeply grateful to my colleagues at the Wiseman Group for their support and understanding when I was more madman than Multiplier while I was confined to my writing cave. In particular, I was greatly aided by Judy Jung for managing my schedule (and me) and protecting my creative space with both grace and loyalty. Sally Crawford bravely managed our leadership development practice and cared for our clients so I could focus on the book.

As always, my very deepest appreciation goes to my family—to Larry, my husband of twenty-seven years, for always believing in me, and to my children, Megan, Amanda, Christian, and Joshua for teaching me as much as I could possibly teach them. I also express deep appreciation to my mother, Lois Allen, who taught me through her example to love learning and teaching.

Lastly I wish to acknowledge those who read, practiced, and championed the ideas in *Multipliers* and *The Multiplier Effect*. Your engagement fueled me and your generosity in sharing the ideas gave me the opportunity to write this book. Thank you for your trust.

# APPENDIX A:
## THE RESEARCH PROCESS

The modes, mindsets, and practices discussed in this book are the product of extensive research over a two-year period. I was fortunate to work with a team of exceptionally capable individuals, many of whom were delightfully new to this particular type of research. The team included:

**HILARY BENEDICK**: Graduate student at Columbia Law School. Holds B.A. degree from Columbia University.

**ELISE CARUSO FOSTER**: Executive coach, and coauthor for *The Multiplier Effect: Tapping the Genius Inside Our Schools*. Holds B.S. and M.S. degrees from Virginia Polytechnic Institute and Ed.M. from the Harvard Graduate School of Education.

**DEEPA KRISHNAN DHALIWAL**: Corporate lawyer and business development executive. Holds B.A. from Princeton University and J.D. from the University of California, Los Angeles.

**NADIA LAURINCI**: European Union citizen and a former investment banker who is now developing young entrepreneurs across Europe. Holds B.S. degree from University of Pennsylvania (Wharton School).

**ALEX PETERSON**: Holds B.A. from California State University Long Beach and an Ed.M. from the Harvard Graduate School of Education.

**A. J. SECRIST**: Investment professional. Holds B.A. from the University of California, Los Angeles, M.S. from the University of Oxford, and MBA from the Stanford Graduate School of Business.

Our research process is broken down into three primary phases: 1) research questions and some definitions, 2) the research process, 3) the development of the rookie-smarts framework.

## PHASE 1: RESEARCH QUESTIONS AND DEFINITIONS

### Research Questions

- When is experience a liability and not knowing more valuable than knowing?

- What allows rookies to at times outperform veterans?

- What are the key characteristics of the successful rookie?

### Definitions

- **Experienced**: someone who had done that type of work at least once before, regardless of age.

- **Inexperienced**: someone who had never before done that type of work, regardless of age.

## PHASE 2: THE RESEARCH PROCESS

*Structured interviews:* We began our research by conducting in-depth interviews with more than fifty people in management positions across a broad array of industries. In these interviews we asked the managers to identify a piece of work and then analyze how a particular individual who was inexperienced and how a particular individual who was experienced approached the work. Both professionals needed to be smart and capable and could be of any age.

The interview format was as follows:

1. Identification of a rookie and a veteran who both approached a similar piece of work

2. General background on both the rookie and veteran as well as description of key character traits

3. Description of the specific actions taken or not taken by the rookie and veteran

4. Description of the assumptions and mindsets that the rookie and veteran held

5. Evaluation of the rookie's and veteran's performance on the piece of work

**Manager survey:** We used the insights from the interviews to identify potentially critical rookie traits and then designed our first contrast survey accordingly. Similar to the interviews, we asked survey respondents to identify a rookie and a veteran who both approached a similar piece of work. We then asked respondents to evaluate the rookie and veteran they had identified on a five-point scale against more than sixty behaviors and characteristics. We analyzed the results from this survey looking for mindsets and practices that were strongly associated with veterans or rookies. In our analysis we also looked for correlations between project success and particular traits and mindsets.

**Self-assessment survey:** We administered a self-assessment survey to more than two hundred people across a broad range of industries. Respondents were assigned at random to either identify a situation where they were brand-new to the type of work (when they were a rookie) or a situation they had encountered many times before (when they were a veteran). We used this survey to identify the different pressures and motivators that rookies and veterans experienced and to learn how they responded to these challenges.

*Time to new challenge survey:* Seeking to identify the traits that are correlated with a rookie mindset , we administered a second self-assessment survey to 987 people. Respondents self-reported on the degree to which they possess an array of rookie traits and on their job satisfaction and effectiveness. We analyzed this data to establish a correlation between difficulty of role and job satisfaction as well as attitudes toward new challenge assignments.

Interview and survey data were collected globally with an effort to represent a cross section of industries and geographies. This was made possible by a research team with diverse networks and the global nature of social media. Specifically, interviews were conducted with leaders in North America, Central America, Europe, Australia, India, Greater China, and the Middle East.

## PHASE 3: THE DEVELOPMENT OF THE ROOKIE SMARTS FRAMEWORK

Through analysis of our more than nine thousand data points, we correlated various approaches with work performance and identified the traits that were unique to successful and less successful rookies and veterans. We then developed the traits of successful rookies that were significant at the 95 percent confidence level into the framework of rookie smarts: Backpacker, Hunter-Gatherer, Firewalker, and Pioneer. We call these four facets the "modes" of rookie smarts. We also analyzed the results from the self-report survey to determine the mindsets that correspond with each mode. We then tested these rookie mindsets and modes against the initial interviews we conducted to confirm accuracy and prevalence.

**Key Terms/Concepts:**

- **Rookie:** Someone who is doing something for the first time (for example, new to the workforce, a career, a work stream, or even a particular type of project), regardless of age.

- **Veteran:** Someone doing a type of work with which they have experience, regardless of age.

- **Rookie Smarts:** How we tend to think and act when we are doing something for the first time.

- **Mindsets:** A state of mind and the assumptions and beliefs that drive specific practices.

- **Practices:** Sets of behaviors common within either the rookie or veteran mode of operating.

- **Rookie Smart Modes:** The common cluster of mindsets and practices of those operating with rookie smarts. These include: Backpacker, Hunter-Gatherer, Firewalker, and Pioneer (as discussed in chapters 2–5).

- **Veteran Comfort Zone:** How experienced professionals tend to think and act. This is the "at rest" mode.

# APPENDIX B: FREQUENTLY ASKED QUESTIONS

## THE RESEARCH

### Q: Is rookie smarts another name for beginner's mind?

Rookie smarts is much broader than what is typically meant by beginner's mind (or beginner's luck). I've joked with friends and family members that anyone who referred to my research as "the beginner's mind project" was getting taken off the Christmas list! Let me explain: Beginner's mind, a concept from Zen Buddhism, refers to having an attitude of openness, eagerness, and lack of preconceptions when studying a subject, even when studying at an advanced level, just as a beginner in that subject would.[1] Beginner's mind focuses on being mentally unencumbered (one critical element of the Backpacker mode), but this is just the beginning of the virtuous cycle. Rookie smarts is not just about our ability to *see* with fresh eyes; it is what we are driven to *do* when we face a significant gap in our knowledge or skill. The determination (if not desperation) to close this gap propels us to reach out, move cautiously but quickly, improvise, and forge through ambiguity to build new value.

### Q: Do successful rookies embody all of the four rookie smart modes?

It is most accurate to say that effective rookies embody many of the four rookie smart modes. The four modes are a synthesis of the aggregate data on how top-performing rookies operate. When you examine individual examples (including many profiled in this book) you will typically see a cluster of two or three of the modes working at once, often with one strong or dominant mode. There were many examples of people who displayed all four modes, but this wasn't the norm (or necessary). Essentially, you don't need all four modes at once, but the more the better.

**Q: How much of the rookie successes (or failures) is personality dependent?**

I cannot offer a precise (or even responsible) answer because this question was outside the scope of our research. Our research focused on the common behaviors and ascertainable mindsets of top-performing rookies but did not delve into deeper elements of personality. No doubt a portion of success in any situation is personality dependent and a number of the rookies that I profiled in the book likely have personality characteristics that amplified their success as a rookie.

While we didn't study personality per se, there were a number of common traits that helped people retain their rookie smarts (despite having years of experience). These traits were: curious, humble, playful, and deliberate. While these characteristics are probably not considered personality traits, they do reflect some of the deeper, shared characteristics.

**Q: Do rookies always outperform veterans?**

Definitely not. Our research showed that rookies perform at par with veterans in many situations and even better in a number of important circumstances. Rookies tend to do well with work that has the following characteristics: 1) Innovative in nature (especially disruptive technologies), 2) Multiple ways to solve a problem, 3) Short time horizons, 4) Too big and complex for any one person to know.

However, there are plenty of cases where rookies can be disastrous. Some of these cases are situation dependent—when the stakes are too high or where a single mistake can end the game. Rookies are also potentially disastrous when they operate with a very similar set of blinders to veterans.

For example, the young, new leader of hermetic North Korea offers an interesting illustration. Under pressure to match the greatness of his grandfather, the revered Kim Il Sung, who lifted the country out of the ashes of the Korean War, Kim Jong Un seems to have something to prove. While Kim Jong Un was educated in Europe and has opened the country's doors to Western business and sports celebrities, he sometimes seems to be leading on autopilot, running the same plays as his father and grandfather. He may be hindered by not only his own rookie blinders, but also a full set of veteran blinders inherited from his progenitors.

### Q: Is one gender better at developing and maintaining rookie smarts?

We found interesting examples of rookie smarts across both genders. However, we did find that women are more cautious about taking on stretch assignments. Women in our survey were 12 percent less likely than men to take a job that was "two sizes too big." However, our data showed that women were more willing to learn from people below them in the organization (humility), interestingly 12 percent higher than men. The data also showed that women tend to operate with higher levels of deliberateness than men. It appears women may need more encouragement to step into a rookie role, but once they are there, they can draw on natural rookie smarts.

## THE IMPLICATIONS

### Q: Do you have to be young and new to the workforce to be a rookie?

You can be a rookie at any age. Being a rookie simply means you are new to a type of work. It is a function of the circumstance. When Elon Musk started the rocket company SpaceX, he was an experienced entrepreneur but an aerospace rookie. When Magic Johnson recently bought a baseball team (a sport he had never played), he stepped up to a rookie role once again.

You can also operate with rookie smarts at any age—even if you aren't technically a rookie. Rookie smarts is a state of mind and a set of behaviors that flow naturally from that state of mind. These mindsets and behaviors enable people to continue to approach their work as if it were their first time. It is a function of attitude.

### Q: If I want to hire people with rookie smarts, what should I look for in the hiring process?

Hire for the perpetual rookie traits (curious, humble, playful, deliberate). Then, once people are on board, coach for the rookie smarts behaviors (for example, ask good questions, listen, make connections, experiment, improvise, etc.). Any of these traits or behaviors could be added to a company's behavioral-based interviewing battery.

### Q: Can rookie smarts be learned?

With most people and with most of the rookie smarts traits and behaviors the answer is yes. To be certain, some people have an advantage— either a natural advantage or a situational advantage. This is much like the world of athletics.

Consider Ziggy Ansah, defensive back for the Detroit Lions, whom you met in chapter 4. At six feet six and 270 pounds, Ziggy has a *natural* advantage compared with a smaller player who is five-nine and 175 pounds. This smaller player has to work harder than most of his opponents to excel at football. But a smaller player, while lacking a *natural* advantage, might have a *situational* advantage through stellar coaching, a strong peer community, and great conditioning.

Similarly, some people in rookie roles have a natural advantage because they already possess the underlying traits for perpetual rookies (curious, humble, playful, and deliberate). Think Ziggy Ansah. Others will have a situational advantage because they've had more coaching or have had more opportunity to practice the behaviors (exploring ideas, seeking input, moving quickly, improvising). Think smaller player.

Those without either of these advantages can develop the traits or behaviors; they will just need to work harder. But working harder isn't the only approach to increase learning. We can manufacture a situational advantage by placing ourselves into an unfamiliar, even uncomfortable, situation where we are forced to think and act like a rookie. Either way—through practice or by putting ourselves in a new situation—rookie smarts can be developed.

## Q: What if you are willing to take a job you aren't fully qualified for, but the hiring manager sees it differently?

If you are presently in a job working for a reluctant manager, this might be one of those occasions when it is best to just show up for the party (and bring something to share) rather than wait for an invitation. You probably don't want to unilaterally seize control of a bigger job, but you can take the initiative to work beyond the scope of your current job. You might ask your manager what work you can take off her plate. Start small and prove yourself. When you show a willingness to stretch, acknowledge your limitations, and open yourself up to coaching, most managers will find it hard to deny you a rookie opportunity. If your manager is still disinclined, you can start a conversation about the advantages of being in rookie mode—explain why people so often perform at their best when they are new and underqualified and share the research behind *Rookie Smarts*. Use the Discussion Fire Starter in Appendix F for guidance. If that doesn't work, it might be time to look for a new boss rather than a new challenge.

If you are a job seeker and the hiring manager is determined to hire the most "qualified" candidate, articulate the value proposition of those who operate with rookie smarts. Let him know that, with the right-size stretch, you'll be even more inclined to collaborate, to work with a lean, agile mentality, and that you'll be cautious but quick to prove yourself and "put some points on the board."

If you are a late-career job seeker who is perpetually told that you are "overqualified" you might refocus your job search. Instead of concentrating where you have abundant experience, pivot and point this experience in a new direction. Sell your value as a rookie rather than as an experienced professional. Even better, articulate the value of combining your veteran savvy with a fresh burst of rookie smarts. If you can show two or three cases where you've been successful as a rookie, the hiring manager will be able to extrapolate and visualize your being successful in this new role.

**Q: How can I tell if I've plateaued and am ready for a rookie assignment or revival?**

You might be ready to get back to your rookie roots if you have any of the signs listed in the chart on page 165 in chapter 7. You can also take the "Are You in the Learning Zone?" quiz at www.RookieSmarts .com/quiz to find out which zone you are in on the challenge gauge:

- Idling zone: Burning out

- Comfort zone: Performing

- Discomfort (learning) zone: Learning and performing at your best

- Red-line zone: Burning up

Or you can simply recall the last time you faced a significant challenge. As a rule of thumb, if you don't currently have your teeth on a meaty problem and can't remember the last time you really struggled, it is time. In surveying approximately one thousand professionals, we found that most are ready for a new challenge every three months! That doesn't mean they are ready for a new job, just a new puzzle to solve.

For leaders, be on the lookout for signs of burnout or idling on your team. When you see these signs, start feeding your team members their next challenge to keep them in the rookie zone.

## Q: How do I get started?

Start small and build a series of successive wins. Most new initiatives (be they corporate change initiatives or personal improvement plans) begin with a bang, but fizzle out in what I call "the failure to launch" cycle.[2] Instead, string together a series of small wins to build momentum and a cycle of success.

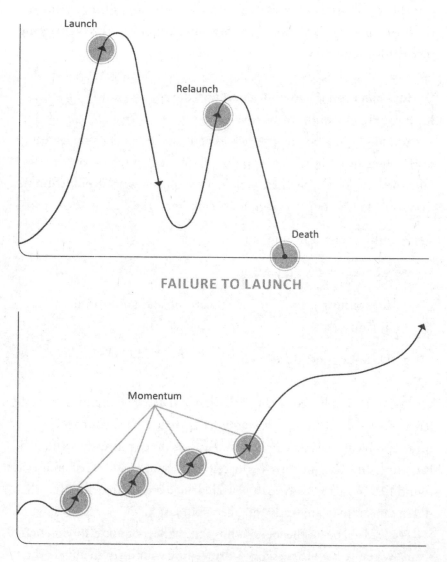

FAILURE TO LAUNCH

SUCCESS CYCLE

The learning experiments outlined at the end of each chapter are all designed as small, doable steps. To help you build momentum, we've organized a number of these experiments into a set of "learning itineraries" (in Appendix D). These itineraries have been created by a number of thought leaders and learning practitioners who have contributed to the ideas in *Rookie Smarts*. Find a scenario that resonates with your reality and get started with the three experiments on the itinerary. Or create your own itinerary by downloading the itinerary template at www.RookieSmarts.com/itinerary and then pick from the full list of experiments (in Appendix C).

**Q: How can I be curious and eager without looking stupid or naïve, especially if I'm midcareer and expected to know what I'm doing?**

Whenever you take a risk, you should make sure there is a safety net underneath you. You can do this by confining your rookie experiment to a safe space—a friendly group or a situation where you have natural credibility. Or you can erect a safety net by simply signaling your intentions—just tell people what you are up to! Let people know that you are intentionally taking a fresh approach and that you'll be taking a "rookie role" in the meeting or process.

## THE PROCESS

**Q: Did Liz write this book as a rookie or a veteran author, given that she's written two prior books?**

This is an interesting tension. Given my experience with the past two books, I found myself naturally drawn to the veteran comfort zone, doing what I know worked in the past. Yet I was keenly aware of the irony (and potential hypocrisy) of writing a book about the rookie mindset from a veteran mentality. Toggling back and forth between the veteran mode of knowing and the rookie mode of learning felt like a furious tango at times.

It took deliberate effort to engage my rookie mindset. I used many of the tactics suggested in the book. I often teleported myself back to my first book experience and contemplated how I approached things when I knew absolutely nothing. I then "forced" myself to do these things again. I tried to wipe the slate, resisting the temptation to draw on the ideas from *Multipliers* to explain what I was learning in the research. I also made deliberate attempts to seek out negative feedback. With my first book, I was eager to hear positive feedback, to find out if I was on the right track. With this book, I had to explicitly seek out early criticism and to ask people to beat me up a bit more than usual. For example, I gave my research assistant Hilary Benedick the job (which she called being "Debbie Downer") of challenging anything that seemed to lack rigor or felt rote.

However, the situation itself pulled me back to the rookie mode, as I was a legitimate rookie to this book's topic. Instead of writing where I have deep expertise, I research and write where I have burning questions but lack answers. I enjoy the chance to move to a frontier, to forge through ambiguity to find some clarity. I sincerely hope my attempt to engage both modes and embody the ideals of the book has produced a tool that will aid you in your own journey.

# APPENDIX C:
# LEARNING EXPERIMENTS

The following is the complete list of experiments and learning strategies (found in each chapter) that you can use to develop rookie smarts. Additional details to help you implement these experiments can be found in the enhanced ebook or as part of the Wiseman Group workshops, which you can learn more about at www.theWisemanGroup.com.

## BACKPACKER

1. **Ask Naïve Questions—*Ask the basic questions that simplify and clarify.*** Consult with the stakeholders for your work and only ask questions. Ask the questions that cut to the core and reveal the fundamental objectives or needs. Ask the questions that a newcomer would ask. Or even better yet, ask a novice to define the questions for you.

2. **Wipe the Slate—*Get a fresh start.*** Implement a semester system where work has a beginning, middle, and an end where victory can be claimed or defeat declared. Then wipe the slate clean and give yourself and your colleagues an opportunity to start fresh, unburdened by past performance.

3. **Let Go of the Monkey Trap—*Release your resources.*** A monkey can easily be trapped in place by placing a banana inside a basket

or container with an opening large enough for the monkey to put his hand in but not sufficiently large to pull the banana back out. He'll wait captive, banana in hand, rather than release the prize and extract his hand. You might not need to actually release your entire staff, but start by rebuilding your budget from the ground up. Or ask yourself, what would I do if I didn't have any staff to consider? What would I do if my title was simply "Team Member"?

## HUNTER-GATHERER

1. **Teleport Yourself—** *Rediscover your newcomer, rookie state.* Transport yourself in time and place to when you were new to an important piece of work or challenge. Remember how you felt, what you did, and how you approached the work. Use this insight to help rekindle a rookie mindset in your current work.

2. **Multiply Your Expertise—** *Build an expert network by seeking expert advice.* The next time you are faced with a challenge that falls within your area of expertise, avoid the temptation to jump in. Instead, reach out to at least five other experts with your questions, thus bringing in new expertise to bear on the challenge at hand. Ask the experts and keep asking them until you find new patterns.

3. **Reverse the Mentoring—** *Ask a junior colleague to mentor you.* Reverse the learning roles. Instead of offering your insights and expertise to a more junior colleague, find someone younger and less experienced who can mentor you. Allow them to teach you new approaches or technologies and give you insights that reflect your consumer base or employee population.

4. **Talk to Strangers—*Expand your network and perspective*.** Eliminate the distortion caused by the echo chamber. Remove your information filters and consider views contrary to your own. For example, if you read the *New York Times*, try reading the *Wall Street Journal*. As Robert Shiller, 2013 Nobel Prize winner in economics, said, "It's like having a good friend who is a devout believer in another religion. You can learn a lot from a friend like that, even if you don't pray in his church."[1] As you change the stream of information you receive and consider contrary views, you will not only expand your thinking but also widen your network.

5. **Make a Map—*Map your terrain*.** Take a step back from your current organization and map the terrain the way a newcomer or a cultural anthropologist might. Map out: Who are players? What are the rules of the game? What is valued in this culture? Who can I align with? Who are the experts who can guide me when I get stuck?

6. **Borrow a Job—*Swap jobs for a day*.** Identify a colleague in an adjacent area and swap jobs for a time period—anywhere from one day to two weeks. Use the exchange to gain new insights and to formulate the naïve questions that a newcomer might ask.

## FIREWALKER

1. **Risk and Iterate—*Remove risk as a blocker by defining a space for experimentation*.** Define two categories of work: 1) those tasks where success has to be ensured and 2) those where failure can be recovered from. This second realm becomes your playground—a safe space for you, your team, or newcomers to struggle and potentially fail without harming your stakeholders or their business. Within the playground, identify a project

where you or your colleagues can take a risk and then in a series of small, calculated steps, iterate until the solution hits the mark.

2. **Get Your Hands Dirty—*Get close to the action.*** Getting closer to the action can help you stay connected with the needs of your customers, stakeholders, or employees. In the world of mining, someone who is "at the coal face" is in the part of the mine where they are actually digging and extracting the coal. As you might imagine, at the coal face, you get your hands (and your face) dirty. When you bypass layers of management (with its share of sycophants, yes men, and plodders) and get to where the coal is being extracted, you can get the information and feedback you need to stay on track.

## PIONEER

1. **Disqualify Yourself—*Move into your discomfort zone by taking on a job you aren't qualified for.*** Is it possible that our best work and greatest career successes come when we are working in a role that is daunting and quite uncomfortable? Perhaps it is time for you to take a job for which you aren't fully qualified. Instead of playing to your strengths, you might consider pivoting from strength, stepping out of your comfort zone into a zone of learning. When you step out, you might feel a pull to step back to the place where you feel capable, even safe. If so, take a lesson from Cortés and burn the boats so your only option is to move through the discomfort. Try any of the following:

   • **Take a job in a new domain—**If you've been running a consumer products marketing team at work, perhaps you need to venture over to the enterprise product division and learn how to lead in this new market.

- **Take on a broader role**—Maybe it's time to take your divisional program to the next level and champion the initiative across the entire company.

- **Take on a stretch challenge**—Take on a challenge that is a size or two too big.

2. **Become a Half Expert**—*See how fast you can get halfway up the learning curve.* While becoming an expert may be a long, arduous process (requiring up to ten thousand hours of deliberate practice in some fields),[2] one can quickly learn the basics and the latest developments through deliberate inquiry. Interview experts and ask them to teach you the essentials of their field or their expertise. Then ask them to tell you about the latest discoveries, debates, and dilemmas. To get started, try studying the field of expertise from the perspective of an actor or journalist doing research. For example, ask yourself: If I were an actor playing an astrophysicist on a TV series, what would I need to know and understand to get into character? If I were interviewing a social media maven, what would I need to know to be able to hold an intelligent conversation?

   Don't just learn enough to be dangerous. Learn enough to stay out of danger. Learn enough to know the right questions to ask. Then find the right people to ask and let the true experts answer them.

3. **Staple Yourself to a Problem**—*Attach yourself to a complex problem and let it drag you to a new space.* Geoffrey Moore, author, speaker, and business adviser, explained to me how he keeps his thinking and his work fresh. Geoffrey counters the temptation to come into a company, speak about what he knows, and then leave, by stapling himself to his client's problem. Geoffrey commits to a challenge and then lets it drag him into unknown

territory. In these unfamiliar places, his current models, theories, and perfunctory answers don't suffice. He must now improvise, think, rethink, and cocreate with his clients. He must not only teach; he must learn. Geoffrey said, "I don't let go of the problem. I hold my breath knowing I will be dragged underwater. But, when I let this happen, it is a brand-new game every day."

Try stapling yourself to a problem. Let it drag you underwater and to a new place. You will not only arrive at new solutions; you too will become renewed.

## PERPETUAL ROOKIE

1. **Try to Get Fired—*Instead of playing it safe, just play.*** Don't overthink or second-guess yourself. Just do what feels right. If you are spending too much energy trying to win, try once again working the way you did when you had nothing to lose. Like Andrew Stanton, you might find that when you push the limits, you will end up doing what is natural, and what you once did easily. If the thought of trying to get yourself fired is too terrifying to face, play a game of make-believe: Ask yourself, "What would I do if I wasn't afraid of losing my job?" Write it down and then go build organizational support for these ideas. With this safety net in place, when you walk out onto that high wire, you are far more likely to get inspired than fired.

2. **Throw Away Your Notes—*Toss out your best practices and develop new practices.*** The late management thinker C. K. Prahalad was repeatedly ranked as the world's top business professor by the Thinkers50 website. At his memorial in 2010, his wife, Gayatri, revealed that C.K. threw away his teaching notes every semester. When she responded with alarm the first time she saw his precious teaching notes in the rubbish bin, he replied, "My

students deserve my best, fresh thinking every time." It is no wonder students at the University of Michigan's Ross School of Business lined the halls trying to listen in to his perpetually oversubscribed classes, creating a fire hazard. Try shredding your crib notes, stump speeches, and the other templates that have you stuck in a rut. As you do, you will offer fresh thinking to others while also renewing your mind.

3. **Surf with the Amateurs—** *Spend time with the amateurs and the young at heart.* Instead of working with your peer group of experienced professionals, spend time with the newcomers. Watch how they work and play: Learn from them. When Sergio Marchionne, fifty-nine-year-old Italian chairman and CEO of Chrysler Group, was turning around the failing automaker, he vacated the chairman's office on the top floor and moved his office next to the design and engineering teams and spent time on the shop floor. He got rid of many senior management positions, combed through the organization, and found twenty-six young leaders who would report directly to him.[3] They kept him close to the action and energized as he reinvigorated the whole company. If you are stuck at the top, go talk to those at the bottom of the organization or those new to the game. How might their ideas shape you and their energy renew you?

## ADDITIONAL ROOKIE REVIVAL STRATEGIES

1. **Keep an "I Don't Know" List—**Make a list of things you don't know but need to understand.

2. **Announce Your Ignorance—**Instead of pretending you know what you are doing, let people know that you're clueless . . . but learning.

3. **Dump Your Assumptions**—Make a list of your core beliefs regarding your work or situation. Then review them and look for evidence to the contrary. Ditch the assumptions that may be obsolete.

4. **Move to the Edge of the Frontier**—You don't need to leave your job; just push yourself to the outer limit of what you know how to do.

# APPENDIX D:
# LEARNING ITINERARIES

The journey of a thousand miles begins
with one step.

—LAO TSU

To help you apply the ideas in *Rookie Smarts*, my colleagues and I have created a set of learning itineraries. These guides are meant to guide your learning journey, much like a recommended travel itinerary might serve as a starting point for an adventure of a lifetime. Each itinerary maps out the first steps in one of eight different scenarios in which you might seek to strengthen your rookie smarts.

The first five scenarios are designed for organization leaders who want to strengthen the rookie smarts across their team, whether that team is a small, growth company, a large established firm, a school, or a faith-based organization. The last three scenarios are crafted for individuals who want to start off strong in a rookie assignment or rekindle the passion they once felt for their work. The list of itineraries is below.

The itineraries have been authored by guest contributors, each of whom brings his or her unique expertise to the concepts explored in this book. It is a group of smart, interesting people whose insights I greatly value. The list includes members of my research/review team, key partners, and thought leaders in related domains. You can find a short biography for each person at the bottom of the itinerary.

## LEARNING JOURNEY

Each itinerary includes a starting point, a destination, and the learning experiments along the way that will get you there. The path moves "up a learning curve," so start at the bottom left and traverse your way up and to the right!

## Itinerary 1
## Keeping Your Young Company Agile as it Grows

*by Hazel Jackson & Hazel Cowling*

**B. Destination**
The company maintains fast growth in revenue and profit by accelerating the pace of innovation and remaining agile. The team moves with a sense of urgency and balances risks by using the relevant management information. Managers read numbers with a rookie mindset, seeing between the lines to find the lurking fresh ideas and opportunities.

**A. Starting Point**
Your company has been growing fast for the last five years but the competition is nipping at your heels. Innovation is taking longer and you fear this will only get worse. Access to timely data is a bottleneck to fast decision making and innovation execution.

**1. Wipe the Slate**
Return to a mental state when you were delighted with the work that each member of your team was delivering. Ditch any baggage you have about disappointing performance. Run your next weekly meeting in this state of mind.

**2. Throw Away Your Notes**
Throw away the agenda for your next strategy meeting and ask the team to bring what they believe is important for you to know. Remain totally open and use Naïve Questions to get deeper into their selection of topics.

**3. Staple Yourself to a Problem**
Spend three days in the finance team, following the existing process. Get into the weeds and learn why it takes so long to pull management information and how to extract information quickly and accurately.

**Hazel Jackson** is CEO and founding partner of biz-group, a management consultancy company based in Dubai, United Arab Emirates, that provides leadership training, team building, and business coaching.

**Hazel Cowling** is partner and consultant director at biz-group responsible for managing accounts and developing the consultant workforce.

## Itinerary 2
## Maintaining Your Edge as a Large, Established Company

*by Sally Crawford & Robert Duplantier*

### A. Starting Point
Your company used to move fast, but has become slow and is settling into "the way we do it here." While your company is enjoying the fruits of earlier labors, more nimble competitors are eating away at your market share. You watch competitors release new features faster than you can coalesce agreement on what features to include in the next product release. How can you move swiftly and re-establish your competitive edge?

### B. Destination
While many parts of the organization are still slow to change, you've built muscle for experimentation and rapid innovation and have proof-points to help mobilize the rest of the organization.

### 1. Wipe the Slate
Ensure your projects have clearly defined beginnings and ends. Implement the agile development method where product development is done in "sprints" –short bursts of work with clearly defined functionality. Clearly punctuating work cycles provides a sense of completion, builds energy and momentum, and enables the company to respond nimbly to changes in the market.

### 2. Get Your Hands Dirty
Examine your business from the outsider's perspective. Spend time with your customers to see how they are using and adapting your products. Let your rookies lead the customer conversations–they will ask questions (and get answers) you never thought of. Examine your business through your competitor's lens. Instead of dismissing their claims, look for areas where you have a competitive vulnerability.

### 3. Risk & Iterate
Experiment with rapidly prototyping in one part of your business. Instead of designing in long cycles, go "straight to making" and get immediate feedback. Start with a small team, but excuse them from the usual procedures and rules. See how fast they can go from idea to prototype.

**Sally Crawford** is vice president of the leadership development practice at the Wiseman Group and leads the education business worldwide. Previously she was the CEO of a firm specializing in technology transfer and adoption.

**Robert Duplantier** is a senior HR leader with 15 years of experience in human resources development, management, and analytics.

## Itinerary 3
## Navigating Cultural and Generational Differences in the Workforce

*by Mario Borghino*

### A. Starting Point
You are the experienced financial leader of a company with many young accountants working for you. You are highly conservative, extremely disciplined, and you believe that to grow within the company, rookies must put in the same time you did to become a VP. Young executives don't last long and are quitting the company out of frustration over lack of growth opportunities.

### B. Destination
Your company will arrive at a place where young executives feel involved in important decisions and know that their personal capacity is being recognized. They will know that they have ownership for results and that the organization is counting on their creativity, initiative, and fresh ideas for the solution to problems.

### 1. Reverse the Mentoring
Ask one of the young executives to lead your next meeting. Rotate the role in following meetings among the team. Ask honest questions with the intention of understanding the idea, not questioning their point of view.

### 2. Multiply Your Expertise
Identify who has the right skill-set to analyze the key points of a project and delegate responsibility. Ask for presentations on advancements in group sessions to be evaluated by the team. Make clear the importance of the assignment and that you are counting on them to deliver.

### 3. Give Rookies a Voice
Identify a couple of areas in your business where there are repetitive problems. Form small groups of young rookies to develop creative solutions.

**Mario Borghino** is an expert consultant and keynote speaker in the fields of strategic planning, leadership, and innovation. He has authored six books (some of the top bestsellers in Latin America). He advises CEOs and government officials.

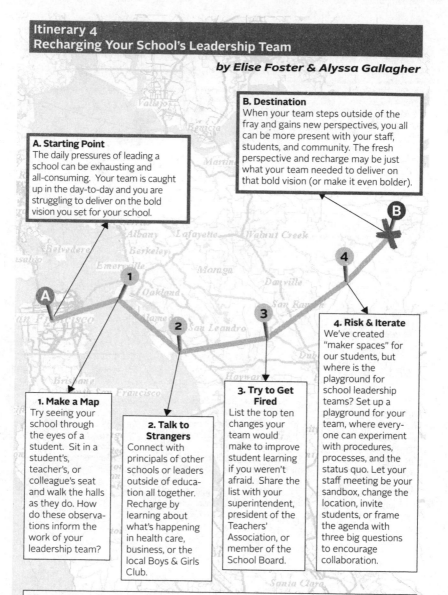

## Itinerary 4
## Recharging Your School's Leadership Team

*by Elise Foster & Alyssa Gallagher*

**A. Starting Point**
The daily pressures of leading a school can be exhausting and all-consuming. Your team is caught up in the day-to-day and you are struggling to deliver on the bold vision you set for your school.

**B. Destination**
When your team steps outside of the fray and gains new perspectives, you all can be more present with your staff, students, and community. The fresh perspective and recharge may be just what your team needed to deliver on that bold vision (or make it even bolder).

**1. Make a Map**
Try seeing your school through the eyes of a student. Sit in a student's, teacher's, or colleague's seat and walk the halls as they do. How do these observations inform the work of your leadership team?

**2. Talk to Strangers**
Connect with principals of other schools or leaders outside of education all together. Recharge by learning about what's happening in health care, business, or the local Boys & Girls Club.

**3. Try to Get Fired**
List the top ten changes your team would make to improve student learning if you weren't afraid. Share the list with your superintendent, president of the Teachers' Association, or member of the School Board.

**4. Risk & Iterate**
We've created "maker spaces" for our students, but where is the playground for school leadership teams? Set up a playground for your team, where everyone can experiment with procedures, processes, and the status quo. Let your staff meeting be your sandbox, change the location, invite students, or frame the agenda with three big questions to encourage collaboration.

**Elise Foster** teaches leadership to and coaches business and educational leaders. She is the coauthor of *The Multiplier Effect: Tapping the Genius Inside Our Schools.*

**Alyssa Gallagher** is the director of strategic initiatives & community partnerships at the Los Altos School District. She was named as the Multiplier of the Year in Education for 2013.

## Itinerary 5
## Keeping Your Church Congregation Vibrant & Hopeful
*by Heidi Brandow & Bill Hybels*

### A. Starting Point
You want to build ministries that bring hope and help to those in need. But you realize you can't do it alone. You must create a vibrant church culture that inspires and engages others to use their gifts, talents, and passions to lead those ministries.

### B. Destination
Your church has a vibrant culture, where ministries are led by engaged staff and volunteers who are empowered to innovate, learn from their mistakes, and bring others alongside them to produce results. The staff and congregation alike are finding fulfillment by using their God-given talents and gifts, and even the newest member has a significant contribution to make.

### 1. Reverse the Mentoring
Determine your area of greatest interest and least understanding. Ask one of your new staff members or volunteers with expertise in that area to help you learn. Ask questions and learn from their answers.

### 2. Talk to Strangers
Humble learners can learn from anyone. Find authors with whom you disagree—and read them. Gather input from people outside your congregation to understand the greatest needs of your community. Take what you learn and see what changes your congregation needs.

### 3. Get Your Hands Dirty
Take a step back and serve in an area that you passed on to someone else long ago. Pay attention to what has changed and find new ways of serving and leading in that space.

**Bill Hybels** is senior pastor of Willow Creek Community Church and chair of the board for Willow Creek Association. He is a bestselling author of more than 20 books, including *Leadership Axioms* and *Simplify: Ten Practices to Unclutter Your Soul*.

**Heidi Brandow** is a senior adviser in leadership development at World Vision International. She is also a master practitioner and learning designer for the Wiseman Group.

## Itinerary 6
## Stepping Into a New, Bigger Job

*by Deepa Krishnan*

### A. Starting Point
You've just been promoted into a management position in your company. The only problem is that the job is about two sizes too big, and you've been asked to take over a function for which you have no direct experience. The business is taking a chance on you, and you don't want to disappoint.

### B. Destination
It's month three at your new job and you are a humble yet confident leader, bringing fresh insight to the organization. Most important you believe in yourself and the job no longer feels two sizes too big. Go get 'em!

### 1. Ask Naïve Questions
In your first few weeks, you have extraordinary leeway to ask questions. Set up meetings with individuals throughout the organization, and ask the same question five different ways, if that helps you solidify the answer in your head. It's a great idea to keep an "I Don't Know" list during this time period, and if a colleague can't answer a specific question, ask them to refer you to someone else who might have the answer.

### 2. Get Your Hands Dirty
There's no better way to understand than to jump in and get your hands dirty. Find out what your team is already working on, and offer yourself as a resource. When you find yourself needing to assign new tasks, keep a few for yourself, so that you can build your domain expertise and simultaneously lessen the load on your team.

### 3. Multiply Your Expertise
By now, having asked naïve questions and gotten your hands dirty, you have built a rough framework for the position. It's time to fill in the holes and add depth to your knowledge. Seek out experts in the field and tap into their brilliant minds. Fight the temptation to jump to quick conclusions, and instead, listen hard until patterns start to reveal themselves to you.

**Deepa Krishnan** is a firm believer in Rookie Smarts, having started her career as a litigator, and then moving to general counsel, business development, and currently, product strategy/development.

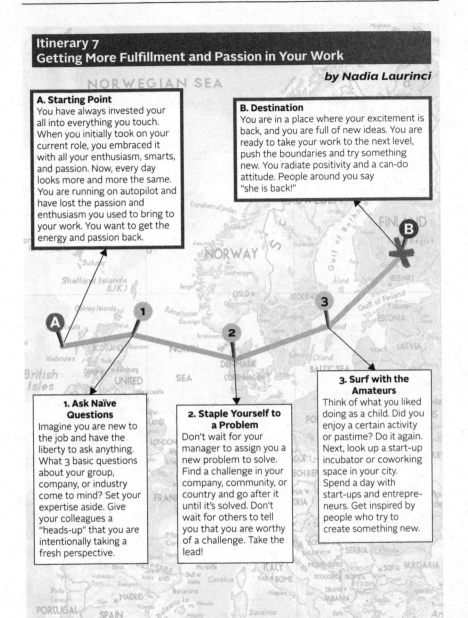

## Itinerary 7
## Getting More Fulfillment and Passion in Your Work

*by Nadia Laurinci*

**A. Starting Point**
You have always invested your all into everything you touch. When you initially took on your current role, you embraced it with all your enthusiasm, smarts, and passion. Now, every day looks more and more the same. You are running on autopilot and have lost the passion and enthusiasm you used to bring to your work. You want to get the energy and passion back.

**B. Destination**
You are in a place where your excitement is back, and you are full of new ideas. You are ready to take your work to the next level, push the boundaries and try something new. You radiate positivity and a can-do attitude. People around you say "she is back!"

**1. Ask Naïve Questions**
Imagine you are new to the job and have the liberty to ask anything. What 3 basic questions about your group, company, or industry come to mind? Set your expertise aside. Give your colleagues a "heads-up" that you are intentionally taking a fresh perspective.

**2. Staple Yourself to a Problem**
Don't wait for your manager to assign you a new problem to solve. Find a challenge in your company, community, or country and go after it until it's solved. Don't wait for others to tell you that you are worthy of a challenge. Take the lead!

**3. Surf with the Amateurs**
Think of what you liked doing as a child. Did you enjoy a certain activity or pastime? Do it again. Next, look up a start-up incubator or coworking space in your city. Spend a day with start-ups and entrepreneurs. Get inspired by people who try to create something new.

**Nadia Laurinci** is the CEO of Laurinci & Company, a talent agency working with leading experts and authorities around the world and spreading their knowledge to places where it is needed and impactful.

## Itinerary 8
## Making a Big Contribution When You are Young and Unafraid

*by Nate Meikle*

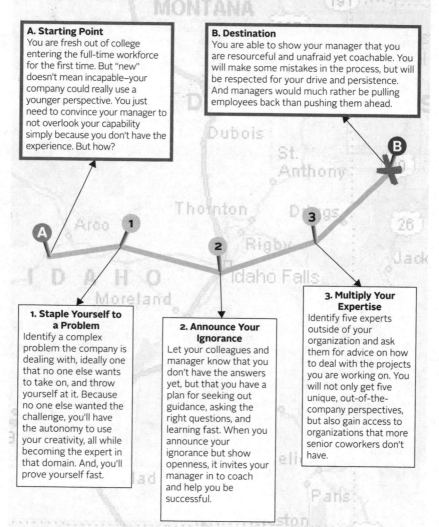

### A. Starting Point
You are fresh out of college entering the full-time workforce for the first time. But "new" doesn't mean incapable–your company could really use a younger perspective. You just need to convince your manager to not overlook your capability simply because you don't have the experience. But how?

### B. Destination
You are able to show your manager that you are resourceful and unafraid yet coachable. You will make some mistakes in the process, but will be respected for your drive and persistence. And managers would much rather be pulling employees back than pushing them ahead.

### 1. Staple Yourself to a Problem
Identify a complex problem the company is dealing with, ideally one that no one else wants to take on, and throw yourself at it. Because no one else wanted the challenge, you'll have the autonomy to use your creativity, all while becoming the expert in that domain. And, you'll prove yourself fast.

### 2. Announce Your Ignorance
Let your colleagues and manager know that you don't have the answers yet, but that you have a plan for seeking out guidance, asking the right questions, and learning fast. When you announce your ignorance but show openness, it invites your manager in to coach and help you be successful.

### 3. Multiply Your Expertise
Identify five experts outside of your organization and ask them for advice on how to deal with the projects you are working on. You will not only get five unique, out-of-the-company perspectives, but also gain access to organizations that more senior coworkers don't have.

**Nate Meikle** holds a Juris Doctorate from Stanford University and is currently a PhD student in organizational behavior at the University of Utah. He is the author of the forthcoming memoir, *Little Miss: a father, his daughter, and rocket science.*

# APPENDIX E:
# ROOKIES AND
# PERPETUAL ROOKIES

The following is a list of the rookies and perpetual rookies that were profiled throughout the book. There are a couple of individuals who appear in more than one chapter, but they are listed only once below, in the chapter that they are featured in most prominently.

| ROOKIE OR PERPETUAL ROOKIE | FEATURED ROLE |
| --- | --- |
| **Chapter 1: The Rise of the Rookie** | |
| Earvin "Magic" Johnson II | Basketball player |
| Gina Warren | VP of diversity and inclusion at Nike Inc. |
| Jim Delaney | A COO and later CEO of Marketwired/ Sysomos |
| **Chapter 2: Backpackers** | |
| Stephanie DiMarco | Cofounder and former CEO of Advent Software |
| Hara Kefalidou | Greek parliament member |
| Bryan Cioffi | Director of innovation at Converse |

| ROOKIE OR PERPETUAL ROOKIE | FEATURED ROLE |
|---|---|
| Bryan Schramm | Cofounder of Sundrop Fuels |
| Navi Radjou | Former researcher at Forrester Research |
| Elizabeth Gilbert | Author of *Eat, Pray, Love* |

## Chapter 3: Hunter-Gatherers

| | |
|---|---|
| Jan Marsh | Teacher |
| Anne Letzerich | Leadership Development Adviser |
| Dillon Lee | Consultant at BTS |
| Salil Parekh | Engineering Manager at Capgemini Group |
| Saum Mathur | CIO of the Software Division at Hewlett-Packard |

## Chapter 4: Firewalkers

| | |
|---|---|
| Mark Carges | CTO and former engineer at BEA Systems |
| Michael Jr. | Comedian |
| Ezekiel "Ziggy" Ansah | Professional football player |

## Chapter 5: Pioneers

| | |
|---|---|
| Sarah Blakely | Founder and CEO of Spanx |
| Henrik Ekelund | Founder and CEO of BTS |
| Jane Chen | Inventor of Embrace Incubator |
| Mark Zuckerberg | Founder and CEO of Facebook |

| ROOKIE OR PERPETUAL ROOKIE | FEATURED ROLE |
|---|---|
| **Chapter 6: The Perpetual Rookie** | |
| Bob Hurley | Founder and CEO of Hurley International |
| Annie Leibovitz | Photographer |
| Peter Drucker | Writer and management consultant |
| Elon Musk | Founder of PayPal, SolarCity, SpaceX, and Tesla Motors |
| Moied Wahid | Senior engineering manager at PayPal |
| Paul Erdös | Mathematician |
| Dr. Tameira Hollander | Physician |
| Andrew Stanton | Screenwriter and director at Pixar |
| C. K. Prahalad | Business professor |
| Sergio Marchionne | Chairman and CEO of Chrysler Group |
| **Chapter 7: Rookie Revival** | |
| Candido Camero | Jazz percussionist |
| Jim Collins | Management author |
| Jim Harbaugh | San Francisco 49ers football coach |
| Sue Warnke | Senior manager of internal documentation at Salesforce.com |
| Jean-Paul Connock | Staff technical writer at Salesforce.com |
| Gabriela Maselli | Psychologist and commercial coach with Grupo Entero |
| Malte Holm | Innovation director at Grupo Entero |

| ROOKIE OR PERPETUAL ROOKIE | FEATURED ROLE |
|---|---|
| Don Kraft | Founder of the Windhorse Foundation |
| François Truffaut | Film director |
| John Donahoe | CEO of eBay |
| Paul McCartney | Musician |

## Chapter 8: The Rookie Organization

| | |
|---|---|
| Peter Hudson | VP of design and innovation at Converse |
| Barkhad Abdi | Supporting actor in *Captain Phillips* |
| Harry Weese | Architect |
| Maya Lin | Architect and designer of Vietnam Veterans Memorial |
| Paul Davies | Principal investigator at the National Cancer Institute |

# APPENDIX F:
## DISCUSSION FIRE STARTER

If you want to spark a group conversation about *Rookie Smarts*, this discussion guide can serve as your fire starter. The questions and activities described below will help you exchange ideas, raise issues, and discuss new possibilities, either as a book club or as a team in the workplace.

### KINDLING FOR THE CONVERSATION

Allow the group to warm up a bit by asking people to summarize the key ideas and their insights from *Rookie Smarts*.

Next, set the tone for the conversation by running the "Teleport Yourself" experiment (found in Appendix C) to help each person in the discussion remember what it was like to be in a rookie role. (Download a template for this experiment at www.RookieSmarts.com/teleport.) To use this "learning experiment" with your group:

1. Ask each person to identify a time when they were a rookie—inexperienced and new to an important type of work.

2. Give people a few minutes to reflect and answer the questions in the "Teleport Yourself" experiment template.

3. Ask the following questions to encourage people to reflect on how they operated when they were a rookie.

- What could you see that others couldn't?

- Who did you seek out for expertise and guidance?

- What did you do to learn quickly?

- How did you prove yourself?

- In what ways did you improvise?

## SPARKING THE DISCUSSION

Once the tone has been set and rookie minds are engaged, use a few selected questions to spark a thought-provoking discussion. Any combination of your own question and those below will work. If you are having a general discussion of the ideas, focus on the questions in chapters 1 and 6–8. If you are discussing the book chapter-by-chapter, include the questions in chapters 2–5. (Tip: Sending selected questions to participants in advance allows everyone to contribute more fully.)

### Chapter 1: The Rise of the Rookie

- How is it possible to be "at our best" when doing something for the first time?

- Who do you know who is an excellent example of a rookie in action?

- Why do we find rookie experiences both very challenging and very rewarding?

- What research findings surprised you the most? Why?

- In what circumstances do you want to operate like a rookie? In what circumstances do you need to use the savvy and wisdom of experience?

- Where can rookies be valuable in your business's or your organization's mission?

- What are the organizational forces that pull us toward the "veteran comfort zone" (operating like caretakers, local guides, marathoners, and settlers)? How can we counter these forces?

## Chapter 2: Backpackers

- What causes us to get weighed down and entrenched in our views?

- How can we unencumber ourselves so we can explore new ideas and innovate?

- What is preventing us from asking the naïve, fundamental questions (the ones that most people are thinking but no one is willing to ask)?

- Where can we "wipe the slate" so we can have more fresh starts?

## Chapter 3: Hunter-Gatherers

- Why do we get stuck in the "echo chamber" where we hear opinions that support our existing views and receive information that validates our current practices?

- How can we escape the echo chamber?

- Where is the echo chamber deafening someone on a critical issue?

- How can we ensure mentoring doesn't just happen top-down but also flows bottom-up?

- What would you like to learn from being mentored by a rookie? What would you like to teach a veteran?

## Chapter 4: Firewalkers

- What's the difference between self-confidence and situational confidence? Why is low situational confidence advantageous?

- Why can it be dangerous to operate at a steady, consistent pace?

- What keeps experienced professionals and managers from getting the feedback they most need? How else might they get the feedback they need?

- How can we create space for people to experiment and quickly test new ideas?

## Chapter 5: Pioneers

- How do we (both as individuals and as a team) benefit from our "settling" behaviors (building secure infrastructure, policies, etc.)?

- How might our existing tools, infrastructure, or protocols be keeping us from innovating?

- What are the signs that someone (or a company) is truly hungry for success?

- Where have we become too comfortable and need a push out to the frontier?

- What might an exciting pioneering expedition look like for you in your current role?

## Chapter 6: The Perpetual Rookie

- Who do you know who is a perpetual rookie—someone who, despite experience and success, can still operate with a rookie mindset? What drives him or her? How do they maintain this orientation? Cultivate it in others?

- How can you tell if someone is intellectually curious? Humble?

- What helps *you* maintain a youthful orientation to your work?

## Chapter 7: Rookie Revival

- What are the signs that you've lost your rookie smarts?

- What helps *you* shift from a mode of knowing into a mode of learning?

- How can we help people rediscover their rookie style of thinking and operating?

- What challenges might you have with balancing your veteran experience with your rookie smarts in your work?

- Why is it easier to see when a colleague has lost their rookie smarts than it is with ourselves?

## Chapter 8: The Rookie Organization

- How can we better utilize rookie talent on our team?

- What do people in a rookie assignment need from their managers and leaders to be successful?

- How can we combine rookie and veteran talent to form powerful teams?

- What conditions need to exist within a team to make best use of both types of talent?

- What can we do as an organization to help all professionals stay in the rookie zone?

- Which of the talent management strategies suggested in the book could have the greatest impact for our team?

- In what parts of our operation must we ensure that we maintain our rookie smarts?

- What is the simplest first step we can take?

## KEEPING THE CONVERSATION BLAZING

To gain more insight into areas where you or your group members need your rookie smarts rekindled, invite discussion participants to take the "Are You in the Learning Zone?" quiz at www.RookieSmarts.com/ quiz. Discuss how each member of the team can get into the green/ learning zone.

If you are interested in digging in even deeper and want to develop the rookie mindsets and practices, you may want to run a Rookie Smarts Experience, facilitated by the Wiseman Group or one of our partners worldwide. You can explore the options at www.RookieSmarts.com or www.theWisemanGroup.com.

If you'd like to join a larger conversation about *Rookie Smarts* and be part of a community of rookies, visit www.RookieSmarts.com to learn more.

# NOTES

## INTRODUCTION

1. David R. Schilling, "Knowledge Doubling Every 12 Months, Soon to be Every 12 Hours," *Industry Tap*, April 19, 2013; "Quick Facts and Figures About Biological Data," *ELIXIR*, 2011; Brian Goldman, "Doctors Make Mistakes. Can We Talk About That?," TED, November 2011; Brett King, "Too Much Content: A World of Exponential Information Growth," *Huffington Post*, January 18, 2011.
2. Edward N. Wolff, "The Growth of Information Workers in the U.S. Economy," *Communications* 48, no. 10 (2005).
3. D. L. Bosworth, "The Rate of Obsolescence of Technical Knowledge: A Note," *Journal of Industrial Economics* 26, no. 3 (1978); Lionel Nesta, "Knowledge and Productivity in the World's Largest Manufacturing Corporations," *Journal of Economic Behavior & Organization* (2011); J. Allen and R. van der Velden, "When Do Skills Become Obsolete, and When Does It Matter?," in A. de Grip, Jasper van Loo, and Ken Mayhew, eds., *The Economics of Skills Obsolescence* (Amsterdam and Boston: JAI, 2007).
4. Michael Alter, "20% of Small Businesses Now Prefer Independent Contractors," *Inc.*, September 3, 2013.
5. Jennifer Sertl, "Our role as conduit is more vital than our role as source in this knowledge economy," tweet, November 29, 2013.
6. Jonathon Colman, "Why I Am Joining the Content Strategy Team at Facebook," *Jonathon Colman*, July 8, 2013.
7. Ryan Mac, "The Fall of Mark Pincus: From Billionaire to Zynga's Former CEO," *Forbes*, July 1, 2013.
8. Horace said, "Atque inter silvas Academi quaerere verum," which roughly means "And seek the truth amid the groves of Academia." From "quaerere verum," which means "seek truth," we arrived at "quaerere eruditionem," meaning "seek learning."

## CHAPTER 1: THE RISE OF THE ROOKIE

1. Alon Marcovici, "A Decade of Parity," *NBA Encyclopedia: Playoff Edition*.
2. "Magic Johnson," *Wikipedia*.
3. "Rookie Makes the Lakers Believe in Magic," *NBA Encyclopedia: Playoff Edition*.
4. Ibid.

5. Ibid.

6. "1980 NBA Finals: Lakers at Sixers, Gm 6," video, YouTube, December 23, 2010.

7. Rick Weinberg, "63: Magic Moves to Center, Beats Sixers for Title," *ESPN.com*, http://sports.espn.go.com/espn/espn25/story?page=moments/63.

8. Ibid.

9. The next day the Associated Press headline read "It's Magic: Lakers Take Title." Magic continued to play brilliantly across a career spanning two decades where he won two more NBA MVP awards, made nine NBA Finals appearances, played in twelve all-star games, played on the 1992 Olympics "dream team," and became the NBA's all-time leader in average assists per game.

10. G. P. Hodgkinson, J. Langan-Fox, and E. Sadler-Smith, "Intuition: A Fundamental Bridging Construct in the Behavioural Sciences," *British Journal of Psychology* 99 (2008): 1–27; Erik Dane and Michael G. Pratt, "Exploring Intuition and Its Role in Managerial Decision Making," *Academy of Management Review* 32, no. 1 (2007).

11. K. Anders Ericsson, Ralf T. Krampe, and Clemens Tesch-Romer, "The Role of Deliberate Practice in the Acquisition of Expert Performance," *Psychological Review* 100, no. 3 (1993).

12. Hillel J. Einhorn, Robin M. Hogarth, and Eric Klempner, "Quality of Group Judgment," *Psychological Bulletin* 84, no. 1 (1977).

13. David Z. Hambrick et al., "Deliberate Practice: Is That All It Takes to Become an Expert?" *Intelligence* (2013).

14. Josh Kaufman, *The First 20 Hours: How to Learn Anything . . . Fast!* (New York: Penguin Books, 2013); Jim Allen and Rolf van der Velden, "The Flexible Professional in the Knowledge Society: General Results of the REFLEX Project," Research Centre for Education and the Labour Market, Maastricht University.

15. Don Peck, "They're Watching You at Work," *Atlantic*, November 20, 2013.

16. Monika Hamori and Burak Koyuncu, "The CEO Experience Trap," *MIT Sloan Management Review*, Fall 2013.

17. The names of all the individuals in this example have been changed.

18. Average rookie performance was assessed at 7.42 on a 10-point scale while average veteran performance was assessed at 7.36 on a 10-point scale.

19. Our research data shows: Rookies listen more (50 percent higher levels of listening); rookies are more likely to ask for help (4 times more likely); believe they have a lot to learn (2.3 times as likely); rookies learn faster (19 percent more).

20. Our research shows: Veterans have higher levels of political savvy (145 percent higher); veterans use more intuition than rookies (60 percent higher); veterans were more likely to default to past behavior (2 times as likely); veterans are more likely to solve the right problem rather than the one presented (2 times more likely).

21. Our research shows: 145 percent higher levels of political savvy.

22. Charles Duhigg, *The Power of Habit: Why We Do What We Do in Life and Business* (New York: Random House, 2012).

23. David T. Neal, Wendy Wood, and Jeffrey M. Quinn, "Habits: A Repeat Performance," *Current Directions in Psychological Science* 15, no. 4 (2006): 198–202.

24. Malcolm Gladwell, *Outliers: The Story of Success* (New York: Hachette Digital, 2008), p. 206.

25. Richard Branson, "Richard Branson on When Inexperience Is an Advantage," *Entrepreneur.com*, November 28, 2011.

26. In our study, managers reported that their rookie employees reached out to an average of six experts, compared to an average of one for their veteran employees—6 times more! Interestingly enough, when professionals self-report, rookies claim an average of three reach-outs compared to one for the veterans. In other words, experienced staff perceives they are seeking input at a much higher frequency than their managers observe. Weighting the two datasets, we calculate a net effect of 5 times.

27. Tomasz Tunguz, "Why Humility Is Essential for Every New Startup Hire," http://tom-tunguz.com/why-humility-is-essential-for-every-new-startup-hire/, February 8, 2013.

28. G. Michael Maddock and Raphael Louis Vitón, "Why Innovation Is Beginner's Luck," *Bloomberg Businessweek*, August 24, 2010.

29. Peter W. Roberts, "New Research Suggests Start-Up Experience Doesn't Help Social Entrepreneurs," *Harvard Business Review* blog, February 14, 2013.

30. Clayton M. Christensen, Jeff Dyer, and Hal B. Gregersen, *The Innovator's DNA: Mastering the Five Skills of Disruptive Innovators* (Boston: Harvard Business School Press, 2011).

31. Sam Teller, "Zuckerberg to Leave Harvard Indefinitely," *Harvard Crimson*, November 1, 2005.

32. Steven Johnson, *Emergence: The Connected Lives of Ants, Brains, Cities, and Software* (New York: Scribner, 2001).

33. James Surowiecki, *The Wisdom of Crowds: Why the Many Are Smarter than the Few and How Collective Wisdom Shapes Business, Economies, Societies, and Nations* (New York: Doubleday, 2004).

34. "Asiana Airlines Flight 214," *Wikipedia*.

## CHAPTER 2: BACKPACKERS: AN UNENCUMBERED MIND

1. Ivy Schmerken, "Advent's Stephanie DiMarco Will Leave a Strong Legacy," *Wall Street & Technology*, January 24, 2012.

2. Alkman Granitsas, Marcus Walker, and Costas Paris, "Greek Premier Faces Revolt," *Wall Street Journal*, November 2, 2011.

3. Suzanne Daley, "A Greek Politician Who Pushed Back Against Perks," *New York Times*, October 28, 2011.

4. Natalie Wolchover, "Breaking the Code: Why Your Barin Can Raed This," *Livescience*, February 9, 2012.

5. K. A. DeLong et al., "Thinking Ahead or Not? Natural Aging and Anticipation During Reading," *Brain & Language* 121, no. 3 (2012).

6. Thomas Wolf, "A Cognitive Model of Musical Sight-Reading," *Journal of Psycholinguistic Research* 5, no. 2 (1975).

7. Richard Branson, "Advice for a Business Studies Student," *LinkedIn*, October 17, 2013.

8. Whitney Hall, "Mobotbolting and So Much Diving," *Houston Chronicle*, August 12, 2012.

9. Daniel M. Curlik II et al., "Physical Skill Training Increases the Number of Surviving New Cells in the Adult Hippocampus," *PlosOne* 8, no 2 (2013).

10. Elizabeth Gilbert, "Your Elusive Creative Genius" TED, February 2009.

11. Ibid.

12. Ibid.

13. Norton Juster, *The Phantom Tollbooth* (New York: Epstein & Carroll, 1961).

14. Ibid.

## CHAPTER 3: HUNTER-GATHERERS: FINDING EXPERTISE

1. Angela Bahns, Kate Pickett, and Christian Crandall, "Social Ecology of Similarity: Big Schools, Small Schools, and Social Relationships," *Group Processes & Intergroup Relations* 15, no. 1 (2012).
2. Adrianna Jenkins and J. P. Mitchell. "Medial Prefrontal Cortex Subserves Diverse Forms of Self-Reflection," *Social Neuroscience* 6, no. 3 (2011).
3. The name of this individual has been changed.
4. Brian Wong, "The Folly of Age as a Number: How We Can All Be Young," *LinkedIn*, December 19, 2012.
5. C. Brené Brown, *Daring Greatly: How the Courage to Be Vulnerable Transforms the Way We Live, Love, Parent, and Lead* (New York: Gotham Books, 2012).
6. Angelina Sutin et al., "Personality and Career Success: Concurrent and Longitudinal Relations," *European Journal of Personality* 23 (2009).
7. Wong, "The Folly of Age as a Number."
8. Rachel Silverman, "Big Firms Try Crowdsourcing," *Wall Street Journal*, January 17, 2012.
9. Jeff Sommer, "Robert Shiller: A Skeptic and a Nobel Winner," *New York Times*, October 19, 2013.
10. Po Bronson and Ashley Merryman, *Top Dog: The Science of Winning and Losing* (New York: Hachette, 2013).
11. Enrica Crispino, *Artist's Life: Michelangelo* (Florence: Giunti Gruppo Editoriale, 2001).
12. Matthew 7:7 (KJV).

## CHAPTER 4: FIREWALKERS: MOVING CAUTIOUSLY BUT QUICKLY

1. "Firewalking," *Wikipedia*.
2. The name of the company has been changed.
3. The name of the leader has been changed.
4. Tomas Chamorro-Premuzic, "Less-Confident People Are More Successful," *Harvard Business Review* blog, July 6, 2012.
5. Ibid.
6. Frank Knight, *Risk, Uncertainty and Profit* (Boston and New York: Houghton Mifflin, 1921).
7. Malcolm Gladwell, "The Sure Thing," *New Yorker*, January 18, 2010.
8. "The Comedy & Magic Club," *Wikipedia*.
9. "Feedback," *Wikipedia*.
10. Jared Lloyd, "NFL Draft: Mendenhall and Washburn Family Talk About Ziggy's Big Day," *Daily Herald*, April 27, 2013.
11. Lindsay H. Jones, "Ziggy Ansah Speeding Through Learning Curve," *USA Today*, April 10, 2013; Jay Drew, "BYU's Bronco: Ziggy's Mom Wanted Utah's NFL Team to Draft Him," *Salt Lake Tribune*, April 26, 2013.
12. Dave Birkett, "Lions' First-Round Pick Ziggy Ansah Bringing Walk-on Attitude," *Detroit Free Press*, April 28, 2013.
13. Ashley Dunkak, "Andre Fluellen Back to Help Shore Up Defensive Line," *CBS Detroit*, September 23, 2013; John Niyo, "Lions Rookie Ziggy Ansah Fits In Quicker than Expected," *Detroit News*, September 24, 2013.
14. Jeanne C. Meister, "Mentoring Millennials," *Harvard Business Review*, May 2010.

15. Allison Hillhouse, "Consumer Insights: MTV's 'No Collar Workers,'" http://blog.viacom.com/2012/10/consumer-insights-mtvs-no-collar-workers/, October 4, 2012.

16. Alina Tugend, "You've Been Doing a Fantastic Job. Just One Thing . . . ," *New York Times*, April 5, 2013.

## CHAPTER 5: PIONEERS: FORGING AHEAD

1. Douglas Perry, "Teaching with Documents: The Lewis and Clark Expedition," National Archives.

2. *Lewis & Clark: The Journey of the Corps of Discovery*, directed by Ken Burns, PBS, 1997.

3. Ibid.

4. Matthew Belvedere, "'My Own Butt' Spanx Inspiration: Billionaire Inventor," CNBC, October 16, 2013.

5. "How'd They do That? Spanx," *Oprah*, February 1, 2007.

6. Kathy Caprino, "10 Lessons I Learned from Sara Blakely That You Won't Hear in Business School," *Forbes*, May 23, 2014.

7. Ibid.

8. Daniel H. Pink, *Drive: The Surprising Truth About What Motivates Us* (New York: Riverhead Books, 2009).

9. "Jugaad," *Wikipedia*.

10. C. Page Moreau and Darren W. Dahl, "Designing the Solution: The Impact of Constraints on Consumers' Creativity," *Journal of Consumer Research* 32, no. 1 (2005).

11. "Embrace," *Extreme: Design for Extreme Affordability*, http://extreme.stanford.edu/projects/embrace.

12. Paulo Coelho, *The Alchemist*. New York: HarperCollins, 1998.

13. Roger Hill, "Demographic Differences in Selected Work Ethic Attributes," *Journal of Career Development* 24, no. 1 (1997).

14. Henry Blodget, "The Maturation of the Billionaire Boy-Man," *New York*, May 6, 2012.

15. "Cortés Burns His Boats," *The Fall of the Aztecs*, PBS, https://www.pbs.org/conquistadors/cortes/cortes_d00.html.

16. Anders K. Ericsson, Michael J. Prietula, and Edward T. Cokely, "The Making of an Expert," *Harvard Business Review*, July–August 2007.

## CHAPTER 6: THE PERPETUAL ROOKIE

1. "Magic Johnson," *Wikipedia*.

2. You can check out all the Disney Dream Portraits by Annie Leibovitz at http://disneyparks.disney.go.com/disney-dream-portraits.

3. "Peter Drucker's Life and Legacy," Drucker Institute.

4. Robert Gibbs, "Tributes to Those We Lost in 2013: Helen Thomas," *Time*, December 9, 2013.

5. David Stout, "50 Years of Tough Questions and 'Thank You, Mr. President," *New York Times*, July 20, 2013.

6. Spencer H. Harrison, Davi M. Sluss, and Blake E. Ashforth, "Curiosity Adapted the Cat: The Role of Trait Curiosity in Newcomer Adaptation," *Journal of Applied Psychology* 96, no. 1 (2011): 211–20.

7. Min Jeong Kang et al., "The Wick in the Candle of Learning: Epistemic Curiosity Activates Reward Circuitry and Enhances Memory," *Psychological Science* 20, no. 8 (2009): 963–73.

8. Henry Cloud (DrHenryCloud), "Certainty is one of the weakest positions in life. Curiosity is one of the most powerful. Certainty prohibits learning, curiosity fuels change," tweet, December 3, 2013.

9. Frederic Kerrest, "Hubris: A Startup's Worst Mistake," *Forbes*, January 9, 2014.

10. Gina Kolata, "Paul Erdös, 83, a Wayfarer in Math's Vanguard, Is Dead," *New York Times*, September 24, 1996.

11. Adrian Gostick and Scott Christopher, *The Levity Effect: Why It Pays to Lighten Up* (Hoboken, NJ: Wiley, 2008).

12. Randy Garner, "Humor in Pedagogy: How Ha-Ha Can Lead to Aha!," *College Teaching* 54, no 1 (2006): 177–80.

13. Tad Friend, "Second-Act Twist," *New Yorker*, October 17, 2011.

14. Luke Vandezande, "Fiat, Chrysler CEO Sergio Marchionne Interviewed on *60 Minutes*," *AutoGuide*, March 26, 2012.

## CHAPTER 7: ROOKIE REVIVAL

1. Alvin Toffler, *Future Shock* (New York: Bantam Books, 1970).

2. Immanuel Kant, *Prolegomena to Any Future Metaphysics*, 4, 260; 10.

3. Abraham J. Heschel, *God in Search of Man: A Philosophy of Judaism* (New York: Farrar, Straus & Cudahy, 1955).

4. Additionally, 39 percent cite workload as the top cause of stress; Nikki Blacksmith and Jim Harter, "Majority of American Workers Not Engaged in Their Jobs," Gallup, October 28, 2011; Sharon Jayson, "Burnout Up Among Employees," *USA Today*, October 24, 2012.

5. Our research shows that those who are the least challenged are 40 percent *less* challenged than the average and those who are the most challenged are 36 percent *more* challenged than the average.

6. Ron Shaich, "If You're Learning, You'll Never Need to Recharge," *LinkedIn*, June 6, 2013.

7. Jim Collins, "Hitting the Wall: Realizing that Vertical Limits Aren't," http://www.jimcollins.com/article_topics/articles/hitting-the-wall.html, September 2003.

8. Bill Hybels, *Axiom: Powerful Leadership Proverbs* (Grand Rapids, MI: Zondervan, 2008).

9. Monte Poole, "Poole: San Francisco 49ers Find Motivation in Past," *San Jose Mercury News*, January 18, 2013.

10. Shane Atchison, "Things I Carry: A List of 7 Things I Don't Know," *LinkedIn*, April 2, 2013.

11. Stephen Blandino, "Becoming an UNlearner," http://stephenblandino.com/2009/06/becoming-unlearner.html, June 8, 2009.

12. Richard Wiseman, "New Year's Resolution Experiment," http://www.quirkology.com/UK/Experiment_resolution.shtml.

13. Jonah Lehrer, "Blame It on the Brain," *Wall Street Journal*, December 26, 2009; "Exercise No Good for Weight Loss?," *Popsugar*, August 6, 2009.

14. Meena Surie Wilson et al., "Grooming Top Leaders: Cultural Perspectives from China, India, Singapore and the United States," Center for Creative Leadership, September 2011.

15. Roger Schank, *Coloring Outside the Lines* (New York: Harper Paperbacks, 2001).

16. Michael Barbaro, Sharon Otterman, and Javier C. Hernandez, "After 3 Months, Mayor Replaces Schools Leader," *New York Times*, April 7, 2011.

17. From interview with Michael Fertik.

18. John Donahoe, "To Beat the Chaos, Take a Thinking Day," *LinkedIn*, July 15, 2013.

19. "Wings (band)," *Wikipedia*.

## CHAPTER 8: THE ROOKIE ORGANIZATION

1. Esteban On, "20 Things You Probably Didn't Know About Converse All Stars," *Refined Guy*, May 29, 2013.

2. Randee Dawn, "Rookie Actor, Limo Driver Barkhad Abdi Upstages Tom Hanks in 'Captain Phillips,'" *Today Entertainment*, October 10, 2013.

3. Ibid.

4. Elizabeth Wolfson, "The 'Black Gash of Shame': Revisiting the Vietnam Veterans Memorial Controversy," http://www.art21.org/texts/the-culture-wars-redux/essay-the-black-gash-of-shame-revisiting-the-vietnam-veterans-memorial-.

5. Ibid.

6. "Maya Lin: A Strong Clear Vision," IMDb.

7. Roy Y. J. Chua, "Innovating at the World's Crossroads: How Multicultural Networks Promote Creativity," *Working Knowledge*, May 24, 2011.

8. Warren Berger, "What Zen Taught Silicon Valley (and Steve Jobs) About Innovation," *Fast Company*, April 9, 2012.

9. M. Mitchell Waldrop, "Physics Meets Cancer: The Disruptor," *Nature*, June 1, 2011.

10. Stephen Simpson, "Biggest Corporate Comebacks," *Forbes*, June 22, 2010.

11. Apple Computer was ranked with a market value of $463.55 billion as of February 11, 2014.

12. The growth-minded trait references the growth mindset from Carol Dweck's work on growth verses fixed mindsets in her book *Mindset: The New Psychology of Success* (New York: Random House, 2006).

13. Thomas L. Friedman, "How to Get a Job at Google," *New York Times*, February 22, 2014.

14. Tomasz Tunguz, "Why Humility Is Essential for Every New Startup Hire," http://tomtunguz.com/why-humility-is-essential-for-every-new-startup-hire/, February 8, 2013.

15. Our research shows that 44 percent of people figured out their role in under a month, 87 percent of people figured out their role in under three months, and 98 percent of people figured out their role in under six months.

16. Our research shows that 35 percent of people are ready for the next big challenge within three months and 60 percent of people are ready for the next big challenge within six months.

17. Our research shows that 35 percent of people are ready for a new job or role within one year and 62 percent of people are ready for a new job within two years.

18. Our research shows that 35 percent of people begin to feel stale within two years and 60 percent begin to feel stale within three years.

19. Individual contributors take an average of 5 percent less time to feel ready for the next big challenge than average and take an average of 10 percent less time to feel stale than average.

20. Middle managers take an average of 8 percent less time to feel ready for a new job or role.

21. Fara Warner, "Inside Intel's Mentoring Movement," *Fast Company*, April 2002.

22. Thomas S. Monson, "The World Needs Pioneers Today," https://www.lds.org/ensign/2013/07/the-world-needs-pioneers-today?lang=eng, July 2013.

23. Dallin Oaks, "Following the Pioneers," https://www.lds.org/general-conference/1997/10/following-the-pioneers, October 1997.

24. Jeffrey D. Sachs, "The End of Poverty, Soon," *New York Times*, September 24, 2013.

25. "2013 World Population Data Sheet," Population Reference Bureau; Hélène Mulholland, "Labour Targets 'School-Gate Mums,'" *Guardian*, April 15, 2005.

26. Ken Robinson, "How Schools Kill Creativity," TED, February 2006.

27. Salman Khan, "Introduction: A Free, World-Class Education for Anyone, Anywhere," in *The One World Schoolhouse: Education Reimagined* (New York: Twelve, 2012).

28. More information about the World Economic Forum Young Global Leaders can be found at http://www.weforum.org/community/forum-young-global-leaders. Information on the Global Shapers program can be found at http://www.weforum.org/community/global-shapers.

29. Bill Keller, "Inequality for Dummies," *New York Times*, December 22, 2013.

30. Viktor E. Frankl, *Man's Search for Meaning* (Boston: Beacon Press, 1959).

## APPENDIX B: FREQUENTLY ASKED QUESTIONS

1. "Shoshin," *Wikipedia*.

2. This failure to launch cycle is from the Multipliers workshop and is a derivative of the Gartner Hype Cycle, which begins with a technology trigger, has a peak of inflated expectations, then proceeds with a trough of disillusionment and then continues in a steady upward climb (enlightenment and productivity). Unlike this broad market cycle, personal and organizational change cycles often get killed rather than progress up this slope of enlightenment.

## APPENDIX C: LEARNING EXPERIMENTS

1. Jeff Sommer, "Robert Shiller: A Skeptic and a Nobel Winner," *New York Times*, October 19, 2013.

1. Anders K. Ericsson, Michael J. Prietula, and Edward T. Cokely, "The Making of an Expert," *Harvard Business Review*, July–August 2007.

3. Luke Vandezande, "Fiat, Chrysler CEO Sergio Marchionne Interviewed on *60 Minutes*," *AutoGuide*, March 26, 2012.

# INDEX

**INDEX**

279

2
2

2

# ABOUT THE AUTHOR

**Liz Wiseman** teaches leadership to executives and emerging leaders around the world. She is the President of the Wiseman Group, a leadership research and development firm headquartered in Silicon Valley, where some of her recent clients include Apple, Disney, eBay/PayPal, Facebook, GAP, Genentech/Roche, Microsoft, Nike, Salesforce.com, and Twitter. Liz has been listed on the *Thinkers50* ranking and named as one of the top ten leadership thinkers in the world.

She is the author of the bestsellers *Multipliers: How the Best Leaders Make Everyone Smarter* and *The Multiplier Effect: Tapping the Genius Inside Our Schools*. She has conducted significant research in the field of leadership and collective intelligence, is a frequent keynote speaker, and writes for *Harvard Business Review* and a variety of other business and leadership journals. She is a frequent guest lecturer and has taught at Brigham Young University, the Naval Postgraduate School, and Stanford and Yale universities. She is an active contributor to forums on health-care and education reform.

A former executive at Oracle Corporation, she worked over the course of seventeen years as the Vice President of Oracle University and as the global leader for Human Resource Development. During her tenure at Oracle, she led several major global initiatives and has worked and traveled in more than forty countries.

Liz holds a bachelor's degree in business management and a master's in organizational behavior from Brigham Young. Liz lives in Menlo Park, California, with her husband and four children, who share her overactive curiosity and sense of adventure.

You can connect with Liz at any of the following:

ᵗ @LizWiseman

in www.linkedIn.com/in/LizWiseman

## ABOUT THE WISEMAN GROUP

The **Wiseman Group** is a leadership research and development firm whose mission is to develop leaders who can take on the world's toughest challenges by deeply using all the intelligence and human capability inside them. The Wiseman Group has a network of partners around the world who offer workshops, keynote addresses, and coaching to help companies build leaders and shape organizational culture.

For inquiries, please contact the Wiseman Group at www.thewisemangroup.com/contact.

# ALSO BY LIZ WISEMAN

## MULTIPLIERS
### How the Best Leaders Make Everyone Smarter
**Available in Hardcover and eBook**

A thought-provoking, accessible, and essential exploration of why some leaders ("Diminishers") drain capability and intelligence from their teams, while others ("Multipliers") amplify it to produce better results. Including a foreword by Stephen R. Covey, as well as the five key disciplines that turn smart leaders into genius makers, *Multipliers* is a must-read for everyone from first-time managers to world leaders.

"A well-organized system that could be used as a personal tool or as a workbook for team-development seminars." —*Booklist*

For more details, visit: www.multipliersbooks.com • Twitter: @LizWiseman

HARPER BUSINESS